LANDINGS

A Crooked Creek Farm Year

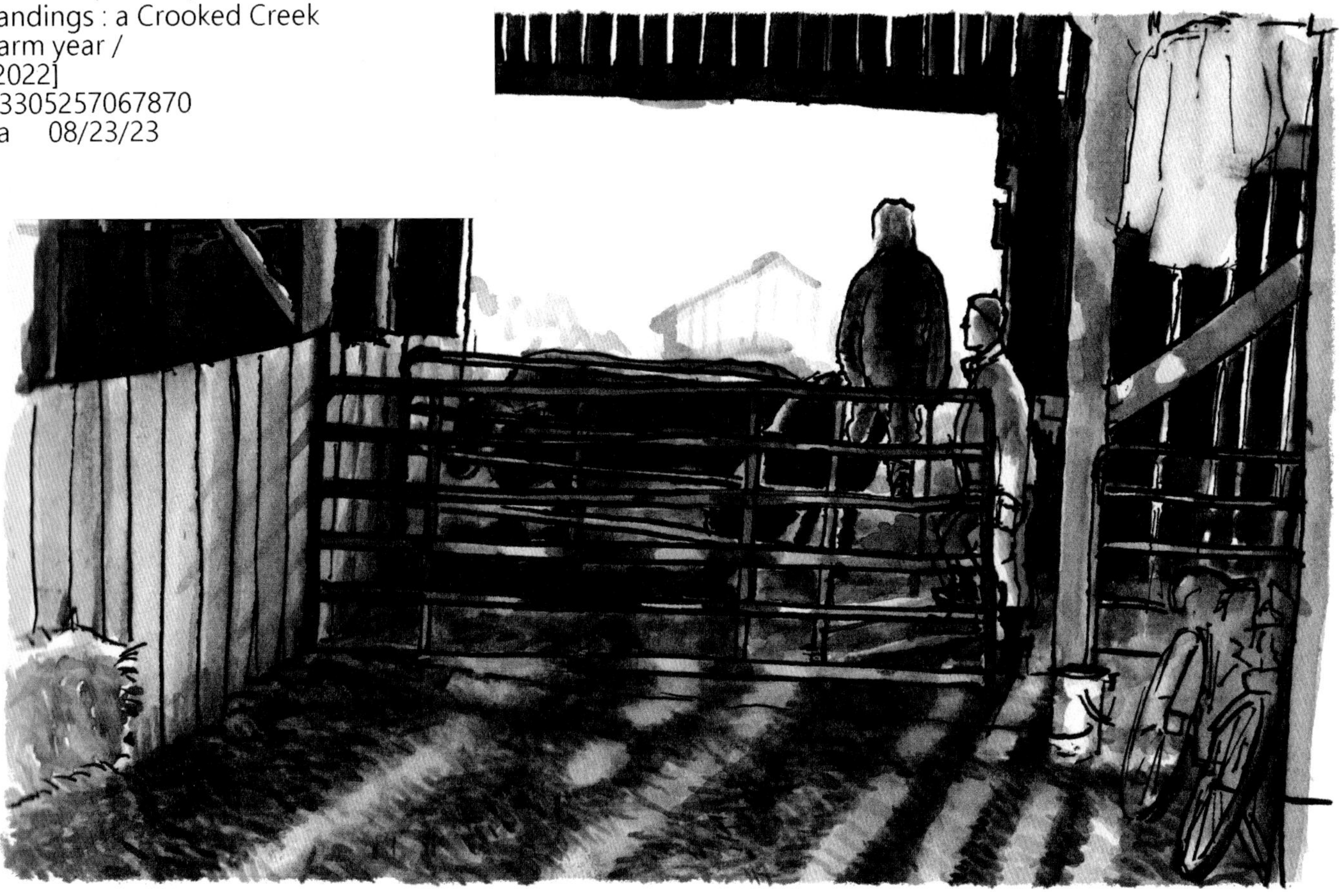

Landings

A Crooked Creek Farm Year

Arwen Donahue

HUB CITY PRESS
SPARTANBURG, SC

Book Design: Kate McMullen
Cover Image: Arwen Donahue
Author Photo: Tina LaDeur Brouwer

INTRODUCTION TEXT: LTC Caslon
BODY TEXT: Evenstar

Library of Congress
Cataloging-in-Publication Data

Names: Donahue, Arwen, 1969- author.
Title: Landings / Arwen Donahue.
Description: Spartanburg, SC : Hub City Press, [2022]
Identifiers:
LCCN 2022019589 (print) | LCCN 2022019590 (ebook)
ISBN 9798885740005 (paperback)
ISBN 9798885740104 (ebook)
Subjects: LCSH: Donahue, Arwen, 1969– | Donahue, Arwen, 1969—Family.
Farmers—Kentucky—Biography. | Farm life—Kentucky.
Classification:
LCC S521.5.K4 D66 2022 (print)
LCC S521.5.K4 (ebook)
DDC 630.92 [B]—dc23/eng/20220610
LC ebook record available at https://lccn.loc.gov/2022019590

Hub City Press gratefully acknowledges support from the National Endowment for the Arts,
the Amazon Literary Partnership, South Arts, and the South Carolina Arts Commission.

Manufactured in the United States of America
First Edition

HUB CITY PRESS
200 Ezell Street
Spartanburg, SC 29306
864.577.9349 | www.hubcity.org

AN INTRODUCTION TO LANDINGS

Time and again as I turned these pages, they brought to mind another book I've loved in my life almost beyond all others: Aldo Leopold's *A Sand County Almanac*. This book, like that one, records a year of mindful work and connection to a modest tract of land. Both authors mark each month's fresh well of surprises, in language charged with the joy of taking notice. They're sanguine about the realities of hard work, while finding peace and pleasure in everyday tasks like splitting wood. The accessible prose of *Landings*, like Leopold's, is informative and poetic, finely focused and transcendent all at once.

Here, though, the text serves as a doorway into the book's deeper offering: more than a hundred daily meditations on farm life, rendered in ink and watercolor. The visual images bring the reader into a direct intimacy with the author and her family, tracking their accomplishments, frustrations, tedium, occasional emergencies, and generous moments of grace. Page by page, the days add up to a layered portrait of modern life as it's lived by farmers in communion with their land. Well beyond revelry in birdsong and dew-damp mornings, it offers a detailed account of food production at the level of soil and rain, laborious planting, watering and weeding, pre-dawn harvests and long market days. The true story, in other words, of a livelihood that underpins all human existence.

That profession gets very little honest representation in contemporary American culture. Stylized, romanticized versions of it are easy enough to find, and so are their condescending opposites. But genuine farm life, as lived in the twenty-first century, is all but invisible in books or film or TV. This is true, painfully so, even for those of us who live in rural, agricultural regions of the country. Even if we subscribe to farming magazines. There is a fair amount of "how-to" out there for those of us who use it, but very little of the "how it is." *Landings* is exactly that: a study and celebration of how it is, how it looks and feels from the ground.

This book was a special delight for me as it offered the repeated shock of recognizing my own childhood. These hills dotted with dark cedars, these meandering creeks, these muddy springs and fecund summers, are a landscape I've never experienced through eyes other than my own. As I turned pages, my nose tingled with the scents of hay and ragweed, and I felt the prickle of cedar burrs in my socks. And oh, those cool, heavenly creeks, where I took off shoes and socks and waded in. Arwen and David's farm is in Nicholas County, Kentucky, an obscure corner of the world where, as it happens, I grew up. Their daughter

Phoebe might have sat in some of the same graying wooden school desks and checked some of the same dog-eared books out of the cash-strapped library. In my day, the high school offered four required years of Home Ec meant to prepare girls for our careers as farmers' wives, and almost nobody ever talked about college. Many of my friends were parents by age eighteen. Times change, but evidently not so much in Nicholas County, I found myself thinking, as I read about ongoing frustrations with the limited curriculum and high school dropout rate.

The economy of these tobacco counties fell apart at least a generation ago, and this is the part of Kentucky where no money trees grew to begin with. It's a struggle common to rural families everywhere, not just Kentucky, to support their children's education and broaden their hopes and horizons. I was glad to read of Phoebe's eventual launch into university life; the world will be lucky to have her. In cultural reckonings of diversity, it's important to remember the unique skills and perspectives of kids raised on the land. I am hugely grateful, myself, for the strokes of luck that combined to get me to college. And while I was wholly unprepared for the math and chemistry classes I met there, I brought values and life experience that have served me in the long run. It's not easy to articulate my debts to my Kentucky origins, but I was moved to find them voiced throughout these pages, as text or subtext: a bone-deep grasp of class, poverty, and privilege; genuine respect for manual labor; an abiding awareness of species other than our own, and their absolute right to share the world with humans.

I live just over the mountains from Kentucky now, in Appalachian Virginia. I could make my home anywhere, as a writer, but I choose to be here on a farm, among other farmers, all of us fiercely attached to this place that some might call "a long way from everything." I can look out my windows at forests, pastures, vegetable gardens, a well that never runs dry, and understand we all have our own ways of defining "everything." Like Arwen Donahue and her family, I feel nourished by this landscape, more deeply than any other I've ever known. I believe this nation's rural communities, with all their beauty, complex challenges, and textured threads of livelihood, deserve better representation. The destructive modern divide between rural and urban America is born, in part, from this frustrating void. Drought, blight, early frost? These hardships we can handle. But it hurts to feel unseen and unacknowledged in the urban power centers where the decisions get made. Especially, I imagine, if one is working on the edge of poverty, and working hard, to grow the food that every soul, everywhere, wants to keep eating every day.

Unfortunately, it's the poverty and toil of farming that still hold a sturdy place in many a family's folklore. Generational memory seems to have fed a modern assumption that manual labor is for the wretched, and farm life is something to be escaped. For those of us who have returned to it, or elected not to leave at all, there is so much more to the story. It's a kind of mission work to explain that land itself holds wisdom, and grace comes from reading it every day. The world needs books like *Landings* to record "the joy, delight, and awe of our creaturely lives on earth." To reveal daily labors like these from the inside out and explain how Efficiency, the god that rules so much of modern life, can be a soul-killing taskmaster. The revelations hold a much-needed redemption of labor itself. For anyone who sees only useless toil in strawberry jam made from home-grown fruits (when a big jar costs only three dollars at Walmart), the author's response is beautifully succinct: "I love to eat of the soil of this place, to know that my flesh and this patch of earth are stitched together. What good is an economy that disregards love?"

It's that sort of simple eloquence, along with cannily expressive ink lines and tonal watercolors, that brings this author's material to life. In one of my favorite entries, she pauses her work to admire an oriole, observing that he seems to be singing the first eight notes of Vivaldi's "Spring" concerto. He does this every year, after his return from wintering on some similar small farm in El Salvador or Mexico. "The oriole carries a long shining thread that stitches us together. Some might call our farm a backwater, but the vast world is present here."

I eagerly invite you into the pages of this book, and that vast world.

BARBARA KINGSOLVER

For David

SATURDAY, DECEMBER 8

This morning I was about to write that after fifteen years of living here, I'm still resisting farm work, as if it can be avoided. Before I could put pen to paper, David noticed the goats were out, so Phoebe and I put on our boots and coats and went to the barn, where we stayed till almost noon: herding the goats back into their paddock, feeding the animals, chopping and stacking wood, carrying water to fill the trough. David came, too, and cleaned up the lower part of the barn. We got back to the house and had our oatmeal breakfast for lunch.

Nothing is better than splitting wood in those moments when you suspect your life lacks direction. It warms the blood quickly and makes you feel stronger than you have a right to feel, since the wood willingly divides if you strike well.

Stop resisting, I tell myself. Be like the wood.

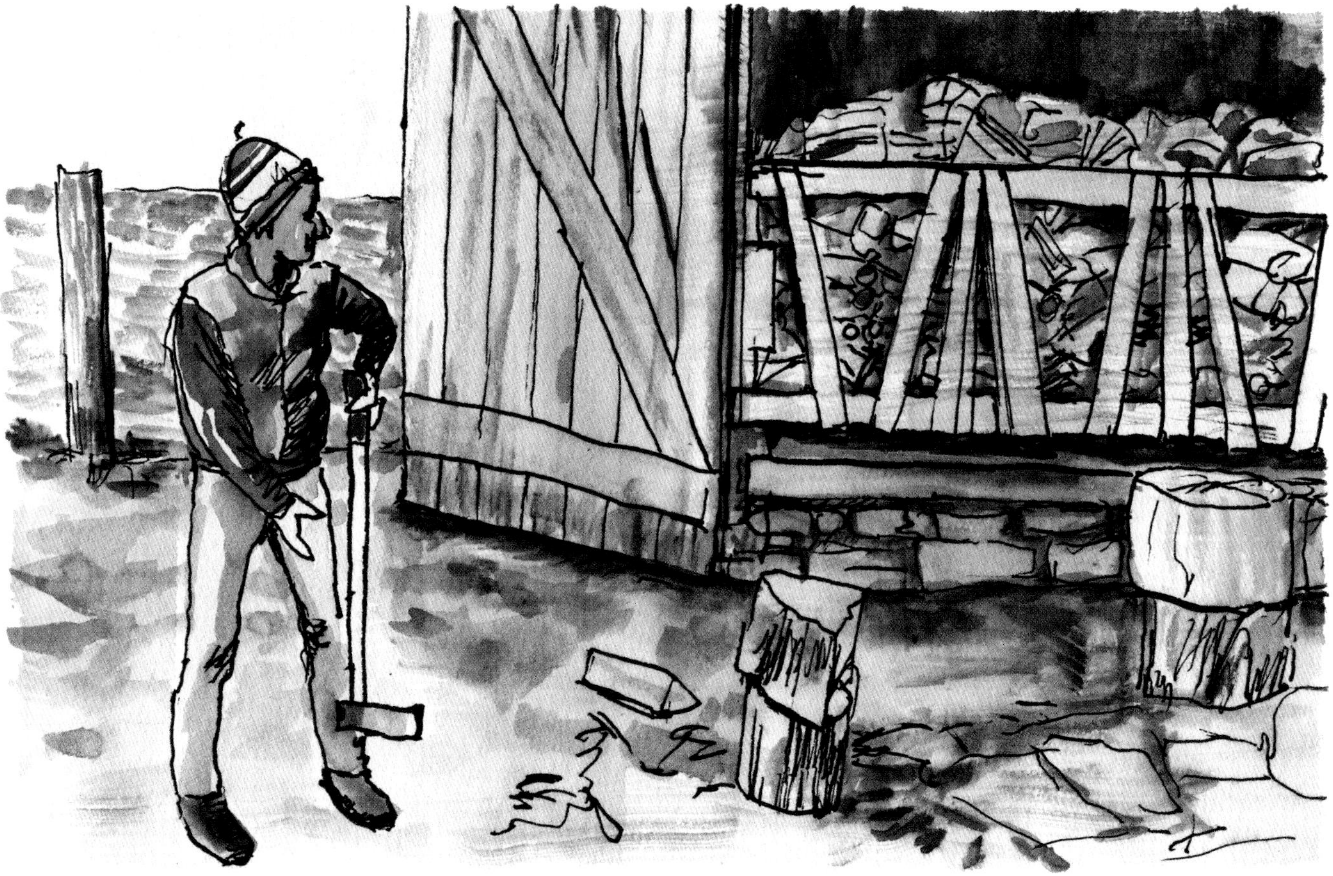

THURSDAY, DECEMBER 13

The laundry's been on the line for over a week. It wasn't dry enough to take down when it started to rain some days ago, so I left it for an extra rinse. That morning, I walked through the drizzle to the barn, fed and watered the animals, and moved the wood I'd split. Back at the house, I sat on the porch, listening to the quiet music that the rain, chickadees, jays, and titmice made together. The birds appeared to be continuously trading places in the trees, as if doing a square dance. When the rain came down a little harder, the birds disappeared, and I came inside. That night, the sky cleared and the temperature dropped. The clothes have been icicles ever since.

This morning, David is cleaning Jerusalem artichokes, carrots, salsify, claytonia, and turnips. He'll pack up the roots and greens and his fiddle, hand the produce off to the chef at a restaurant in Bourbon County, about 30 miles away, and stay to play some tunes for the diners. It was cold when he started harvesting, and now his scarf is draped over the digging fork. Maybe I'll get to take down the laundry this afternoon.

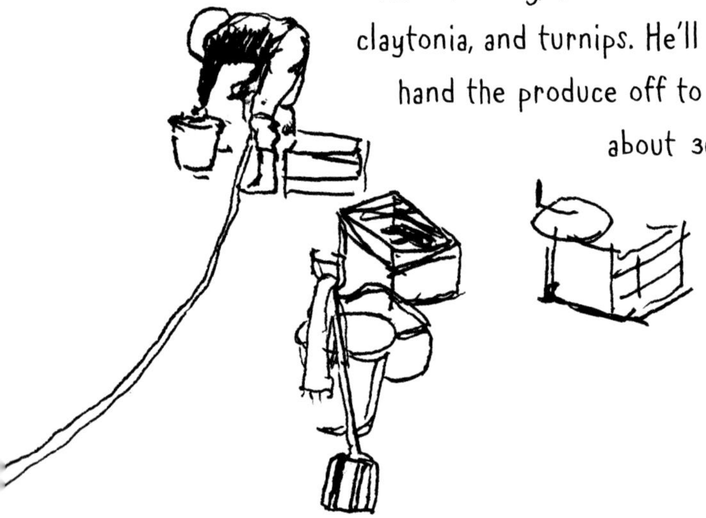

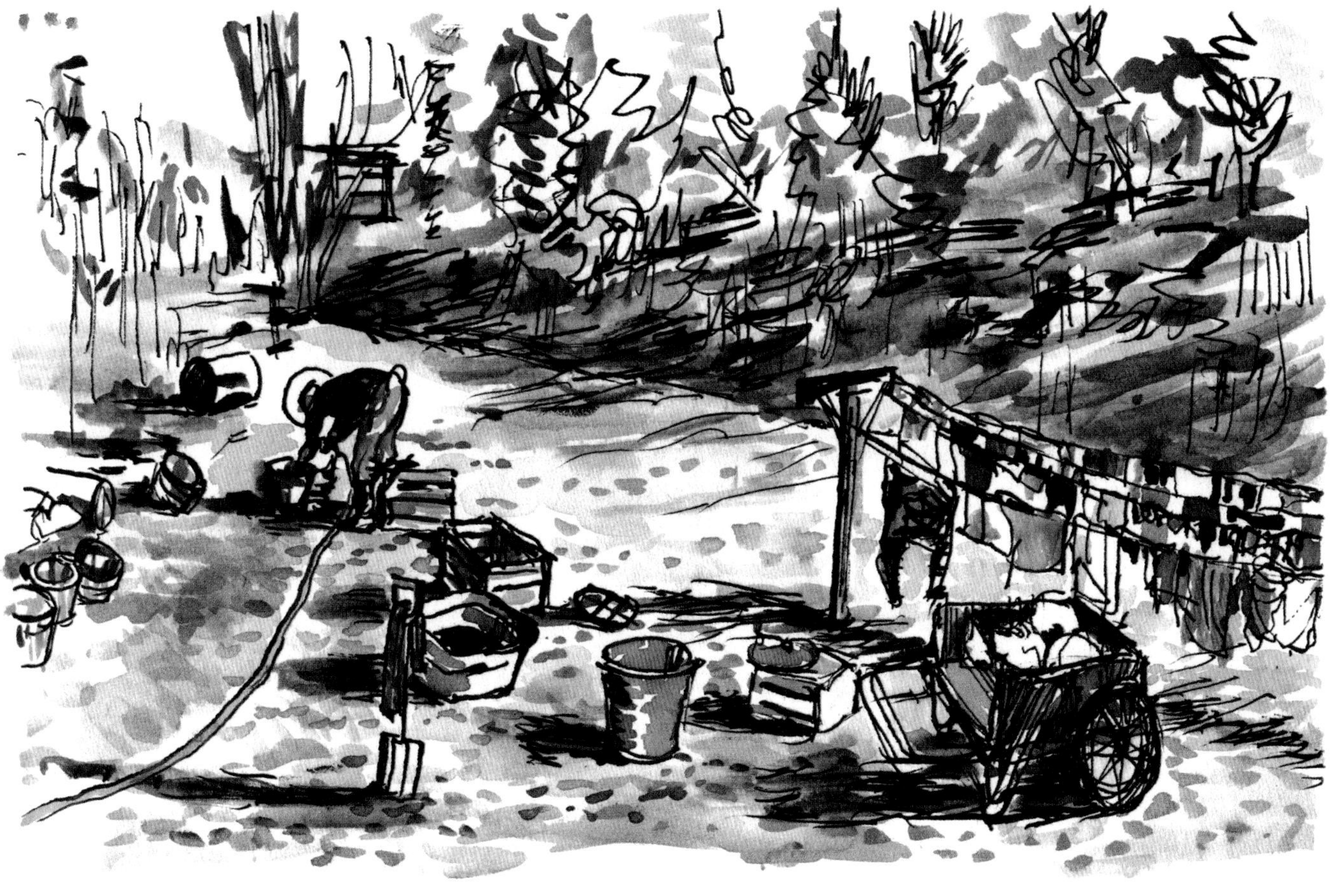

FRIDAY, DECEMBER 14

Vegetables call us out of quiet introspection at the start of the growing season and bind us from early spring to late fall to our community of CSA shareholders, a group of people who pay a lump sum at the beginning of the year to receive a weekly share of the farm's harvest.

They also bind us to our interns. Each year, people come to the farm and work for virtually no pay. Vegetables attract them here, call out to something in them that needs airing. Almost all of our interns have been well-schooled. Our Kentucky farm has been a stop on the way to Stanford and Cornell. Before coming here, though, most have never learned how to plant a seed and shepherd it to harvest.

All of the interns are gone. Now, only a scattering of root vegetables and hardy greens remain in the fields. I notice, drawing this, the quietness of the season. The sound of a fork striking soil, sinking in, prying up roots. The cover crop of winter wheat is a bluer green than the yellowish grass. I can sit and draw, and no one will see me but David, as he digs carrots on a warm December day.

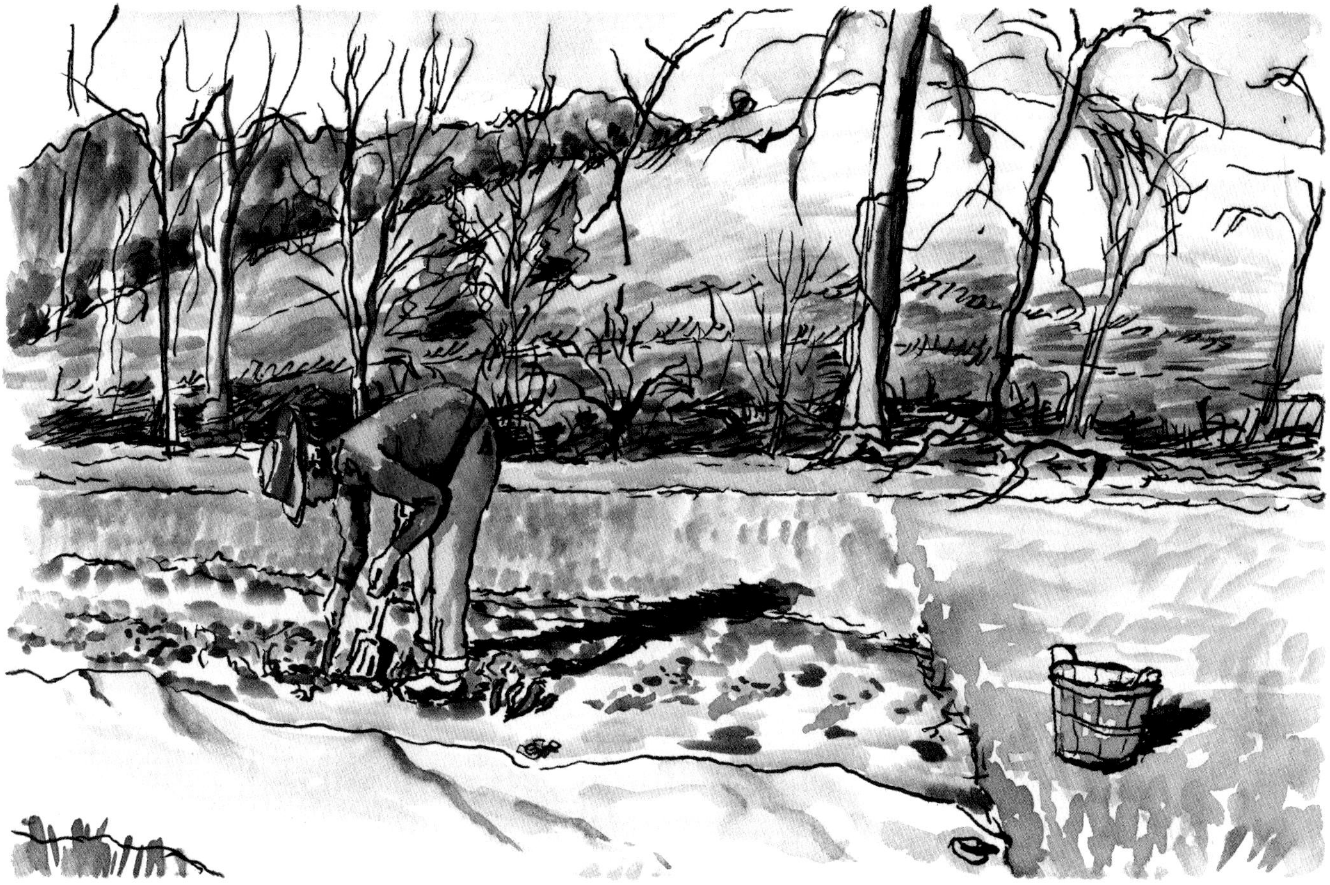

Monday, December 17

I'm just back from a visit with Sandy, two miles up the road. I pass by the Barnes's place on the way. Dirt tracks uphill echo the bluish pavement of Johnson Road. Old appliances and junk cars frame the tracks. Rotting rolls of hay mix into muddy ruts down by the gate. Sights like this, of land that's broken and raw, are common along Crooked Creek.

Sandy is an Episcopal minister and opened the Cedar Hill Retreat Center some years ago. I called her because I wanted to find out what she's up to. She has eleven dogs, twelve goats, a bunch of hens. For many years she was a vegetarian but began to eat meat when she realized it was a good way to support small local farms. She is one hundred percent convinced, she says, that eating meat makes good sense, and even though she's slaughtered and processed her own chickens, she's tender-hearted and has trouble killing animals herself. Her attachment, she says, holds her back from being more than a novice farmer. She's held a variety of retreats at Cedar Hill, including one in which people speak with trees. "I hug them," she confesses. "I tell them I love them and thank them for what they do for me and the world."

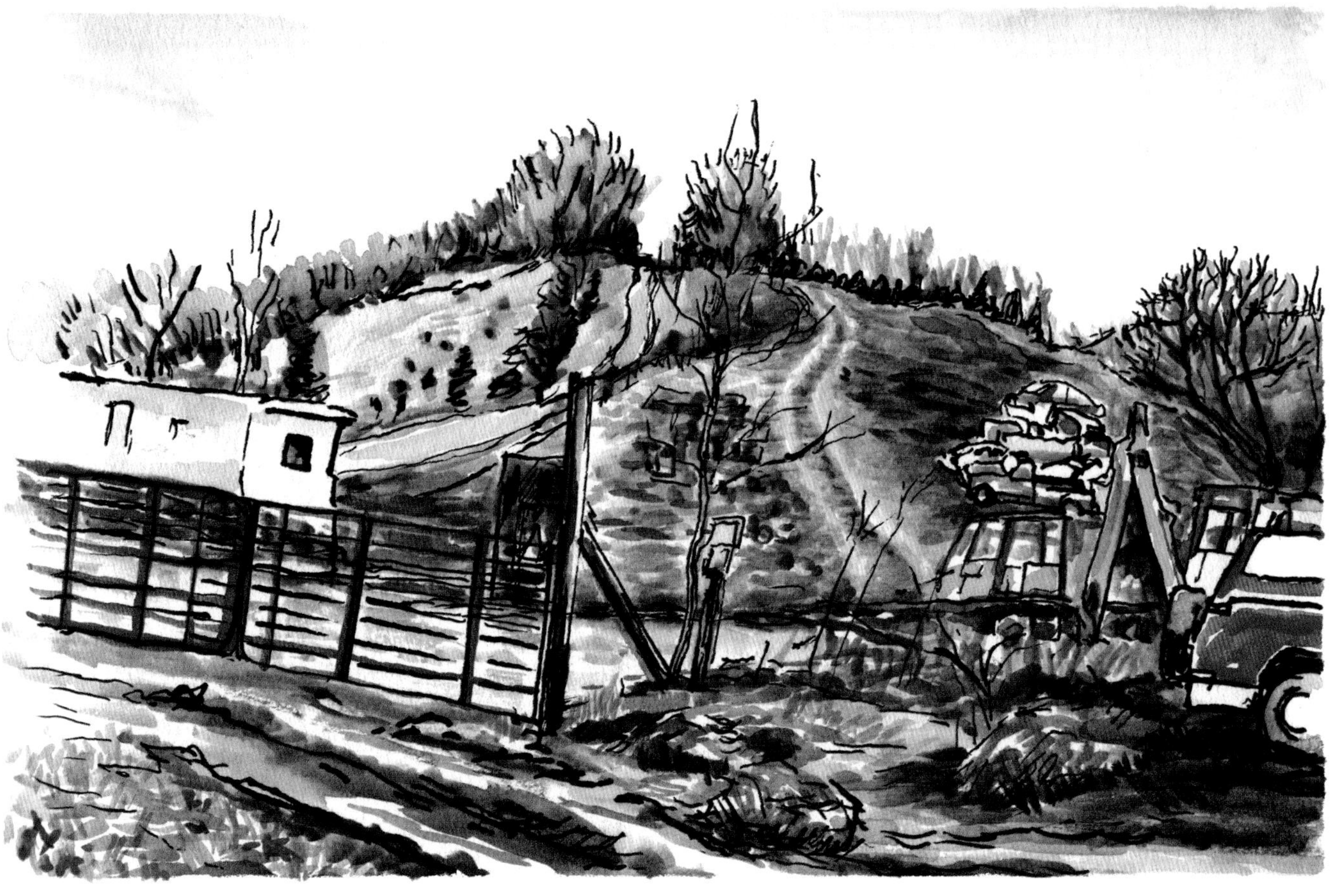

FRIDAY, DECEMBER 21

Snow blows outside. Phoebe is on her second day of winter break. She drops loose wads of hay over the steel gate for the cattle, Lily, Cassie, and Lou, then goes out and throws snowballs with David. I split some wood and cart two loads back to the house.

Last week, a man shot and killed twenty children at a school in Connecticut. The administration at Phoebe's school responded by instituting a policy on Monday in which no one other than students, teachers, and staff would be allowed into the building. For weeks, Phoebe has been practicing a fiddle tune that she was invited to play for the school's holiday program. "I might need to cancel," the principal told me.

In the end, we and other parents protested enough to make the program go forward as planned. Phoebe kicked off with the tune she'd been practicing, Cripple Creek. Students in colonial outfits danced the Virginia Reel. The band included another student and a teacher on guitar, David on upright bass, and the principal on banjo. Then the children sang carols of peace and celebration.

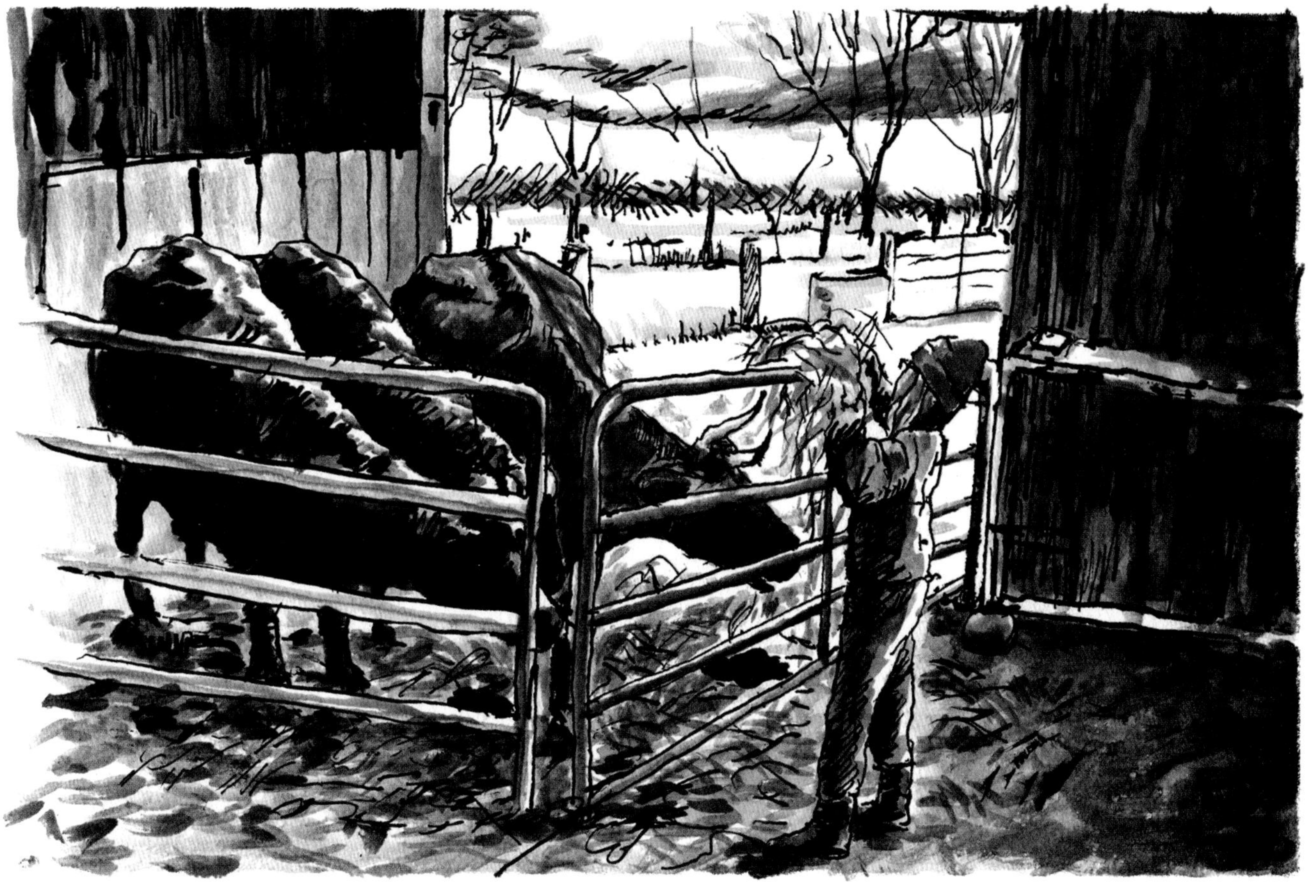

Sunday, December 23

It takes about ten trips to the creek with two five-gallon buckets to fill the water trough. I only made four trips today: I have Christmas treats to make.

A week ago, we celebrated Hanukkah, and now we'll celebrate Christmas. When I volunteered recently at Phoebe's school book fair, I relaxed into conversation with other moms about food, farming, parenting, and facing the death of our own parents. All of us grow gardens, and we compared notes about what we'd put up this season. The librarian, who has always been kind and friendly to me, said, "Oh, I like everyone, I think everyone's okay, as long as you believe in Jesus."

Her words conjured my Jewish mother's face, my connection to maternal ancestors whose lives were upended or destroyed by antisemitism. I hope Phoebe will gain strength from that same connection, even when someone's friendly smile has a dark undercurrent.

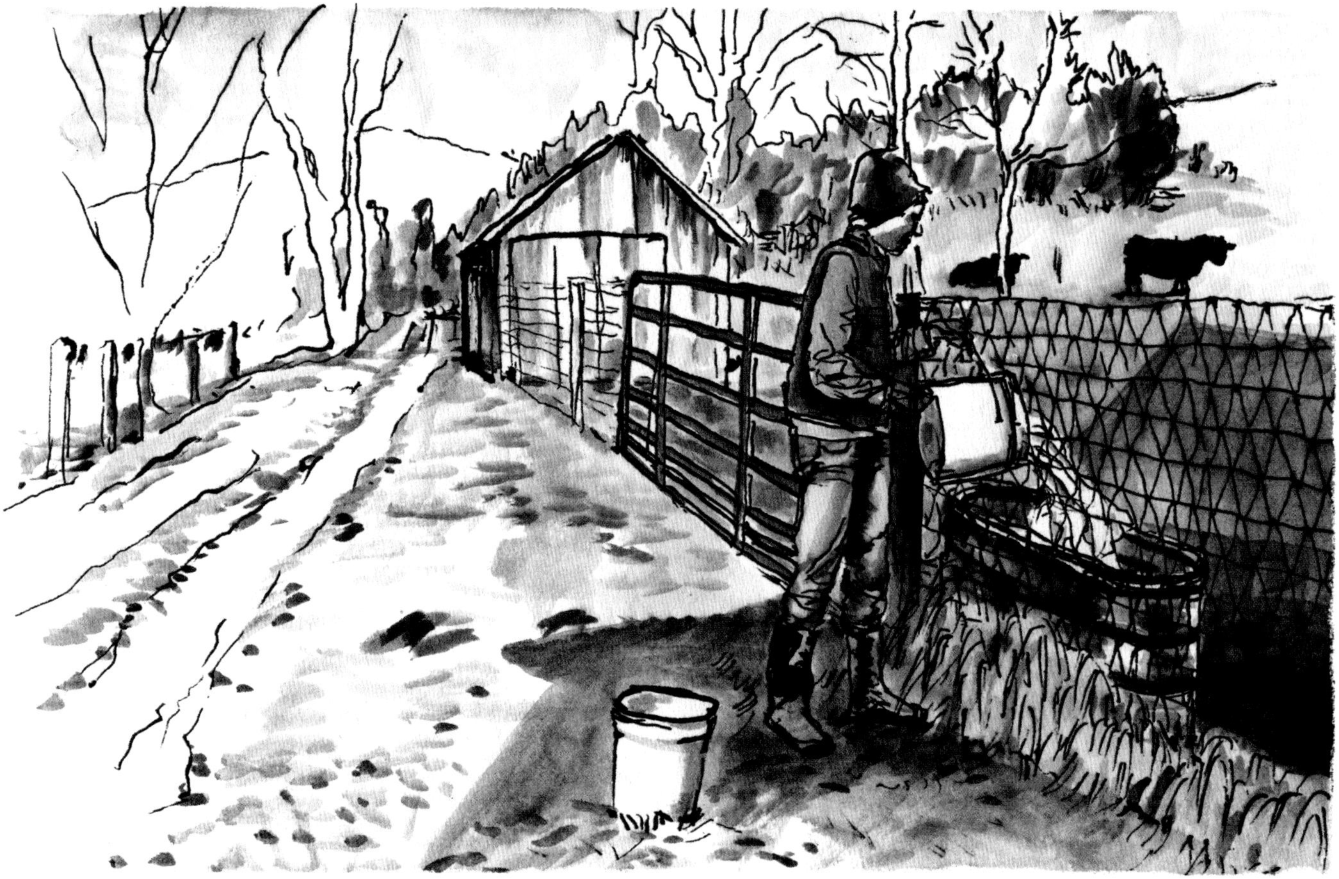

WEDNESDAY, DECEMBER 26

We've suddenly entered a more solitary season. All day, cold rain. I straighten up the house, and then the day decides to think about ending. The three of us go for a walk near dusk. We gather some branches full of juniper berries: I've heard they're good for seasoning sauerkraut. We'll dry them slowly beside the woodstove and keep them in a jar on our pantry shelves for next year's cabbages.

On the ridgetop, sleet bounces off our jackets and stings our cheeks. By the time we get back to the house, the air swirls with thick clusters of snowflakes. We go to the barn and haul a load of firewood to the house. Phoebe's already gone in and is warming up by the fire.

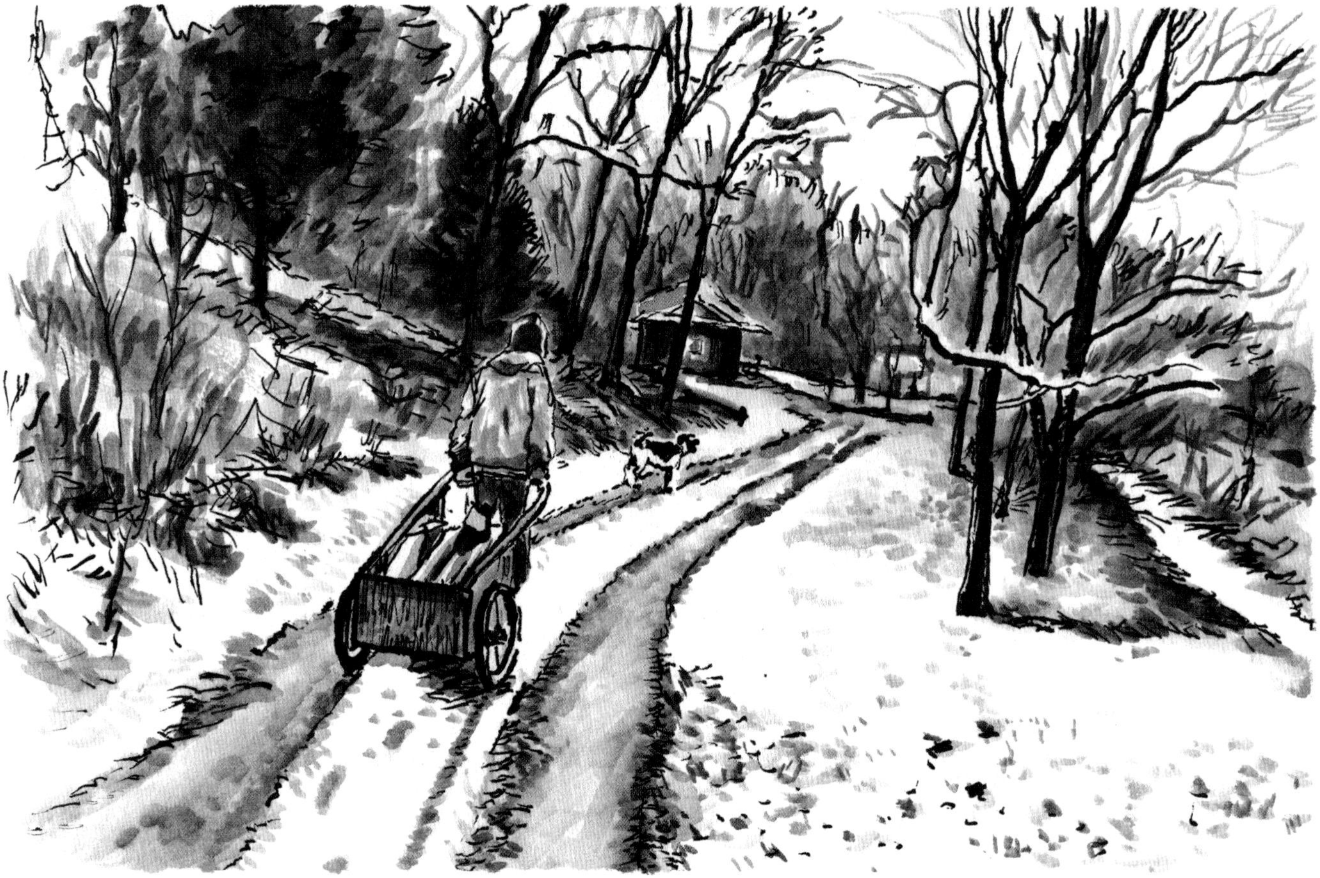

MONDAY, DECEMBER 31

On New Year's Eve, the farm fields and pastures are blanketed with snow. More than half of our two hundred acres are wooded. The snow lies in patches here. David has been enjoying his winter break from field labor by building this tiny cabin. He's using only materials gathered from within a hundred yards or so of this spot, apart from a handful of screws purchased at the hardware store in Carlisle. A fallen barn in the creek bottom has supplied the metal sheets for the roof and boards for the floor; young Eastern red cedars, notched and stacked, form the walls. We joke that when we tire of the hustle and bustle of the farmhouse, we'll retire back here.

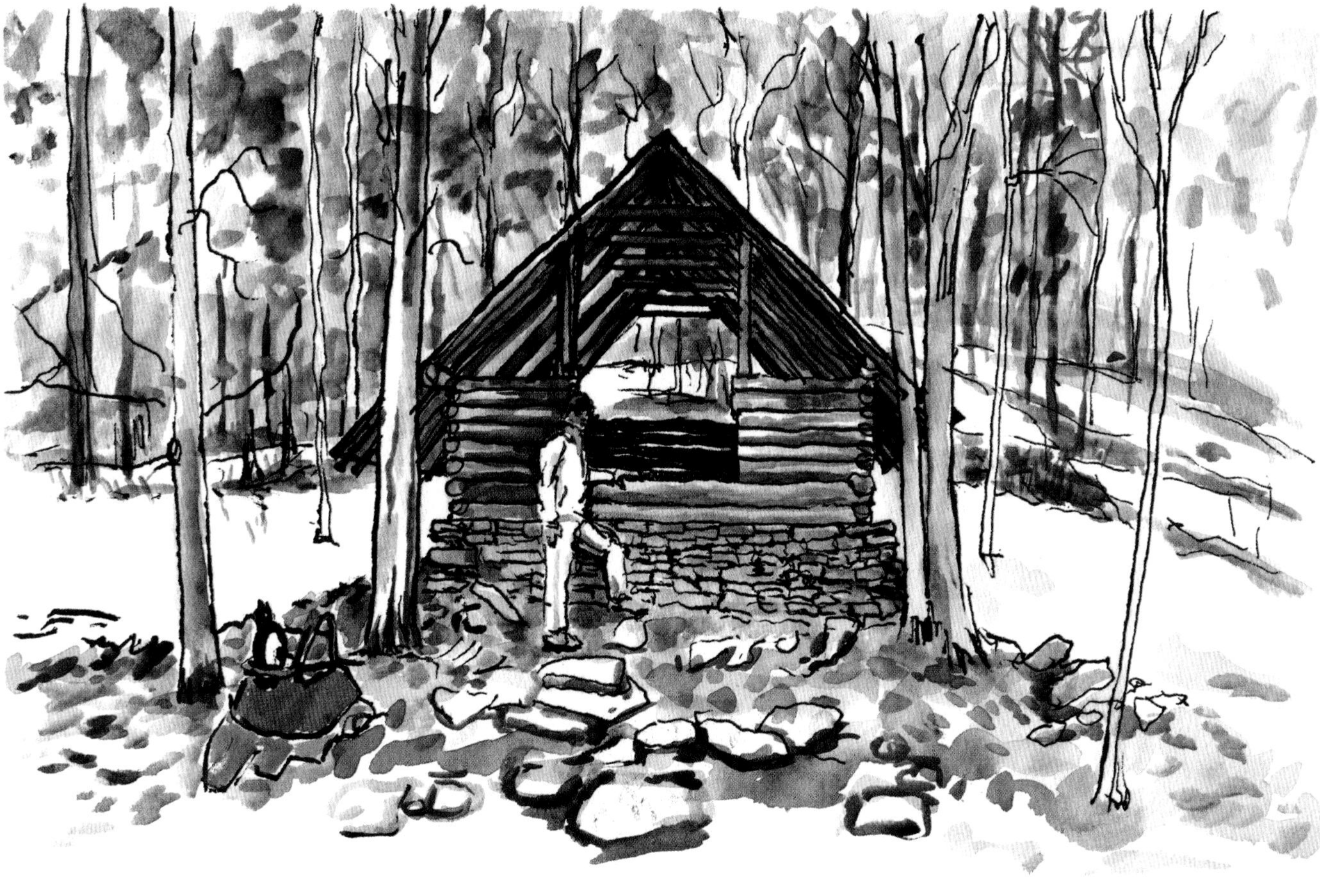

FRIDAY, JANUARY 4

Winter work: cutting wood, fence mending, brush clearing, repairs, and maintenance. A lifetime could be spent trimming trees: along the road, near the power lines, around the deer fence. David limbs up some on Crooked Creek, ahead of the crew with the slope mower that chews branches to a ragged pulp. If it's clean enough when they arrive, they'll skip our section of road.

Neighbor Steve comes by on a four-wheeler, pistol in his holster, searching for someone who he says has trespassed on his place. Every time Steve goes by, he says something to one or the other of us about trespassing and guns.

"It's cold out here," Steve observes.

"Probably not as cold for me as it is for you, riding on that four-wheeler," David replies.

"Yeah," says Steve, "but I'm out here for a *reason.*"

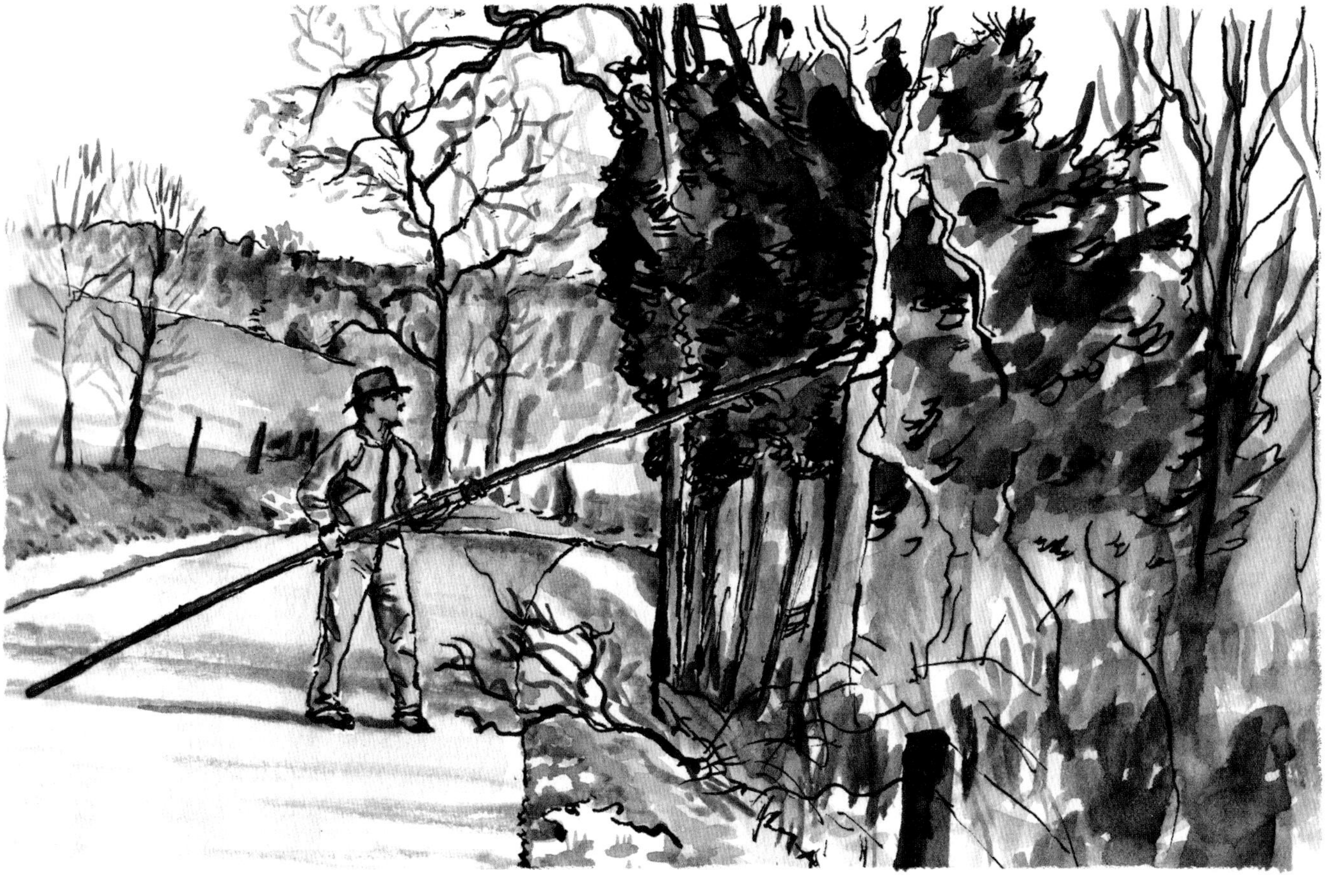

Saturday, January 5

Our new shredder makes mulch of the branches David has finished cutting along Crooked Creek. We haul cut bundles to it from the narrow bottom between creek and fence, then pick up creekside trash. Bando the dog sits in front of the next round of branches to be dragged to the shredder.

Creek trash tells a more intimate story than the roadside variety. Crap tossed from car windows—bottles, cans, fast-food wrappers—seems sprung with hostility. If fragments of Styrofoam cups we gather from the roadside had voices, they would say, *I don't give a shit.* Items we find in the creek, though, especially after a heavy rain, are laced with regret: a child's mud-caked white dress, with a pink ribbon sash; a hummingbird feeder; the plastic roof of a playhouse. I found a NO TRESPASSING sign once, defying its own mission. About a year ago, in a frantic hurry to get somewhere, we left a willow-ware plate on top of the car, full of scrambled eggs. I found a fragment of that plate wedged into the creek bank today.

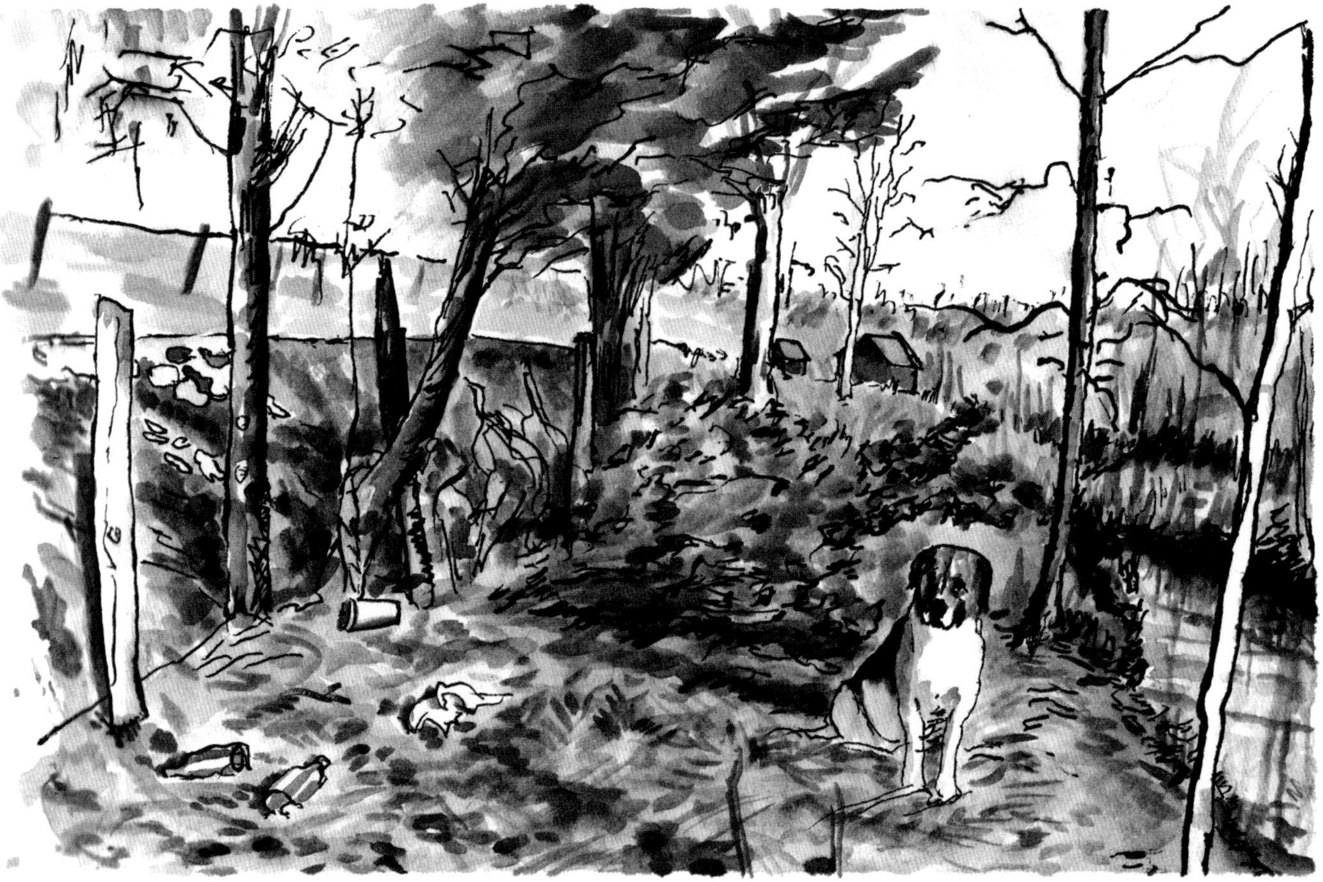

SUNDAY, JANUARY 6

We live in tobacco growing country. The chicken house was once the farm's stripping room. It contained a wood stove that kept a family warm while they spent winter days stripping tobacco leaves off of their stalks. An older friend, a writer raised in a tobacco-farming family, told me that storytellers spent all year honing their craft in preparation for hours spent in the stripping room. This, my friend thinks, has something to do with why Kentucky has been home to so many great storytellers.

We've cut a small door in the side of the house for the hens to come and go during the daytime. I left that door open yesterday, assuming David would close it when he came in from evening work. But he didn't see it open and told me this morning after doing barn chores that four chickens of our ten are gone. The culprit could have been a fox, raccoon, or mink, but it was more likely our dog, Bando, who is a rascal. I come out to view the damage, and here is the steer, Lou, on the wrong side of the fence. The white feathers on the lane are so plentiful they remind me of when the plum tree—which is right above this spot—drops its blossoms in spring.

I've had an ink accident, so let's say Lou pooped while out.

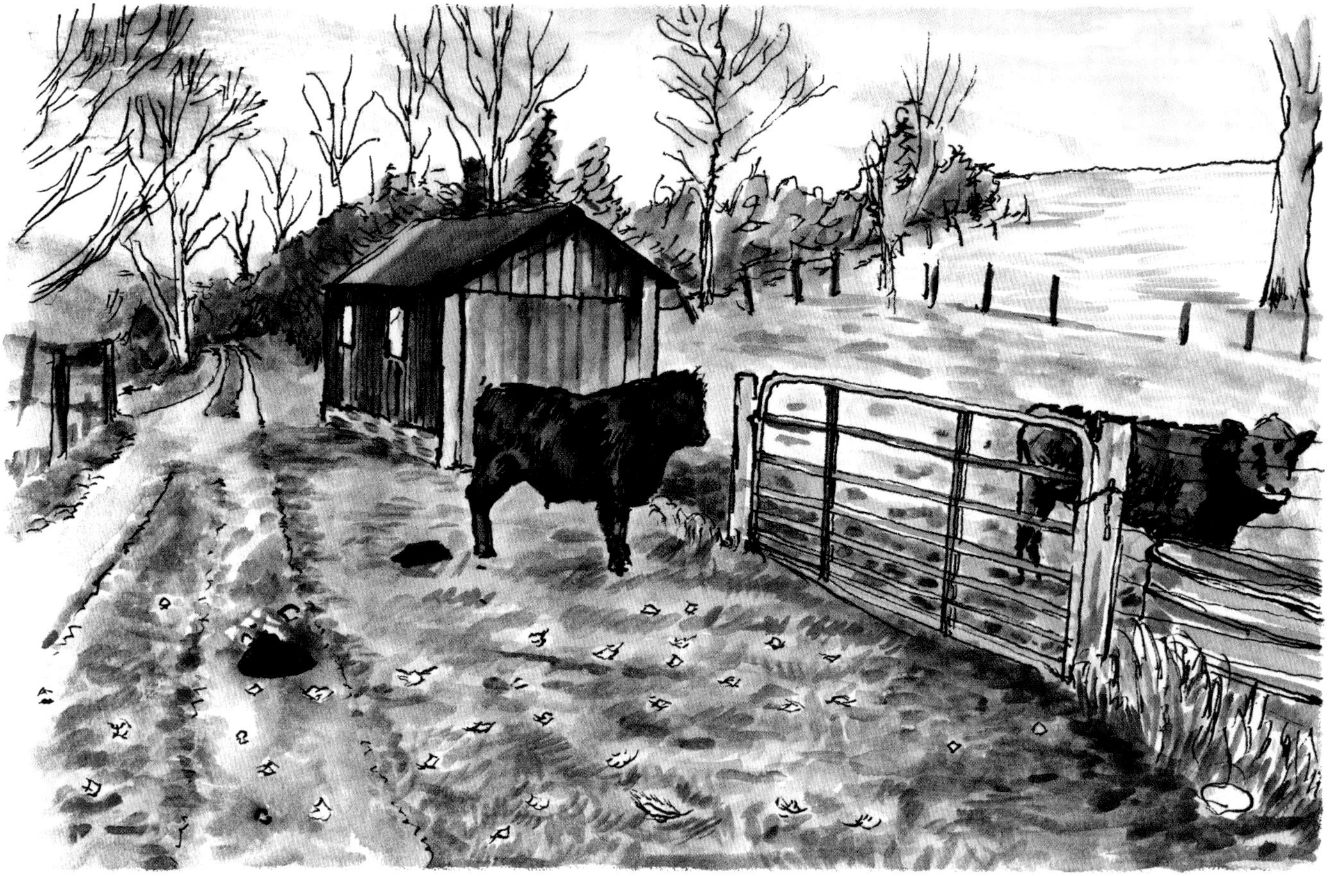

MONDAY, JANUARY 7

This house was once a one-room tenant shack. The kitchen, a long narrow shotgun affair, was tacked onto its backside. Upon cutting an opening between the kitchen and the older part of the house, we found a layer of newspaper glued onto the rough oak boards that once formed the house's exterior walls, pasted over with layer upon layer of wallpaper. We salvaged one scrap with a date and a partial headline, which we've since lost, but I remember it was from 1906 and said something about Teddy Roosevelt.

I've spent much of the last fourteen years of my life here, cooking, washing dishes. We've made some improvements, but it's still a homely room, with a floor of partially rotten, splintery wood boards, a sagging low ceiling, holes here and there patched up with plywood or even cardboard. The kitchen lays bare much that we ought to do, but have not yet done. I sometimes feel ashamed that I've settled for its shabbiness, but I can step outside when I want beauty. When guests come, I employ the stopgap skill of transforming the space through the magic of cookery. A room filled with the scent of baking bread, of roasting vegetables, of onions sizzling in olive oil, grabs on to the hem of loveliness and takes a brief ride.

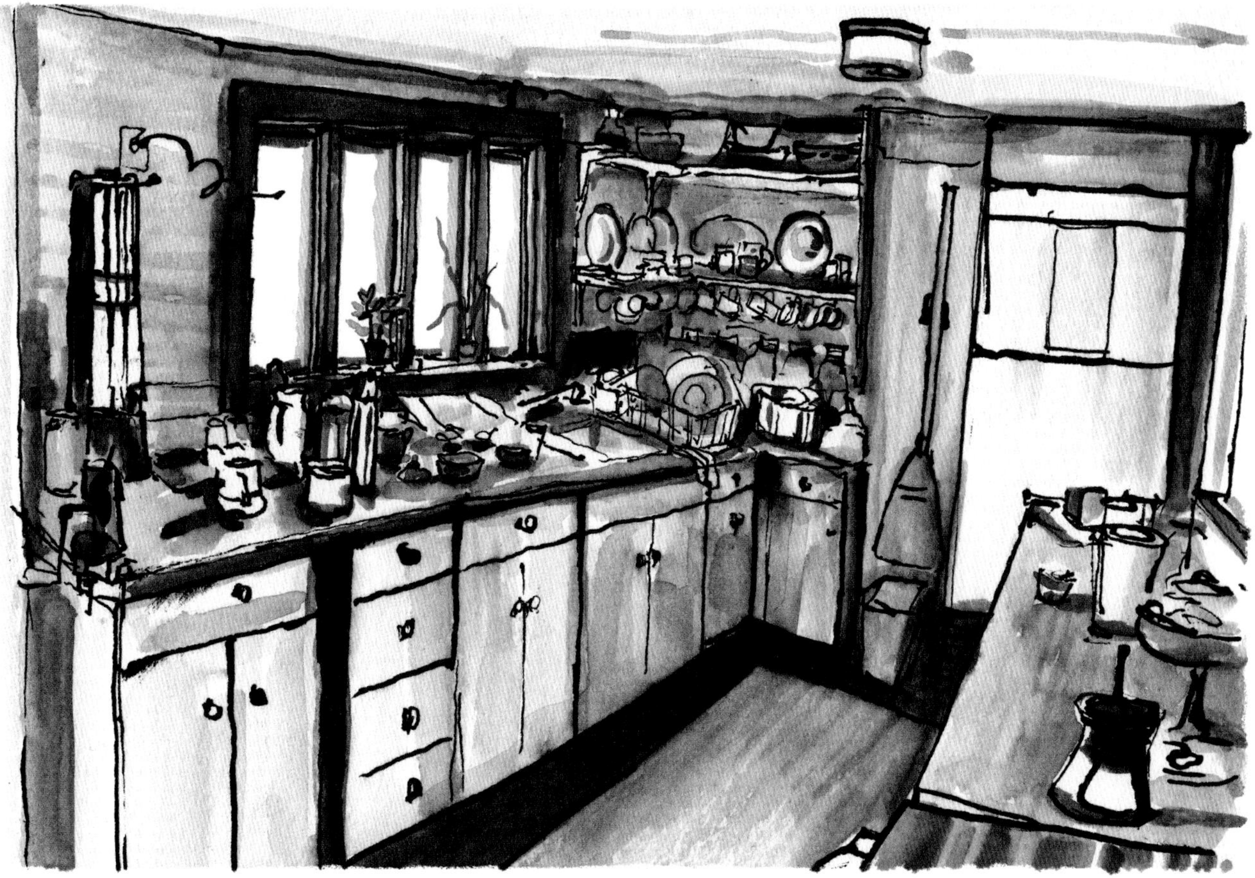

FRIDAY, JANUARY 11

At 3:30 I go to the bridge to meet Phoebe's bus. The snow is gone, and Crooked Creek is flowing. I've just found a package from a friend in the mailbox that contains a few funny hats: one fuzzy, with droopy rabbit ears, another the shape of a limp knitted ice-cream cone. Phoebe immediately chooses the red one with black devil horns.

Her math teacher quizzed the class today on what they ate for breakfast, Phoebe tells me, on the theory that those who skip it and those who misbehave are largely the same population. The results were charted in a Venn diagram. "I told her I had oatmeal," Phoebe laughed. "I didn't tell her what I put on it." The oats were steel-cut, seasoned with tamari, rice vinegar, toasted sesame seeds, chile flakes, and seaweed.

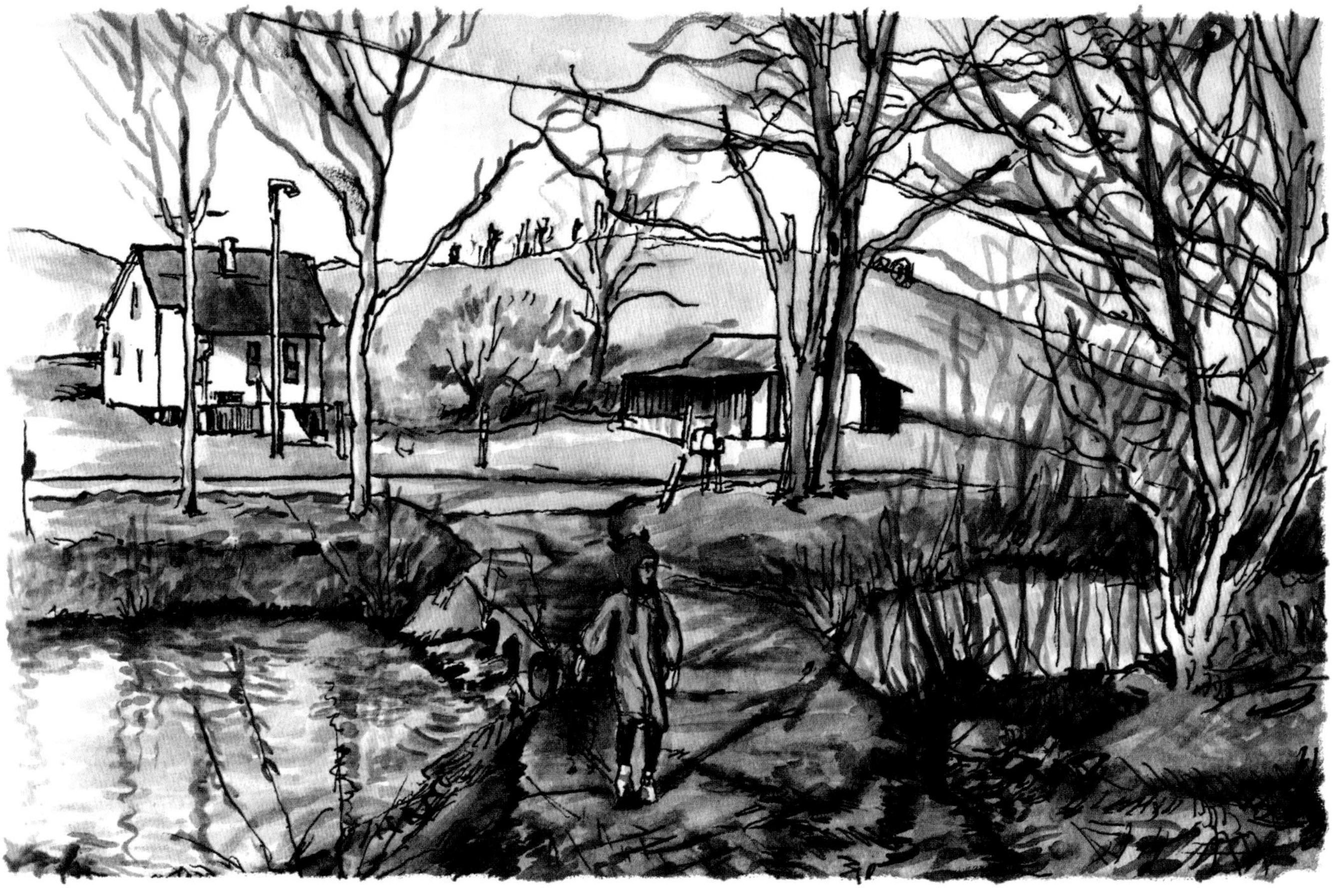

SATURDAY, JANUARY 12

The cedar cut from the hill behind the house and decorated in December has had all of its ornaments removed. We drag it to the barn and put it in the goats' trough. Myrtle and Hermione nibble on it halfheartedly. They prefer fresh trees. Roma the cat peers down from her nest atop the hay.

Each December we cut one of the thousands of cedars that darken our hills. When Europeans began to colonize this land, their lives were consumed with felling trees. Cedars are pioneers: they grow quickly, providing cover for the deciduous species that follow, with no help from us: hickories, black walnuts, tulip poplars, sassafras, sugar maples, redbuds, oaks, cherries, pawpaws. Our neighbors frowned when we allowed cedars to claim the steeper hillsides. Local farmers traditionally grow tobacco in the bottomlands and keep the hills in pasture.

We arrived here with a sense of urgency to do our part to oppose the planet's deforestation. As trees claim a little more of our horizon each year, though, I feel an urge to apologize to our forebears for letting the trees have their hard-earned land.

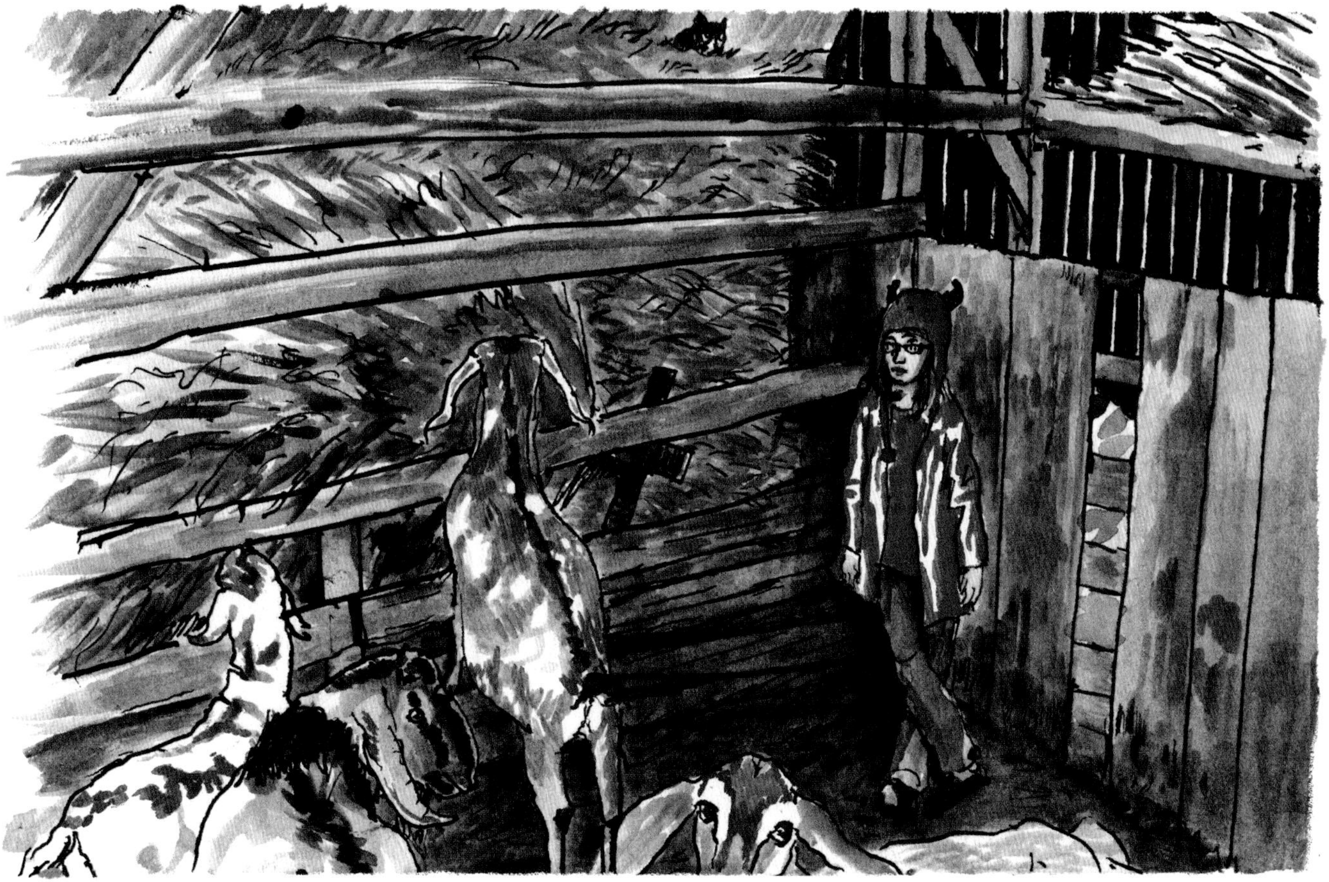

SUNDAY, JANUARY 13

About a month ago, friends who were visiting for the first time called by phone from the road, saying they didn't see the bridge they were supposed to cross. I biked out the lane and immediately saw why they were confused. It had been raining that day, and like today, the water just covered the concrete bridge by an inch or so. It's safe enough to drive across, safe enough to allow our little devil to wade into. She stands there for a long time, perfectly still, with her hands held up beside her shoulders. As a baby, when she got fussy, I carried her here to listen to the water rushing through the culverts. It tended to calm her down, and now, I think, the sounds of this particular place are nestled deep in her inner ear.

A few times a year, the creek gets so high that we can't cross. David's cousin Cay warned us about this before we bought the farm from her fifteen years ago. "We usually like it when that happens," she said. "We have a good excuse to stay home." She knew her audience: we were not discouraged. Since then, though, I've sometimes worried about what would happen if we needed to get out in a hurry during a flood. Especially when I was nine months pregnant.

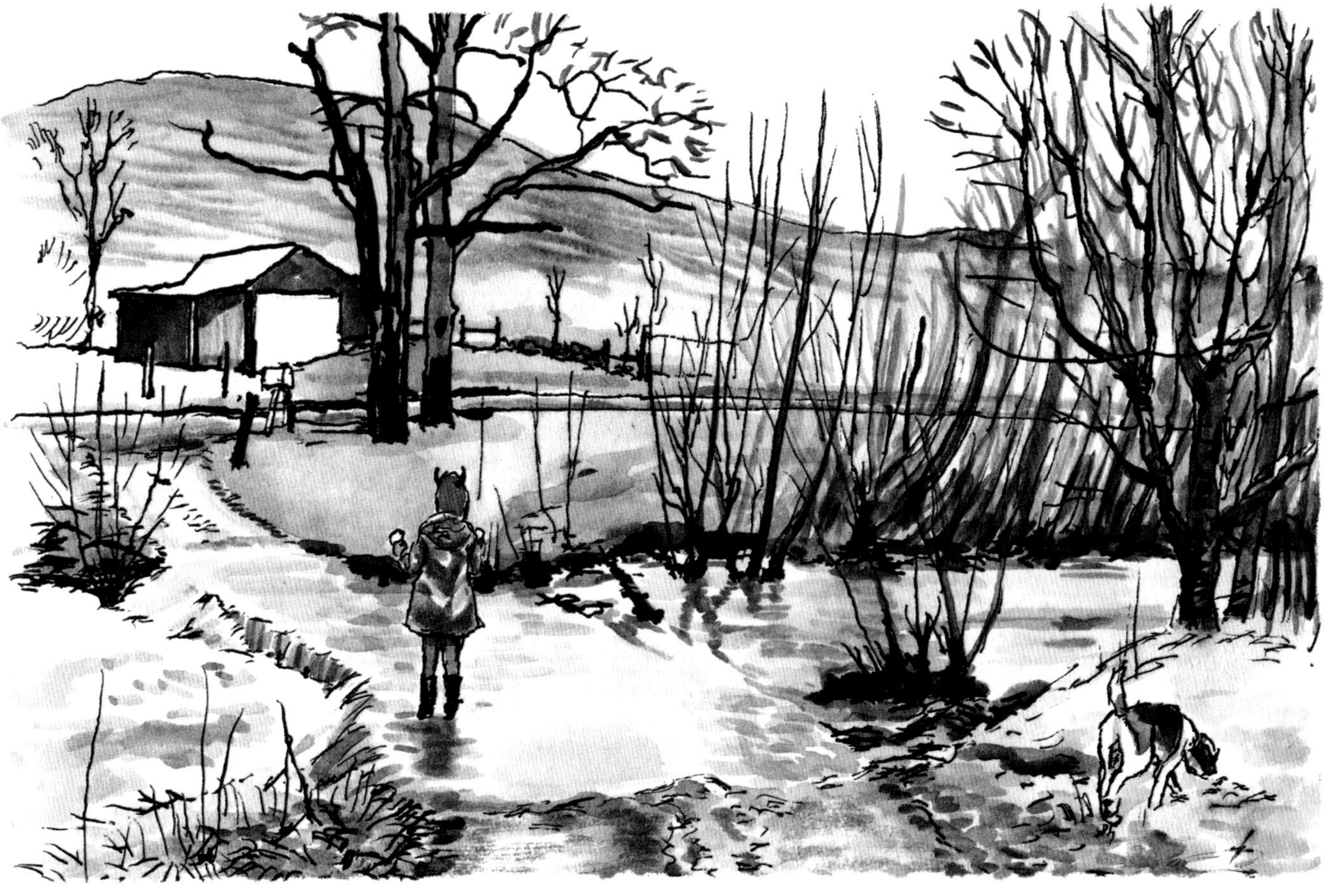

SATURDAY, JANUARY 19

Father and daughter are having a philosophical argument about eating the steer, Lou, who is soon to be slaughtered. After darkness falls, Phoebe and I sit together in the hayloft talking about Lou. She's angry, she says, and afraid, and sad. I understand, I tell her. My first introduction to the world of farm animals was through *Charlotte's Web* and *Watership Down*, books in which animals are virtually human, and farmers are among the villains. It has taken becoming a farmer myself to learn just how closely woven life and death are on the farm, how a farmer can be bound by affection to animals, even while killing and eating them.

Like most farmers, we feel the role of economic necessity in nearly all of the decisions we make. I want to protect my child from the stark requirements of that necessity, so that she explores the outer reaches of her own imagination. I also want to teach her about it, so she will know her own privilege, respect the limits of our lives, and know in her bones the feeling of hard work. As it is, she only works on the farm under duress.

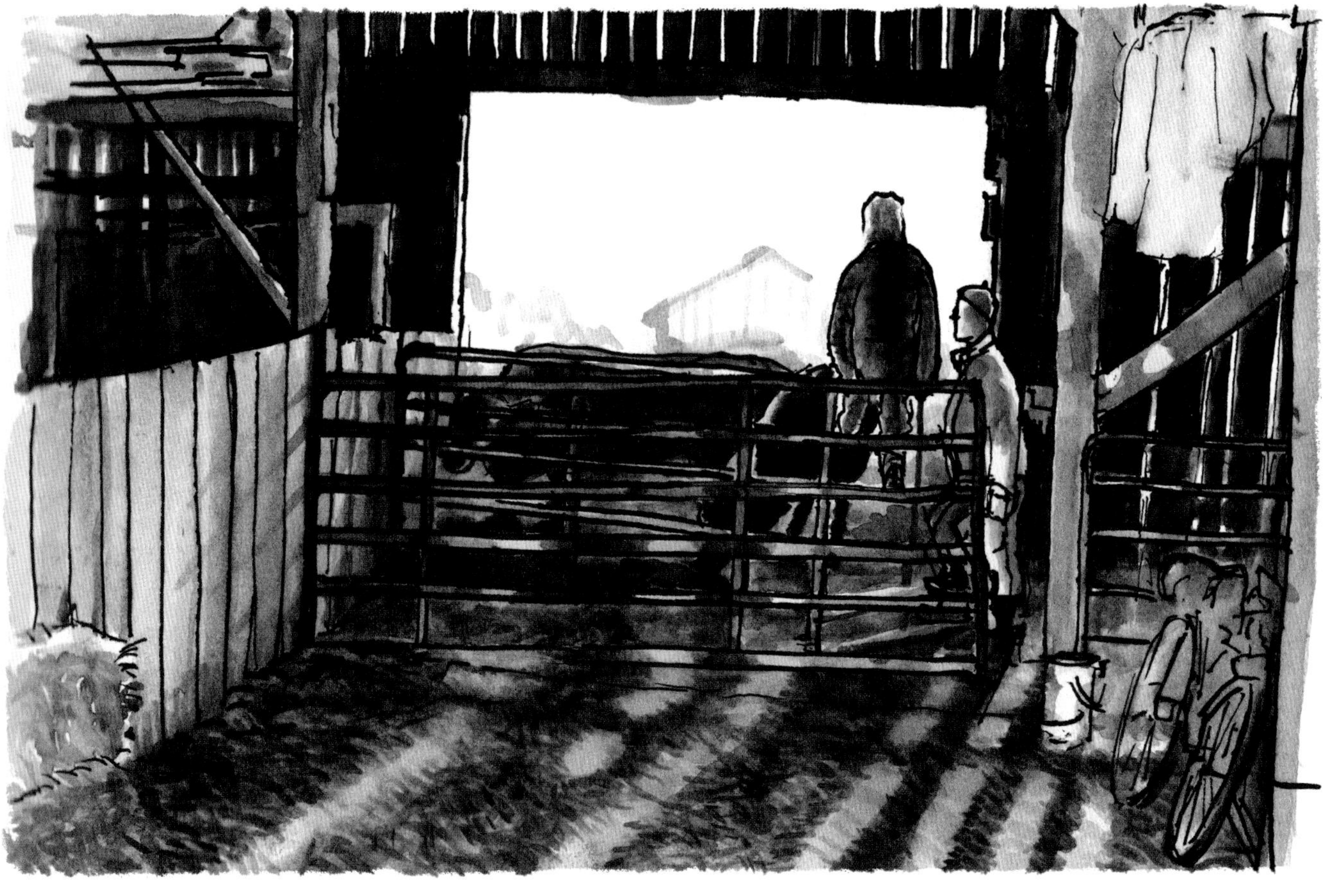

TUESDAY, JANUARY 22

"A swarm in May is worth a load of hay; a swarm in June is worth a silver spoon; a swarm in July isn't worth a fly." So goes an old beekeeper's saw. These two hives were August swarms. What's worth less than no fly? Yet after an hour or two of humdrum hoeing in the late summer heat, the electric buzz of a cluster of renegade bees on their flight in search of a new home made us drop our tools and follow, even though catching them meant that we'd have to feed and coddle them through the months ahead. (A swarm is not hard to catch, if it lands in the right place: the bees cluster around their queen, and if you can shake her into a box, the others will follow.)

Our porch thermometer measured six degrees this morning before dawn: the coldest of winter so far. David has wrapped the hives in an old torn tarp to keep the bees from freezing. Because we captured the swarms too late in the season for them to build up their own honey stores, he gave them some excess frames of comb from our more established hive.

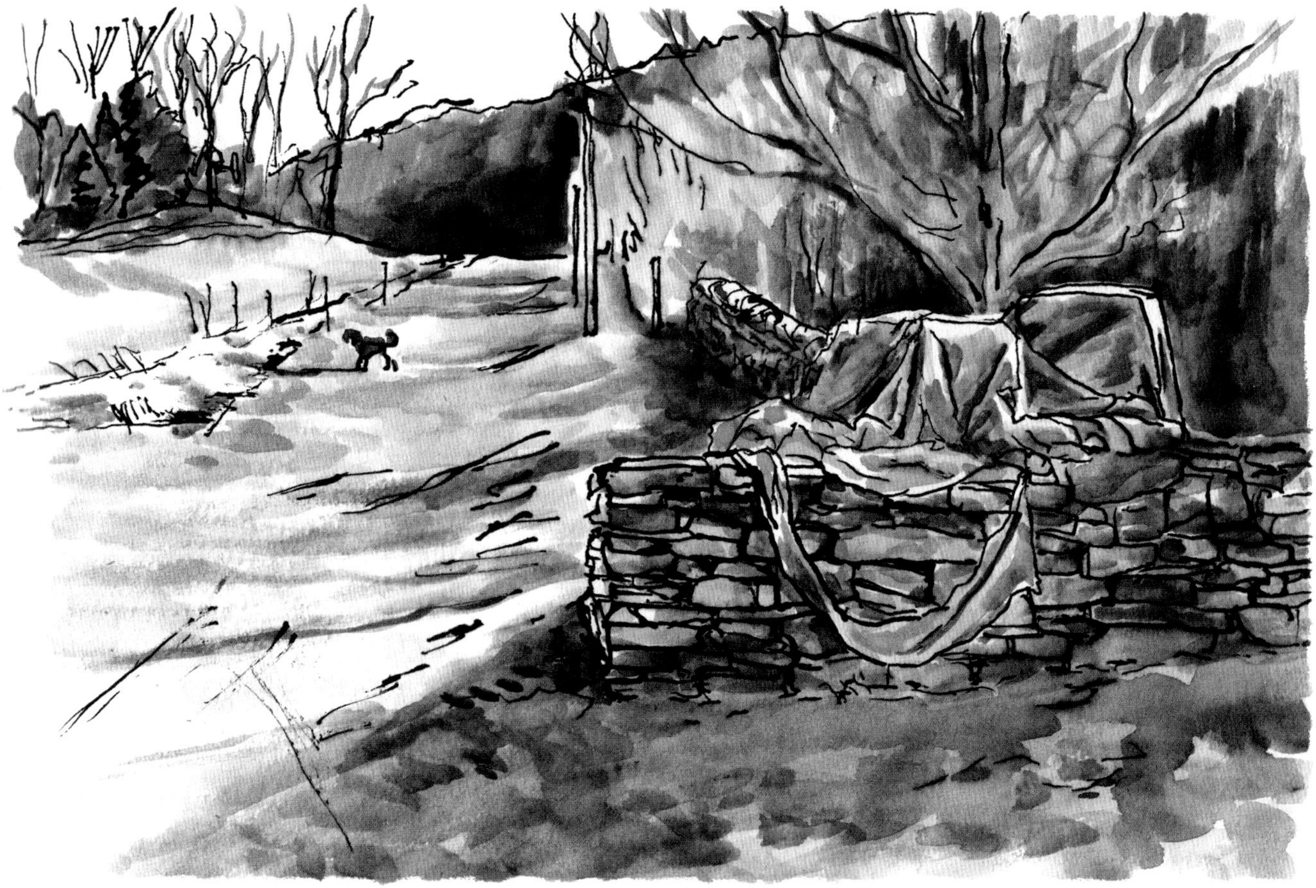

THURSDAY, JANUARY 24

A branch of Crooked Creek bisects our hilly farm. An old-timer who once lived here told us it was known as Straight Run, so it seems we live at the junction of the direct and the meandering. The run has created, on either side, a long narrow stretch of fertile bottomland where our crops are grown and where our house and barn sit.

David and Phoebe skate on the frozen run. David finally gets to try out the skates he scored at Goodwill. We haven't found any thrift-store skates in my size, so I slide on the slick ice in my muck boots. Phoebe's in the skates she got as a Christmas gift from Grandma Cate a year ago: this is the first thick ice we've had since then. On the banks are willow stubs and trunks that David recently pollarded to keep them from growing into the power lines above. We'll use the willow whips for staking peas in spring, and the stumps will soon sprout again.

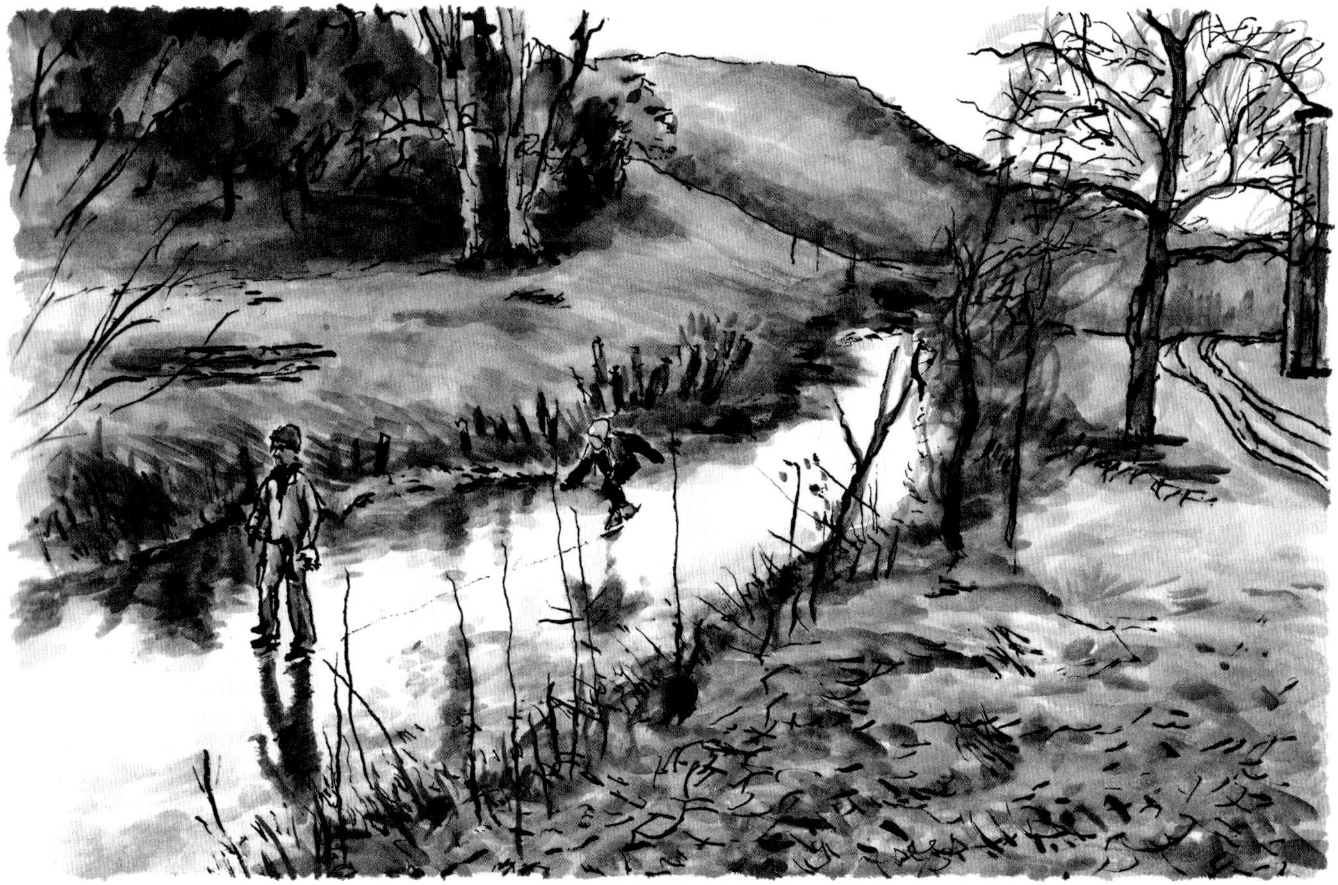

SUNDAY, JANUARY 27

We walk in the woods in the late afternoon. Phoebe is down in the run, stomping on crunchy, wet ice. It's beginning to melt but is still strong enough to hold her. David stands behind a pile of four offset chunks of wood, in the center of the circle he has made of the mess of fallen trees and branches that once lay around this spot, and looks up at the treetops.

I am happy that he felt compelled to make this impractical thing. The rigors of farming and the stark calculus of a farm's economy can wreak havoc on the practice of art. Since we moved to the farm fourteen years ago, I've attempted to protect that practice by segregating art and farming, by building a moat around my artmaking and retreating to it as a refuge from the farm's demands. Farming was David's dream, not mine. Art has been an act of resistance to the reality of my life on the ground.

But what is happening here? David's making art from fallen trees, and I am drawing the lines of our daily lives. I'm still defiant of the farm's relentless need (See a mess? Draw it!), but these drawings are also leading me deeper into my life in this place.

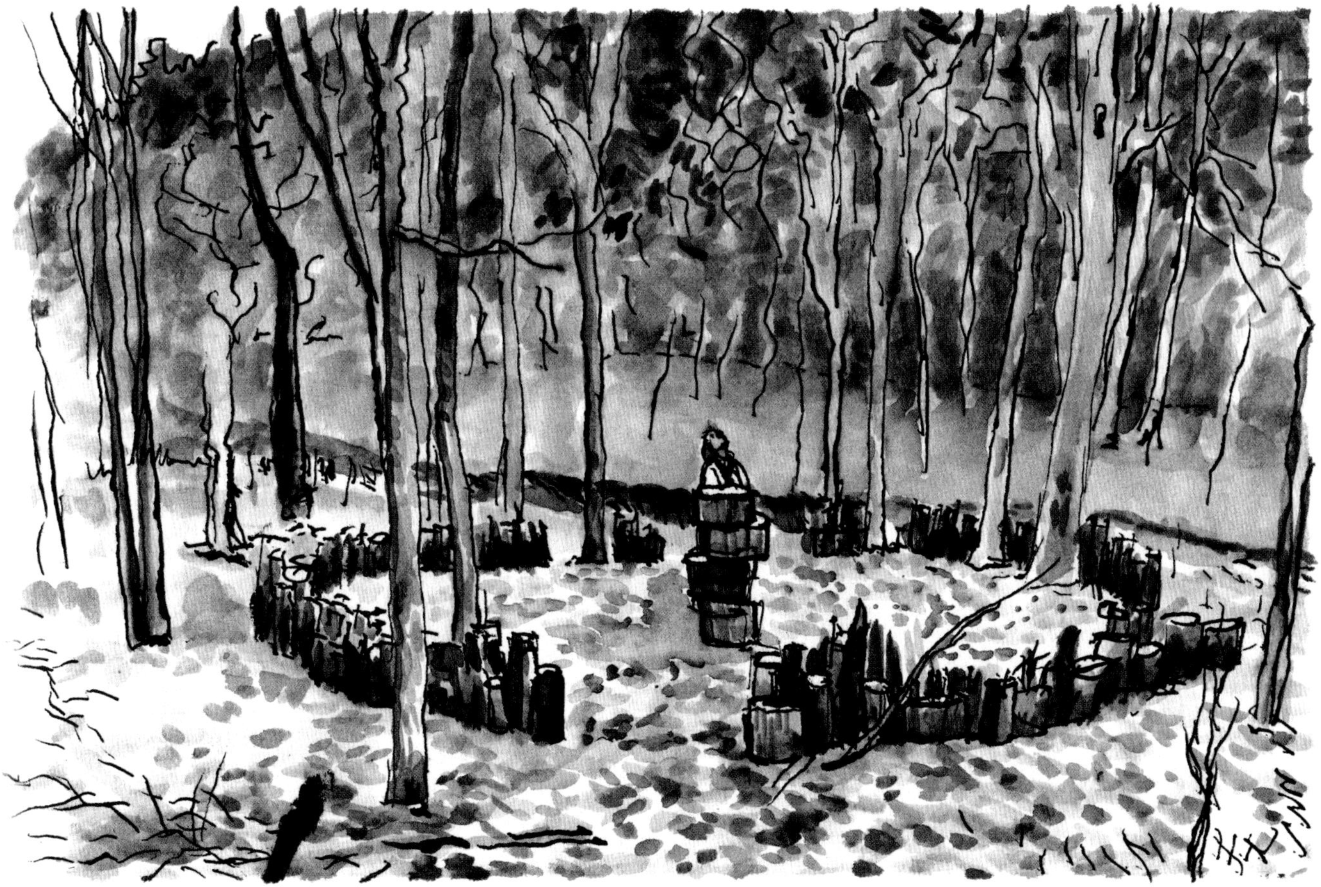

THURSDAY, JANUARY 31

It's late morning. Lou and the buck, Footsie John, are both in the trailer, and David's about to drive off to the slaughterhouse. He borrowed the trailer from a neighbor down the road, who uses it for hauling horses.

When her dad arrived home last night driving this unfamiliar rig, Phoebe immediately knew what was about to happen. "I'll never forgive you!" she yelled at David, who went into the house without a word. I scolded her for speaking to him that way, and tried, again, to talk her through it. She couldn't settle on whether or not to accept comfort from me. Whose team was I on?

"I agree with Dad," I told her. "Then I won't forgive you, either," she said. "You're not being fair," I said, and she threw her arms around me and burst into tears. Later, when we sat together for dinner, she said, "I love you, Daddy, but I hate some of the things you do."

After David leaves I do the barn chores. My hands are so cold I feel nauseous. I warm myself by bringing Lily and Cassie, the two remaining cows, plenty of hay. They do not seem at all troubled by Lou's departure. By the time I finish, it has started to snow.

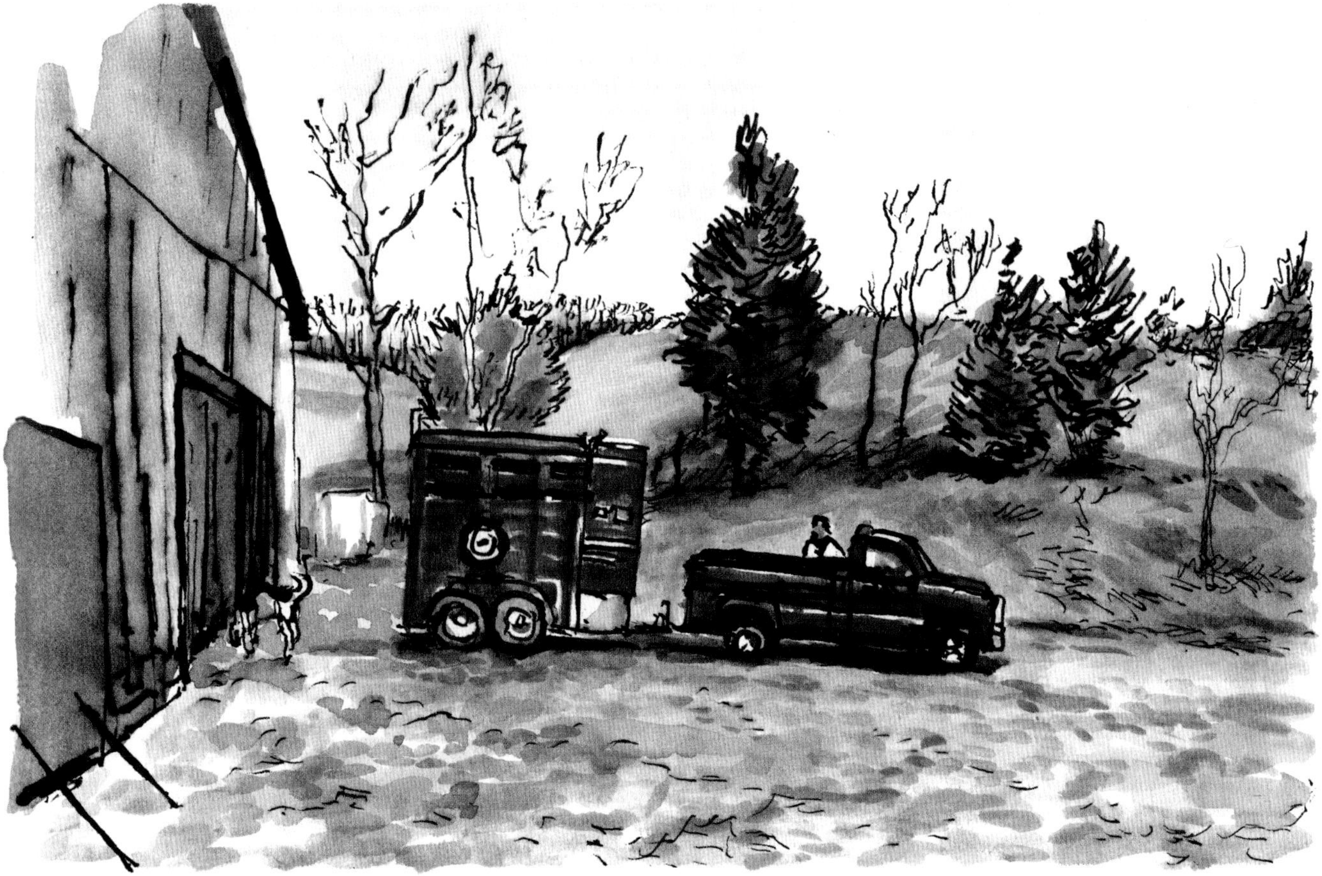

SATURDAY, FEBRUARY 2

All day, fine snow sifts down. We clean house, then take an evening walk. At the swimming hole, water from an underground spring seeps into the snow-covered pool, mimicking the black branches and white sky above, as if the creek can't quit its habit of reflecting.

During our first year on the farm, we met a man named Luther, whose family once owned this land. He lived on Crooked Creek, while tenants occupied the two-room shack that is now the heart of our house. Before he dug the well out back, Luther told us, the tenants would walk the hundred yards to draw water from this spring for their household needs.

When laborers worked at the north end of the farm, near Crooked Creek, they drank from another spring. We too now drink from that cold spring on hot days when we're working in the fields nearby. After learning this history, we named our new home Three Springs Farm. The third spring for which our farm is named feeds the well that Luther dug. These three springs have sustained human life on this farm for many generations.

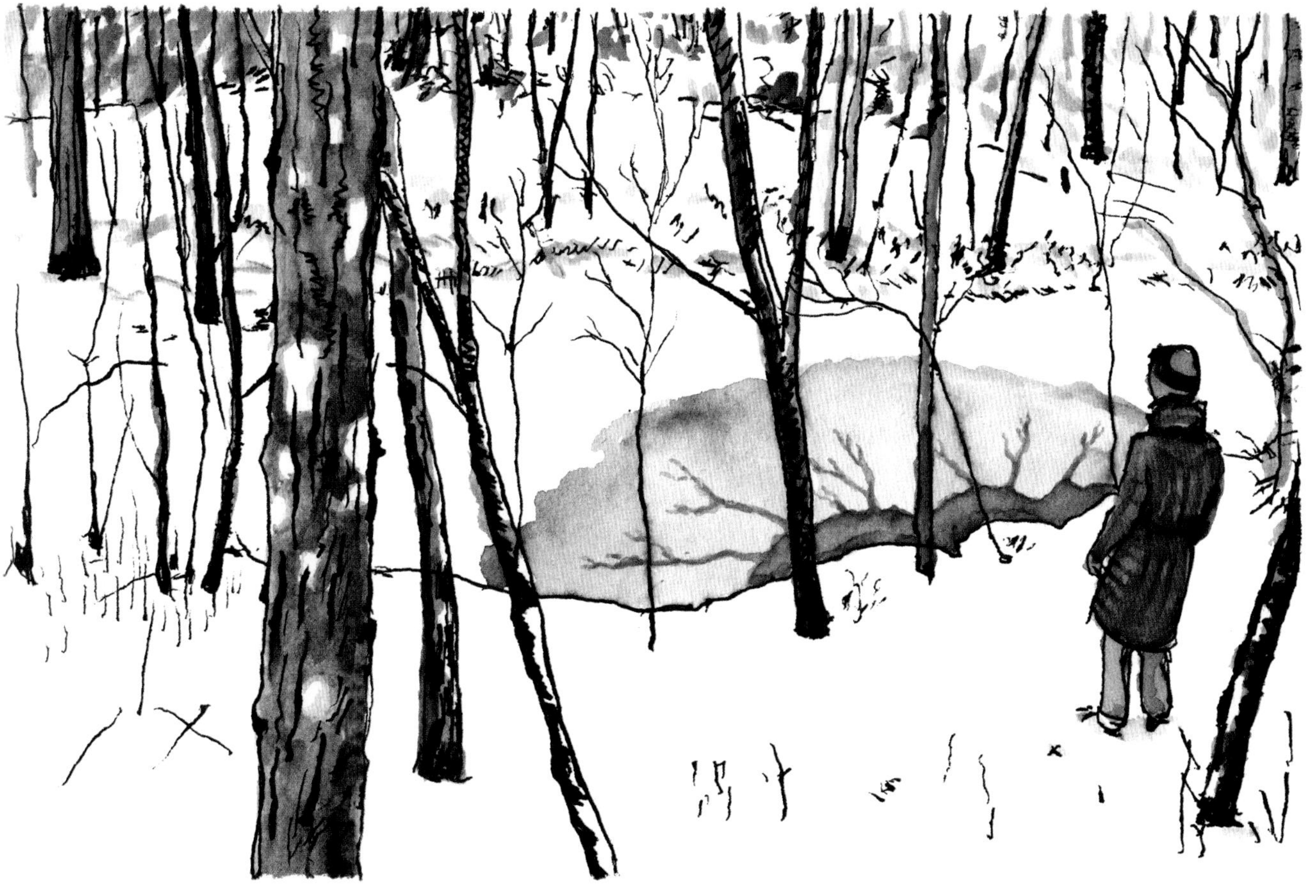

Sunday, February 3

Driving back from town earlier today, I noticed the particular snow of late winter along Crooked Creek. This snow throws the topography of the landscape into sharp tonal relief. It illuminates the corrugated paths on the hillside that malnourished horses have trod and cropped, glows in tire ruts, wreathes and crowns the junk scattered in peoples' yards. It glitters, embroiders the wreck, drapes over and spoons up against the things that usually make me sad.

Back at home, I stay in the barn, splitting wood until it is too dark to see clearly. I step outside, and the snow tells a story of our recent movements—prints and paths of sleds, carts, feet, paws, car tires—a story written days ago, but only now revealed, as if it had been written with invisible ink.

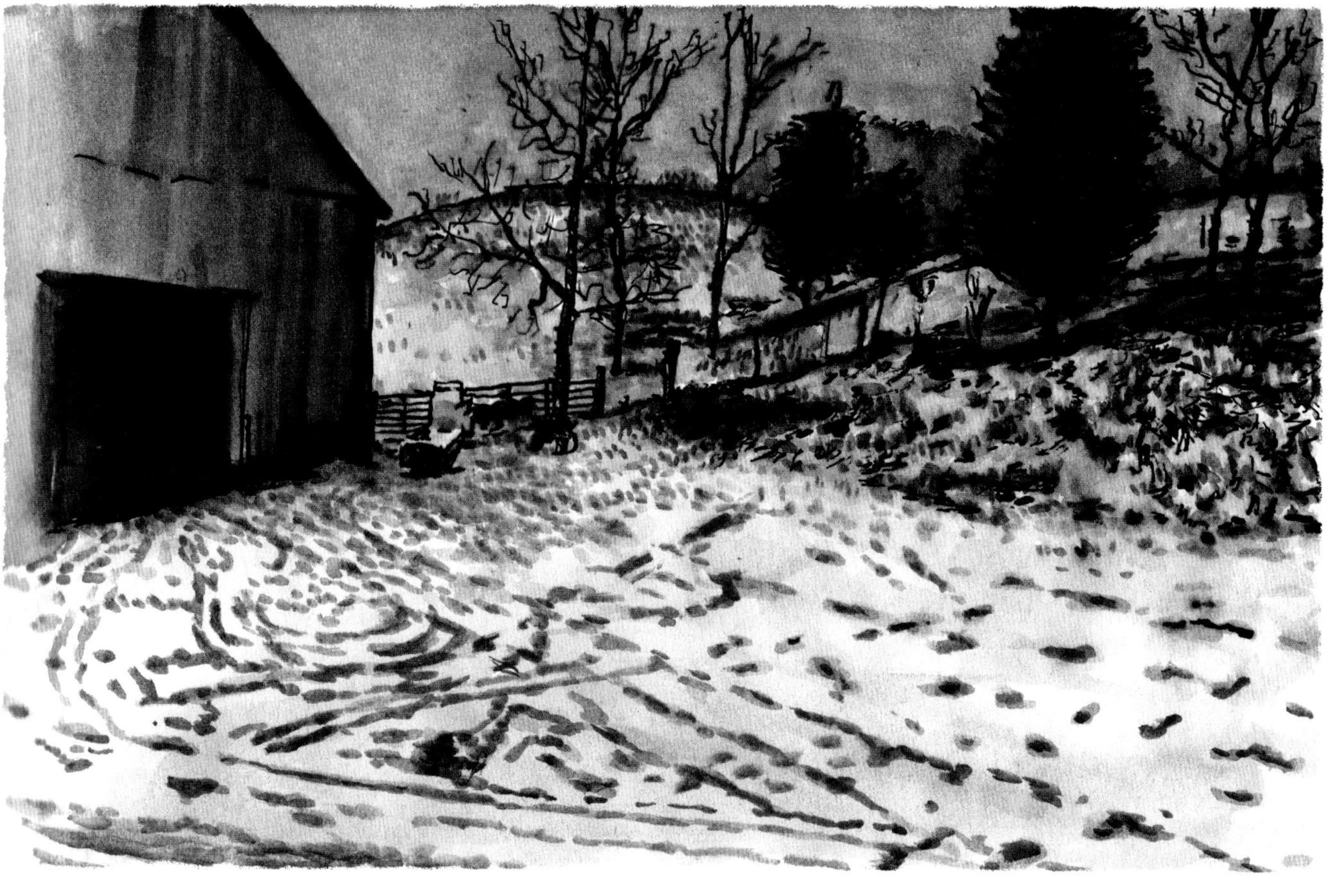

FRIDAY, FEBRUARY 8

I spend the afternoon hauling firewood from barn to porch. The chickens come over, looking for scratch. David returns from the field, where he's been digging carrots. He tells me he wants to farm this year without the help of interns, or any other hired help. He loves working in solitude. I say that it will be too much work for us. "It's always too much work for us," he says. "It doesn't matter how much help we have."

I've got a few freelance gigs to help pay the bills: these days, I go to Lexington once or twice a week to work on an oral history project for an educational nonprofit. I've got a couple of illustration jobs lined up. It's just enough to help us scrape by. But there's something I want to preserve about this year that's got nothing at all to do with money.

"I want to keep doing drawings of our lives on the farm," I say. I sound like a whining child. "Do them," David says. He doesn't expect me to fill in for the interns' absence: I can plan to help on harvest days, as I always do, and otherwise work intermittently on the farm, as usual.

I might spend the year drawing a slow wave of ruin, but I am curiously happy.

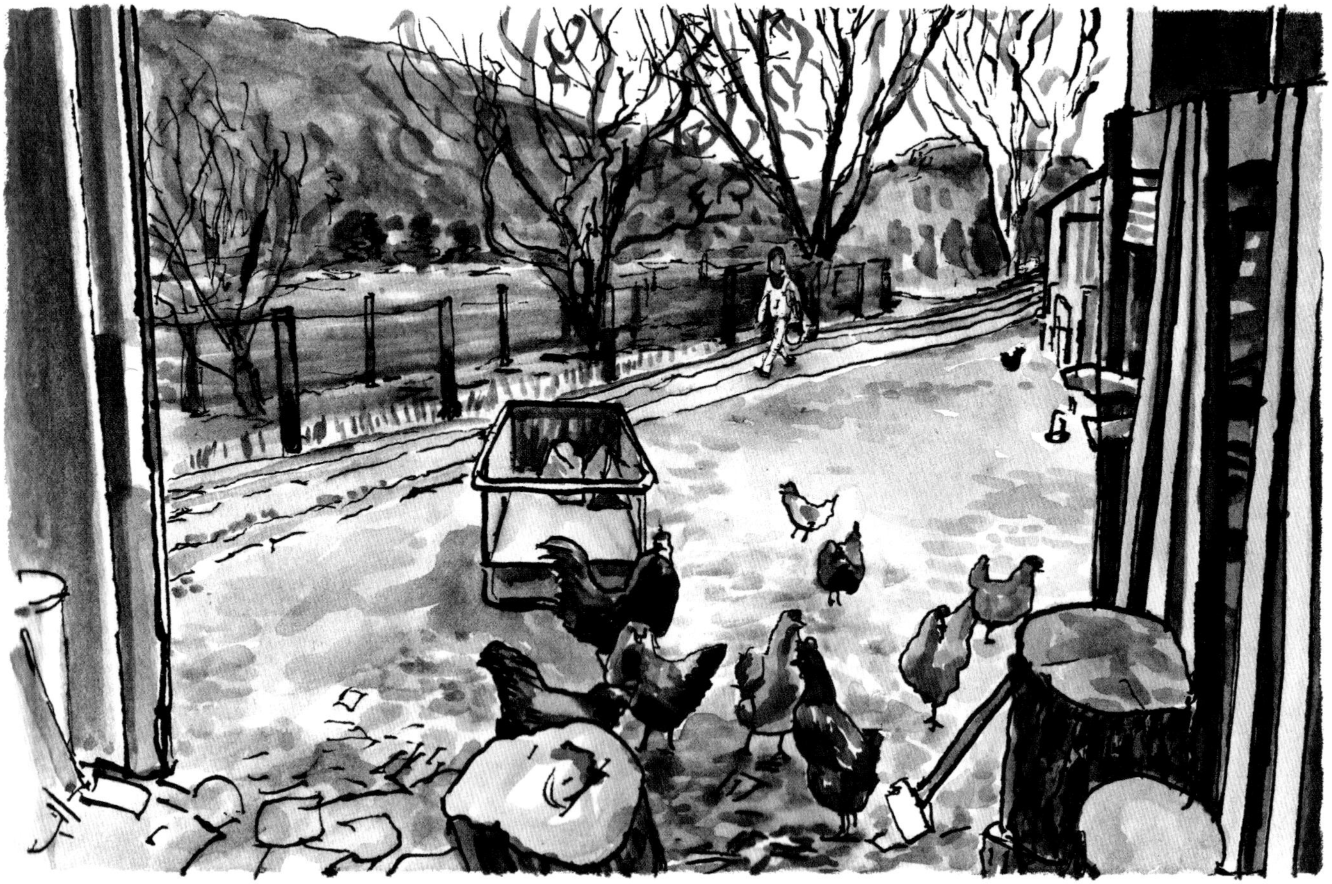

SATURDAY, FEBRUARY 9

David's loading the piles of wood chips he's been making all around the farm. Now we have mulch for blueberries, gooseberries, currants. We ordered more berry bushes to plant this spring.

Last night, David went to Windy Corner to play music. Phoebe and I stayed home together. She had an assignment to write a bill for a proposed new law, and she sat at the computer typing while I sat on the sofa nearby. "Art for Everyone," she proposed: all children should have art lessons in school at least twice a week. The art program has been completely cut from her school's budget. The times I have volunteered to teach art classes at Phoebe's school, I've been stunned at the students' exuberant hunger during their hour of imaginative making, as if they had been starved of some essential nutrient.

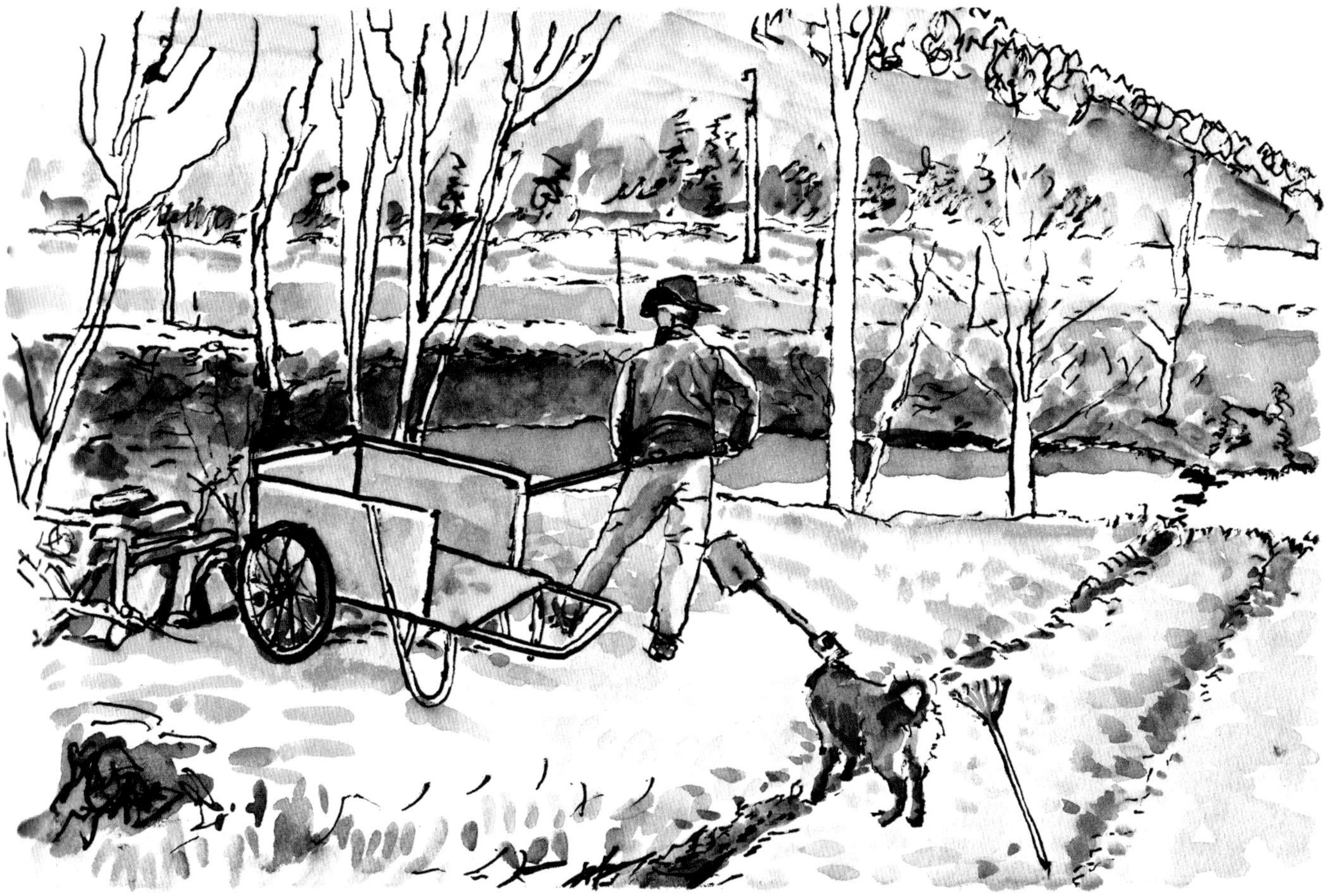

THURSDAY, MARCH 7

I've spent much of the last week working on our tax returns. Each year, this task reminds me that our family lives well below the poverty line. This goes to show how inadequate numbers can be in defining wealth. In terms of global history, we are among humanity's most privileged members. We own enough land to make a modest living. We produce enough food to provide much of our family's needs. We are supported by a community of customers who value what we do enough that they are willing to pay for an entire season of produce in early spring. If we were to get very sick, though, we might lose everything, because we cannot afford health insurance until the Affordable Care Act kicks in next year.

Our so-called luck is the product of a history of violence. Our ancestors killed or drove off this land's early inhabitants. Our skin color and sexual orientation provide a kind of cover that gives us a measure of ease in our lives. We quietly accept it, like cash slipped into our palms on the sly.

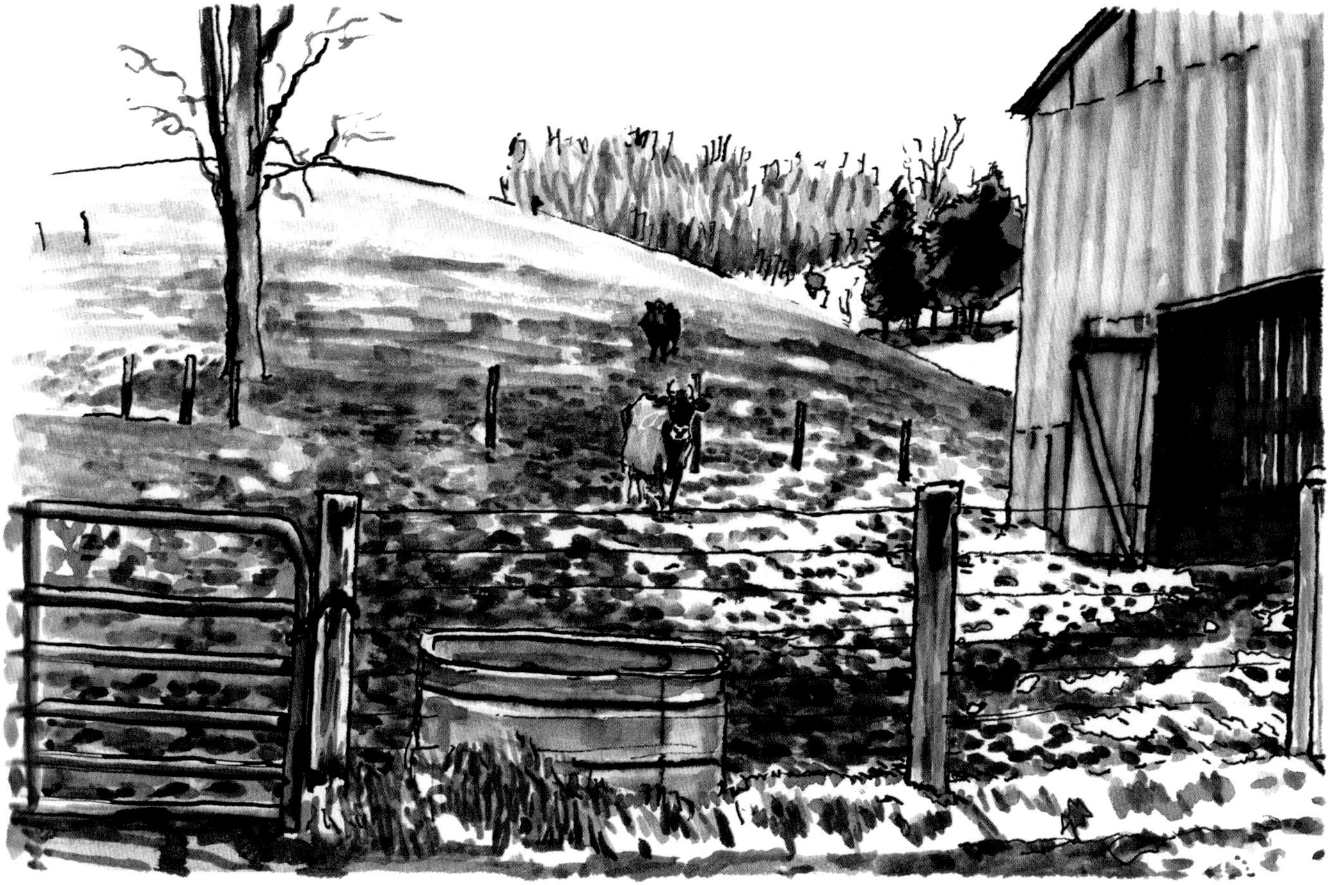

SUNDAY, MARCH 10

Farm production is stepping into high gear. The sky is blue for the first time in many days. After pancakes, the three of us head out to the fields with a wheelbarrow bearing a sack of onion sets, a roll of row cover, and a few tools. We cover a bed of cold-hardy salad greens—claytonia, minutina, and mache—then squat to plant onions.

The row cover, made of gauzy white polypropylene, is a wonder of plastic technology. It's one of the many ways we, as small farmers who aim towards sustainability, fall short of our ideals. This fabric is an occupation and a preoccupation during the shoulder seasons of spring and fall, when frosts threaten tender crops, and when the strong winds that mark the changing seasons hoist the covers up from the earth, make sails of them, rip them to shreds, and deposit their remains in trees and creek.

David cuts a sixty-foot length of fabric from the roll, and the three of us work together to spread it over the bed and anchor corners and edges with the limestone rocks that abound on our farm. The fabric is so pure when it comes off the roll— lightly perfumed, even, as if freshly laundered—that throwing a muddy rock on it feels scandalous, like stepping on a bride's train with your muck boots.

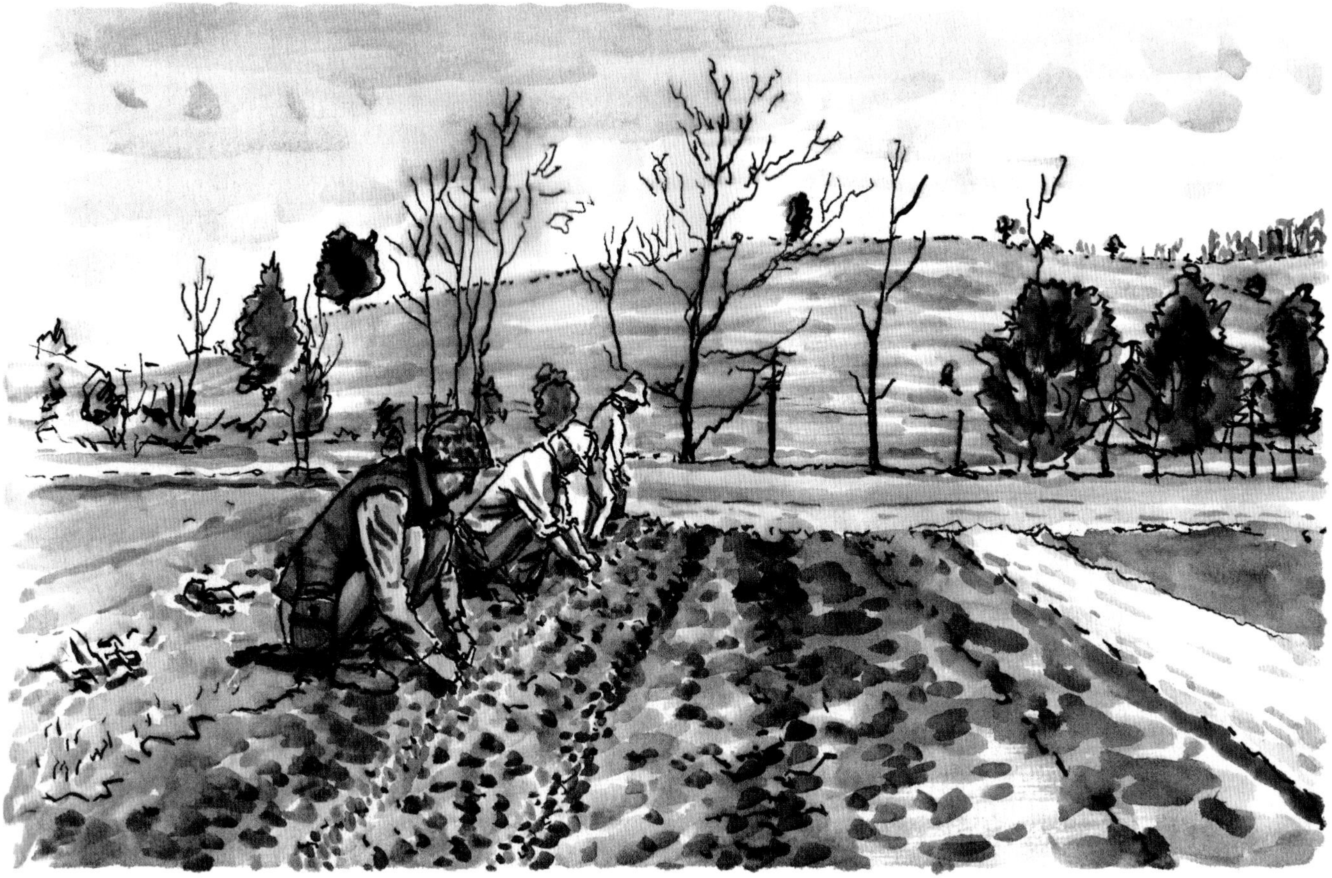

MONDAY, MARCH 18

After David arrived home from his trip to the post office in Carlisle, where he picked up our shipment of twenty-five newly-hatched chicks, he put the box down by the woodstove to keep it warm. He told me he'd just spotted a newborn calf up the road that had been separated from the herd by the high water. It snowed yesterday, and rained through the night. Water stands in the garden beds, and our gravel lane is one long puddle. Crooked Creek is brown and swollen.

The absentee owner is unlikely to discover this calf in time. We get in the truck and find him lying in a ditch, soaked in icy water, mud-caked and shivering. He is the herd's firstborn and was left behind when the cows went to graze, not strong enough to ford the stream and follow. We've brought a bunch of old towels with us; we rub him down, put him in the truck, and drive down the road, where the cows have wandered. His mother, a young heifer, claims him, licking and nudging until he comes to his feet.

Our neighbor John comes over and watches the calf with us. He says he's seen big cows carried off by the creek when the water gets high.

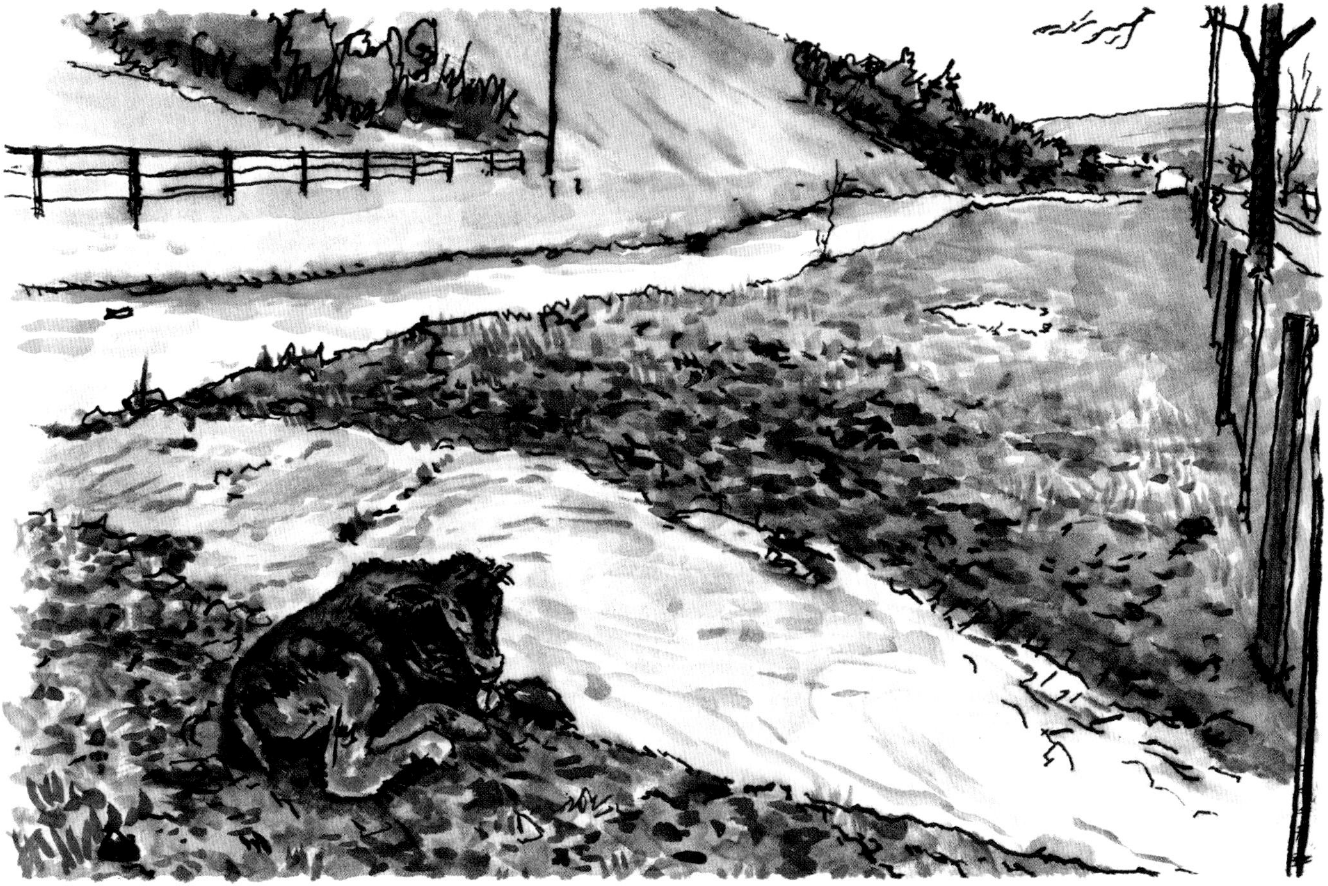

FRIDAY, MARCH 22

The long box behind the woodstove contains twenty-two chicks, about a week old: araucanas, barred rocks, buff orpingtons, Rhode Island reds, black australorps. We've lost three to accidents already. I just sneezed, which sent them into a cheeping, flapping frenzy.

It's been cold, ten degrees last night, and the chicks need to stay warm, so the house is full of their peeping. Lights shine on them for additional warmth. Laundry racks flank the stove.

Payments trickle in from customers subscribing for produce shares this season. Subscriptions will flow in more quickly after the grass starts greening. It takes sunshine to move the money. Things look pretty much the same as they have for the last month: mud interspersed with patches of melting snow. When Phoebe and I walk by the barn in the afternoon, Lily and Cassie come galloping down the hillside, hoping for hay. There's not much to be gleaned from the pasture, and the hayloft has gotten quite low.

We're all ready for spring.

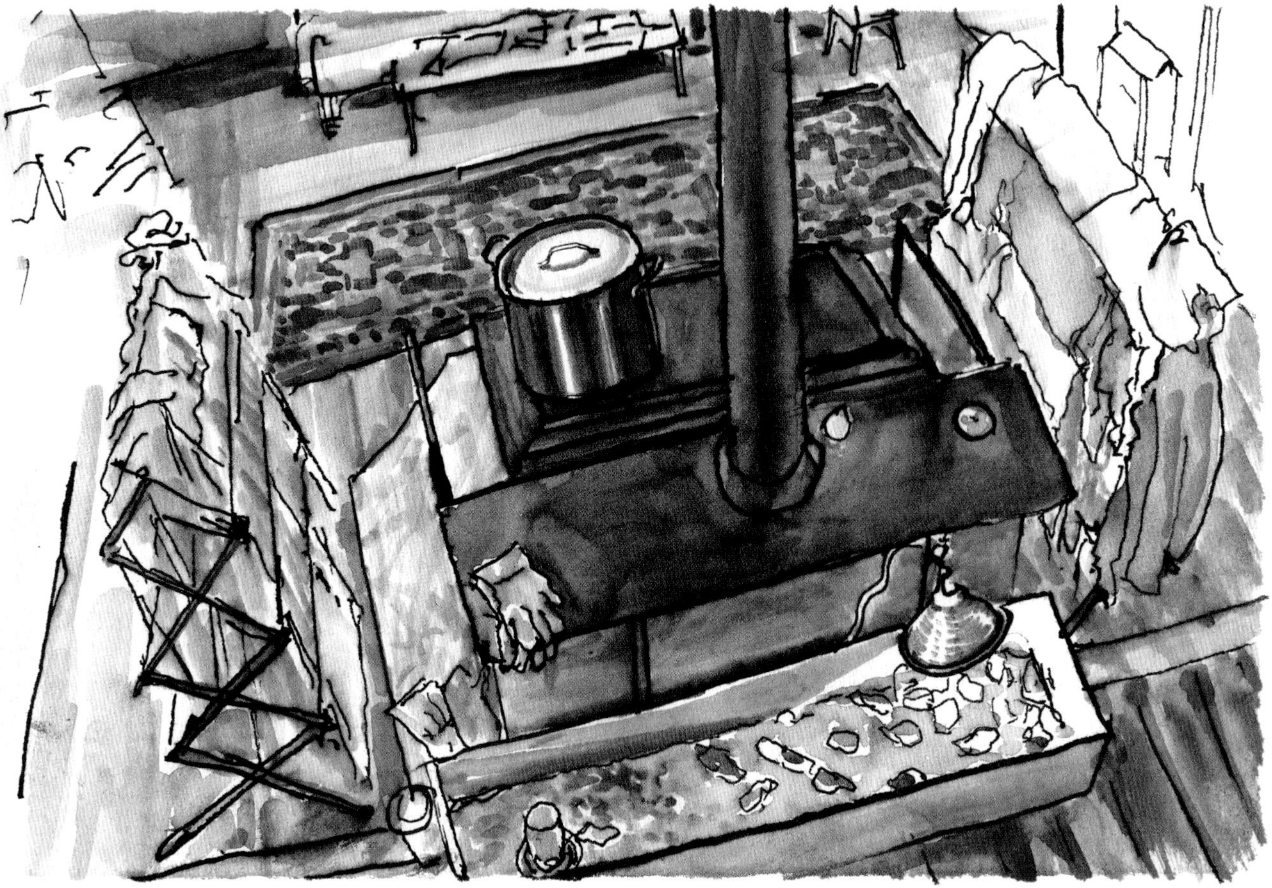

SATURDAY, MARCH 23

We didn't get our garlic planted last fall. Finally, today, Phoebe and I pull four paper bags of garlic heads from the closet, divide them into cloves, and head out to the garden to plant them. I break up the beds with a wheel cultivator, while Phoebe loosens the soil with a broadfork.

This morning, I walked out in the frosty grass to pee, and though it was cold, it was spring. The cold had spring in it, I thought I'd say, but rather the spring had cold in it. Everything has switched around. Although this morning may have been as cold as one was a month ago, it's a different cold. I could smell the earth. Wild turkeys called to each other in the field. The moon was in the east, above the house. It pleases me to see it when it's not any shape in particular—not round, not crescent, not halved, not quartered—it's a tongue being stuck out at my need to name its shape. But oh, I've done it again: it *is* tongue-shaped.

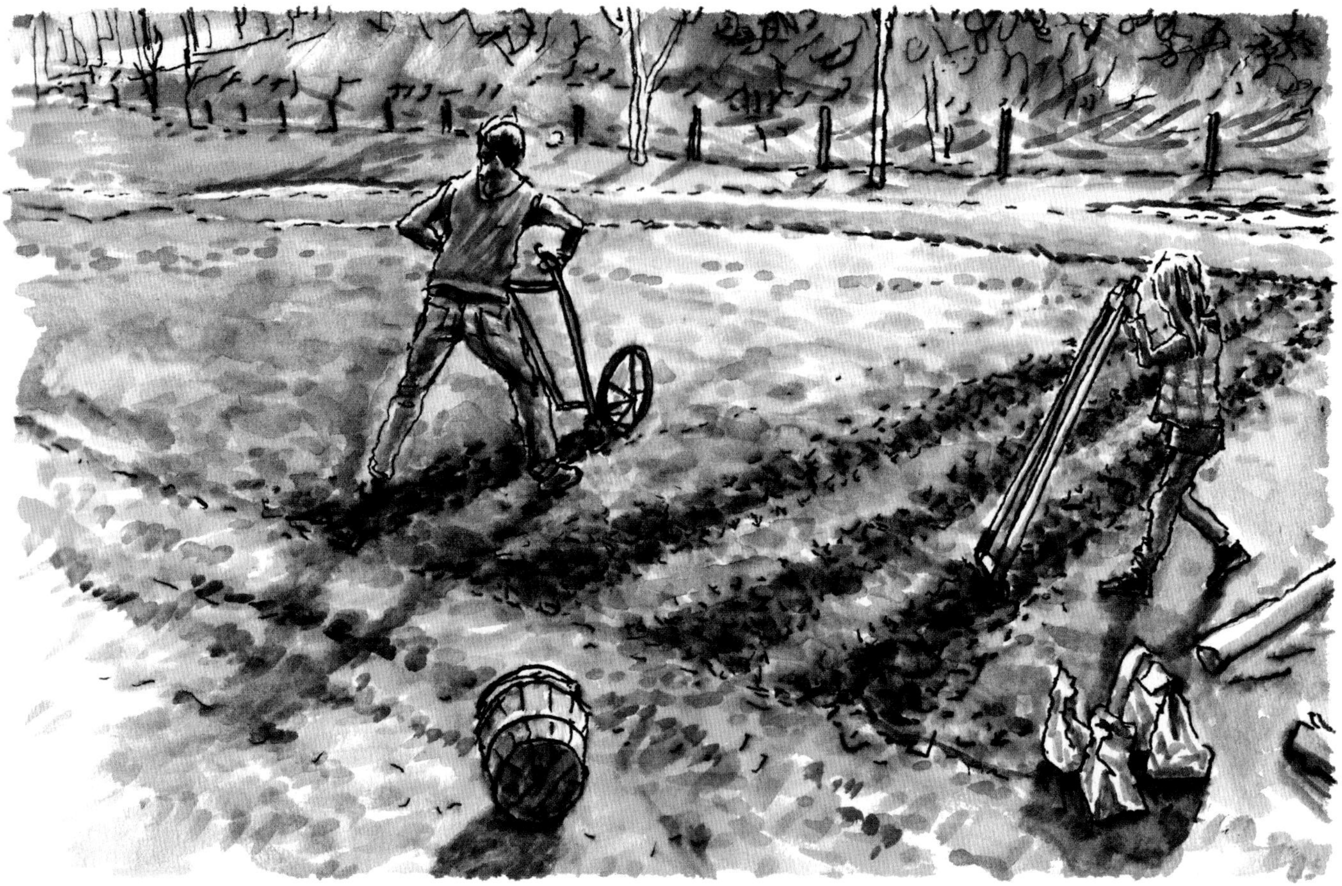

MONDAY, MARCH 25

Only half of the garlic got planted before rain returned, then snow. Back to chopping wood.

It strikes me, in watching how the wood is willing to split, that there is a central point from which rays emerge, each ray a potential fault line, and that in this way the wood is like sunlight in solid form. The tree, made by the sun, mirrors the sun in its heart. Striking the wood, it's clear the fault lines are waiting inside it, like sections of an orange, because sometimes a not-too-strong tap in just the right place sends one section flying from the block.

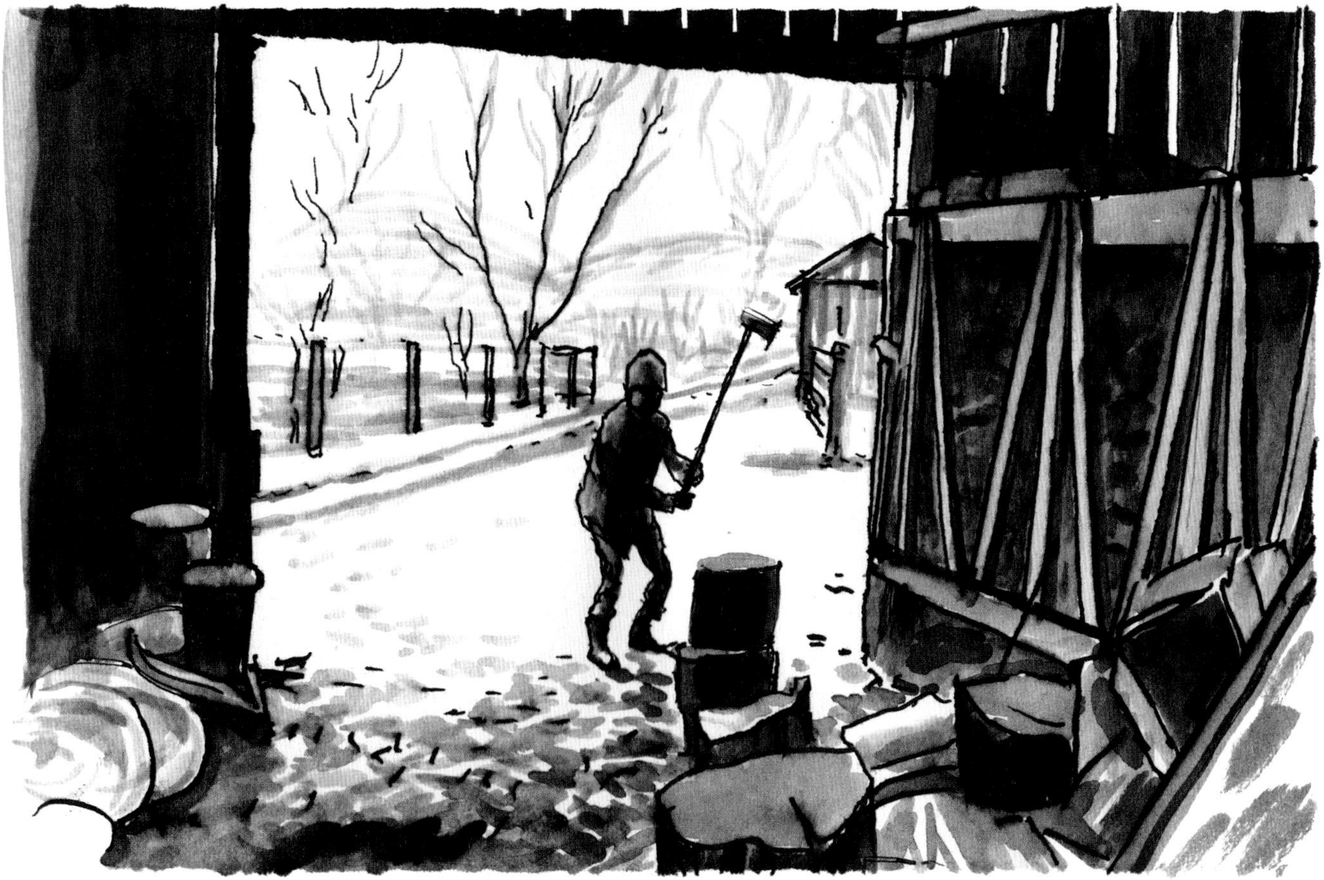

TUESDAY, MARCH 26

Phoebe was born a little more than ten years ago, just inside the house, not more than six feet from our front porch. ("I can't believe I'm already ten years old, and I've accomplished so *little!*" she bemoaned on her birthday.) I felt, then, the pendulum-swing between winter and spring, the wild heave of a season's change, mirrored in my own body. I was in labor for around thirty-six hours, during which time I walked up and down, up and down the farm's lane, interrupted by contractions that felled me to my knees. I also sat in the barn with the goats, my covey of doulas. They are masters at birthing: I've watched them drop a kid midstride after a half hour of labor. They sniffed at me with mild concern, then flicked their ears and settled back into chewing their cud. *All in a day's work, honey*, they seemed to say.

A grip that tightens and releases, a holding and a softening, a thrashing struggle and an easing glide: this is how spring is born. There's nothing gentle about it.

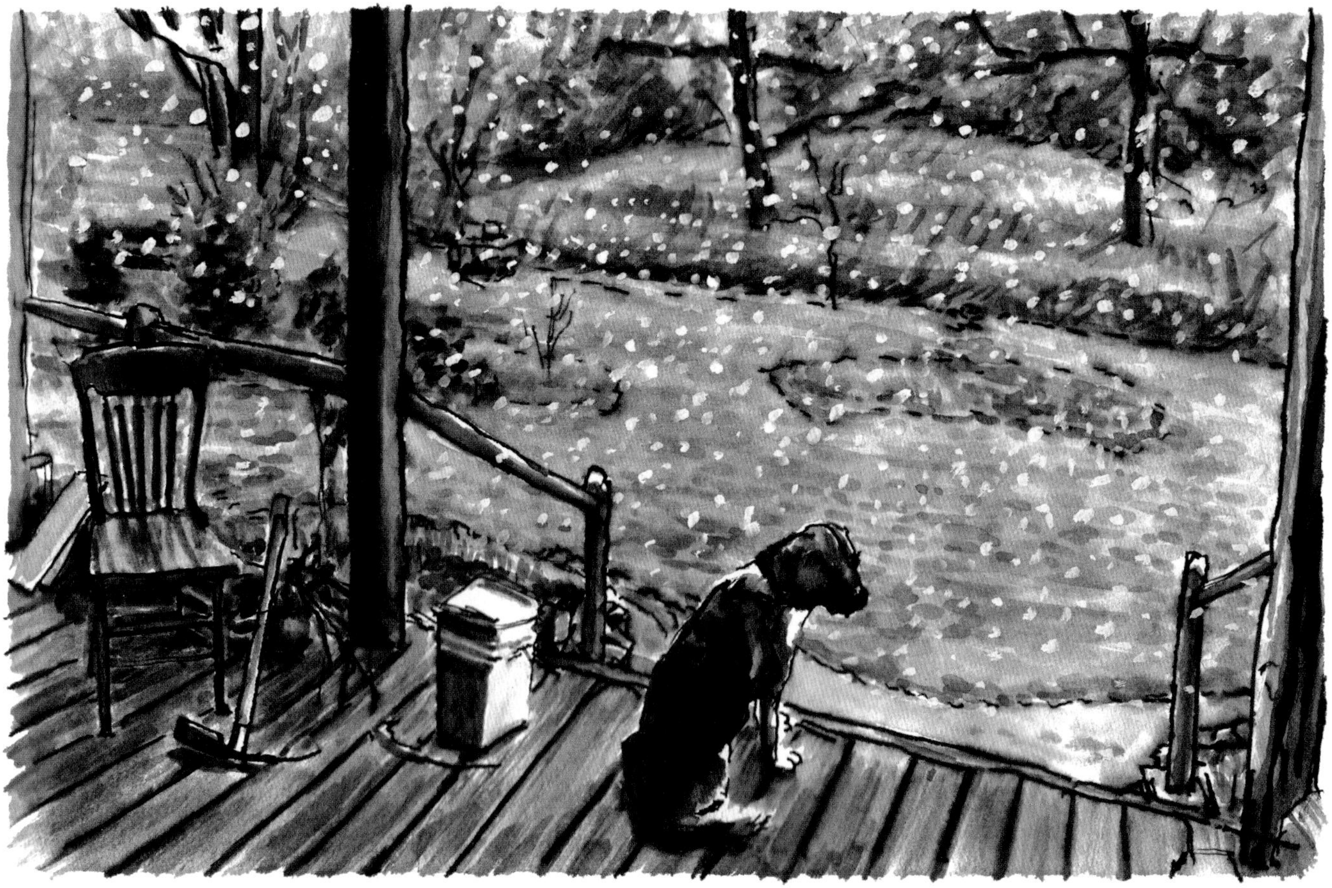

THURSDAY, MARCH 28

A good, cool day. I plant the rest of the garlic. When Phoebe gets home from school, she tells me she's miserable. So much class time is spent disciplining children who misbehave. She does what her teachers tell her to do, but students often get punished as a group, she says. She feels trapped.

At a council meeting last fall, just after the school's low test scores were released, teachers expressed frustration at how little these scores actually reflect. One talked about having to teach a six-year-old girl how to brush her teeth. "These things take time," she said. Fewer and fewer students live with their parents anymore, and the teachers have noticed a decline in their health and stability. Our county, it was recently reported, has the highest high school dropout rate in the state.

Not knowing what else to do, I put the girl to work. She rakes last year's flower stalks from the space we've staked out for her own garden and hauls the stalks back to the compost heap.

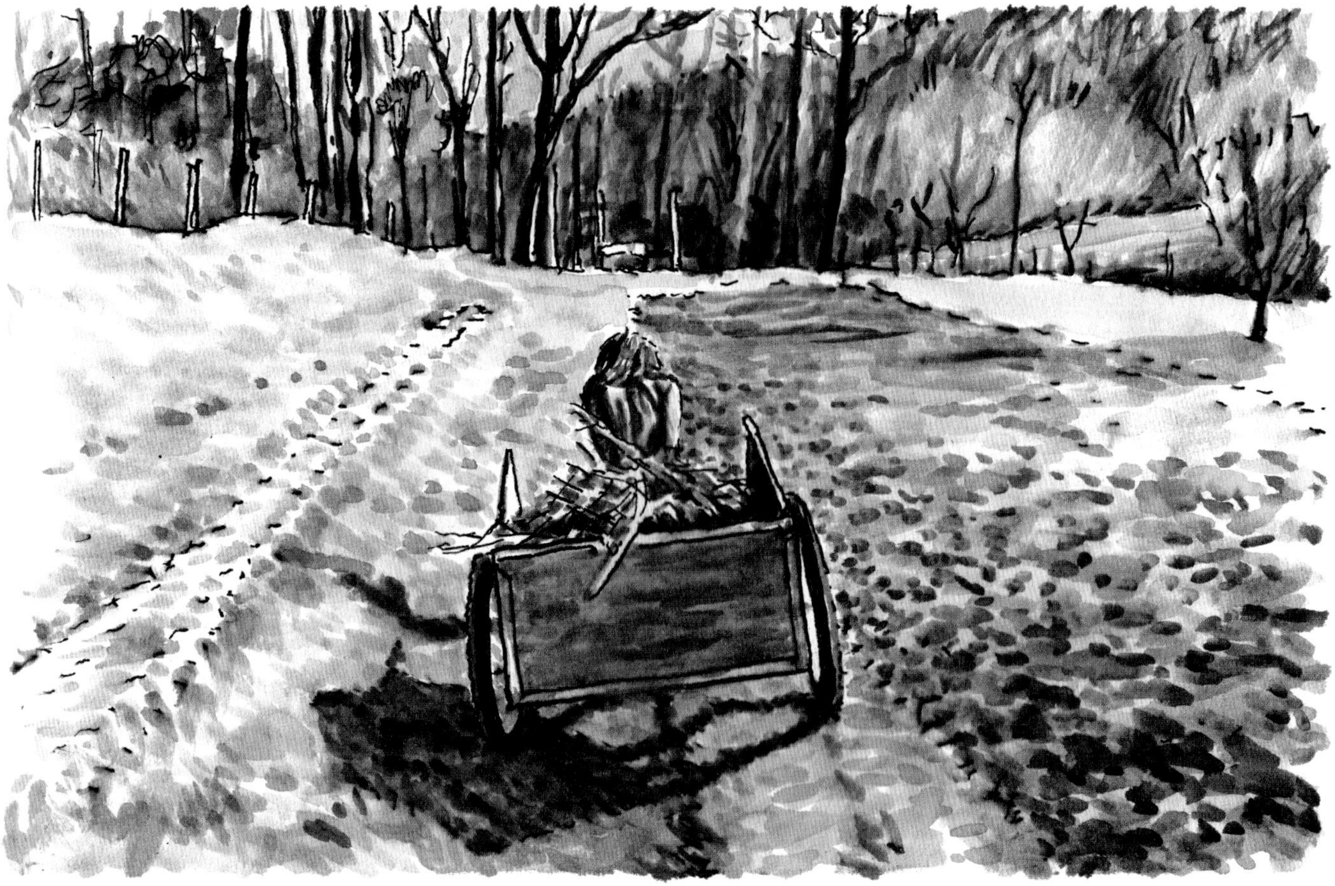

SUNDAY, MARCH 31

While sowing peas, we hear the peepers singing from Pond Hill. We cover the furrows with a thin blanket of cold soil then walk up to listen. The little frogs go silent as we draw near, and the pond fizzes with plops, as if some farmer had enough of sowing peas and slung her last handful into the water. Once we settle in, the frogs tentatively start to peep again. Something strange soon starts to happen: the song worms into your ear and plays the instrument of your hearing. Peeps morph into percussive croaks, clicks, rasps, and taps, like Morse code. These sounds seem to be formed in the caverns of the inner ear and travel outward, tapping on the eardrum from behind. Meanwhile, the peeps keep seeping in, until they merge into a song of one note, simmering with rhythmic variations. It's a musical score for the drifting clouds, for the swerve of a flock of red-winged blackbirds. The birds illuminate the frogs' song: they are many, but they are one. Communication contracts to communion.

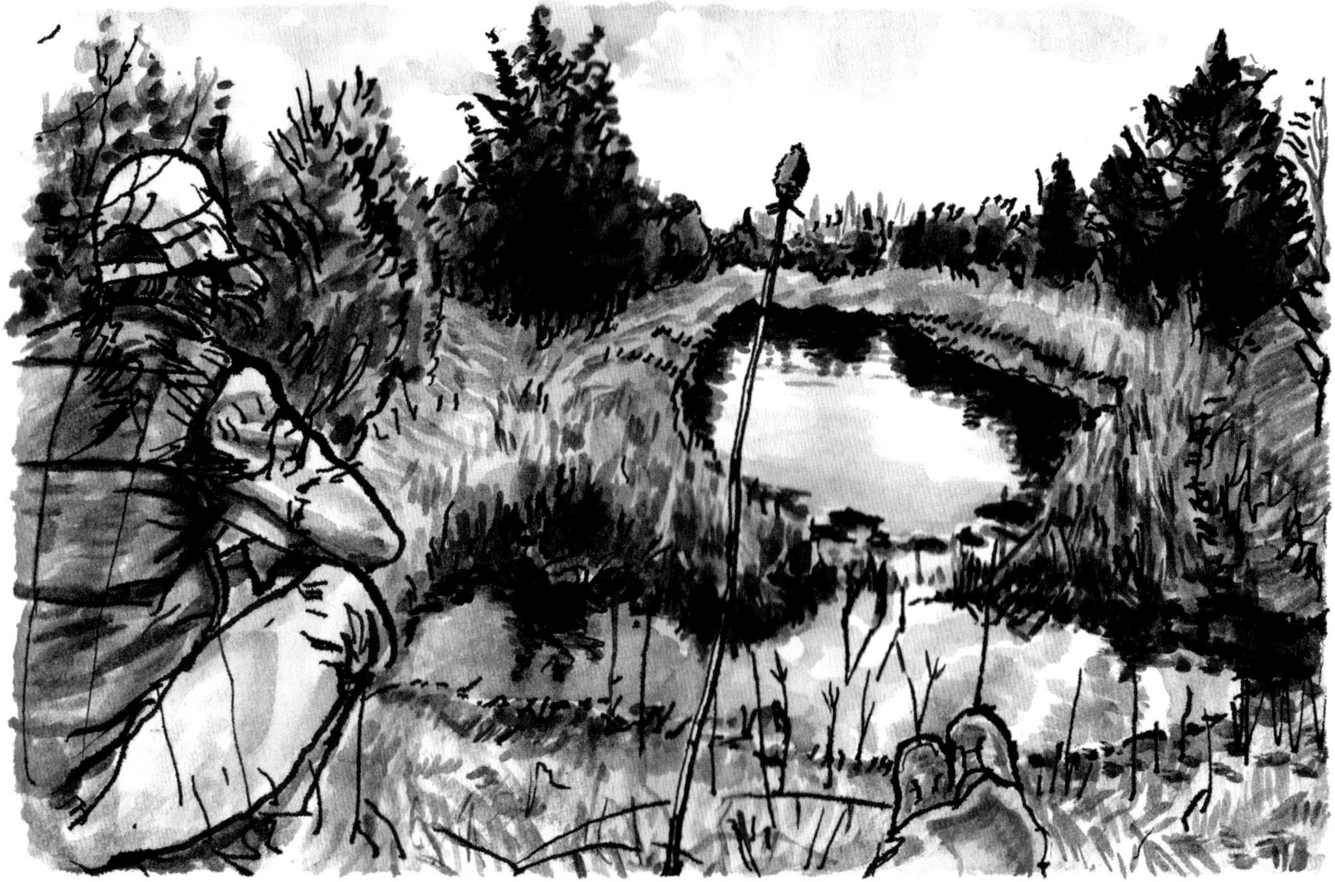

TUESDAY, APRIL 2

It's finally warm enough to bring the stinky box of chicks out into the greenhouse. I make a pen out of chicken wire, and they have a great time all day, pecking at the lush mat of claytonia, chickweed, and henbit that has seeded itself all across the greenhouse floor. When the sun goes behind the hill, back into the box, and the house, they go. Nights are still in the teens: way too cold for them.

It's spring, which means that the greens wrap around your limbs and tether you to the earth and tighten their grip if you get distracted by mere ideas. But here I am, writing and drawing, while the seeds grow plump on all the early weeds in the flowerbeds, the herb garden, the strawberry patch.

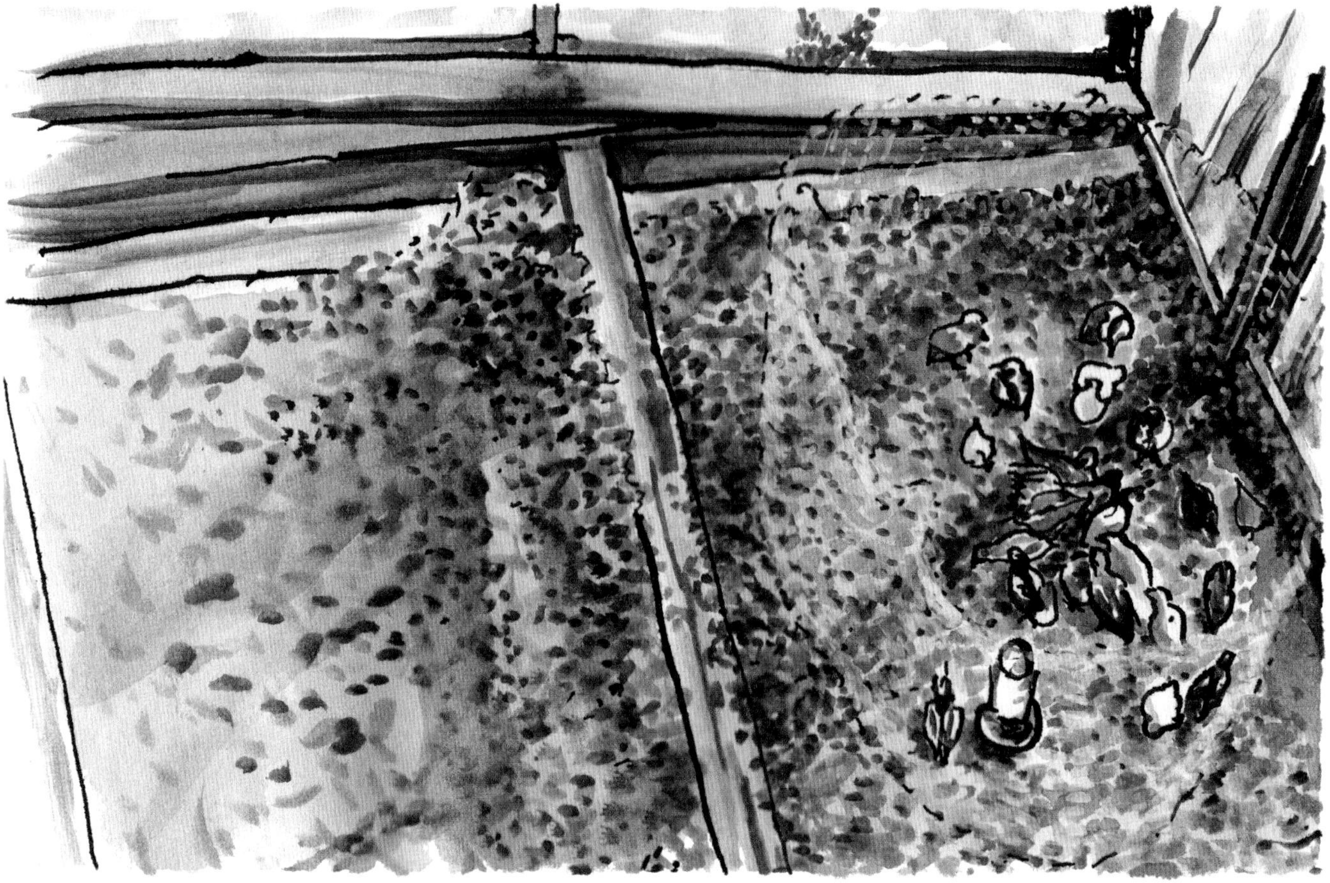

THURSDAY, APRIL 4

All winter, the woods are white, brown and black, with smudges of green. The year's first flowers open in March: tiny, tentative, black, and white embellishments on the pattern of winter's fabric. *Harbingers of spring,* they're called: symbols of spring, not spring itself. This evening, running in the woods, I see pale gold buds swelling on the spicebush: small spots where winter is torn.

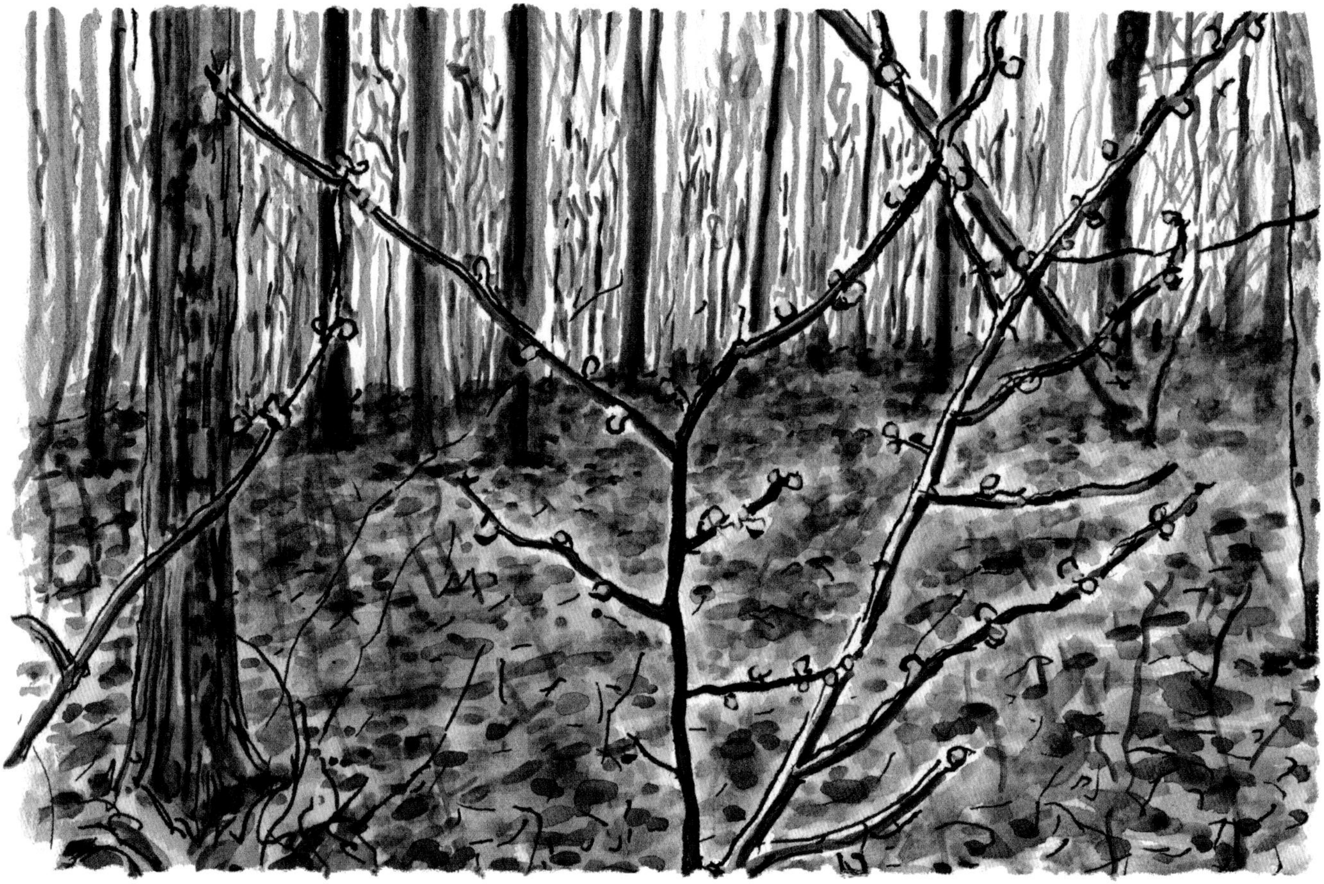

TUESDAY, APRIL 9

The first gift of shit we ever received was from Mr. Otte, who owned a service station we once frequented. It was our first April on the farm. We'd gone to church that morning with our neighbors. There, a guest speaker talked about the various Bibles his organization distributed to churches around the state. I hadn't been to church many times in my life, and I came home feeling deflated. Had I gotten so irritated by the parade of Bibles that I missed the deeper message? What was I doing with my life, anyway? I had quit my job in Washington, DC, and moved to a farm in Kentucky. I wasn't sorry, but I also wasn't sure why I'd done it.

David asked me, then, to go with him to pick up a pile of cow droppings that had been slow-cooking on Mr. Otte's farm for five years. Later, as we pitched the shit onto our new garden plot, something in me opened, as if a key had slid into a lock and turned.

Big Red, the 1978 Ford F-250 that came with the purchase of our farm, has hauled many tons of manure since then. Each load eases the questions of *why* and *what's next*. This year's load came from a neighbor who was cleaning up an old cow barn, and it's aged to a fine fecundity. David and Phoebe spread forkfuls in the furrows, while I begin planting leeks.

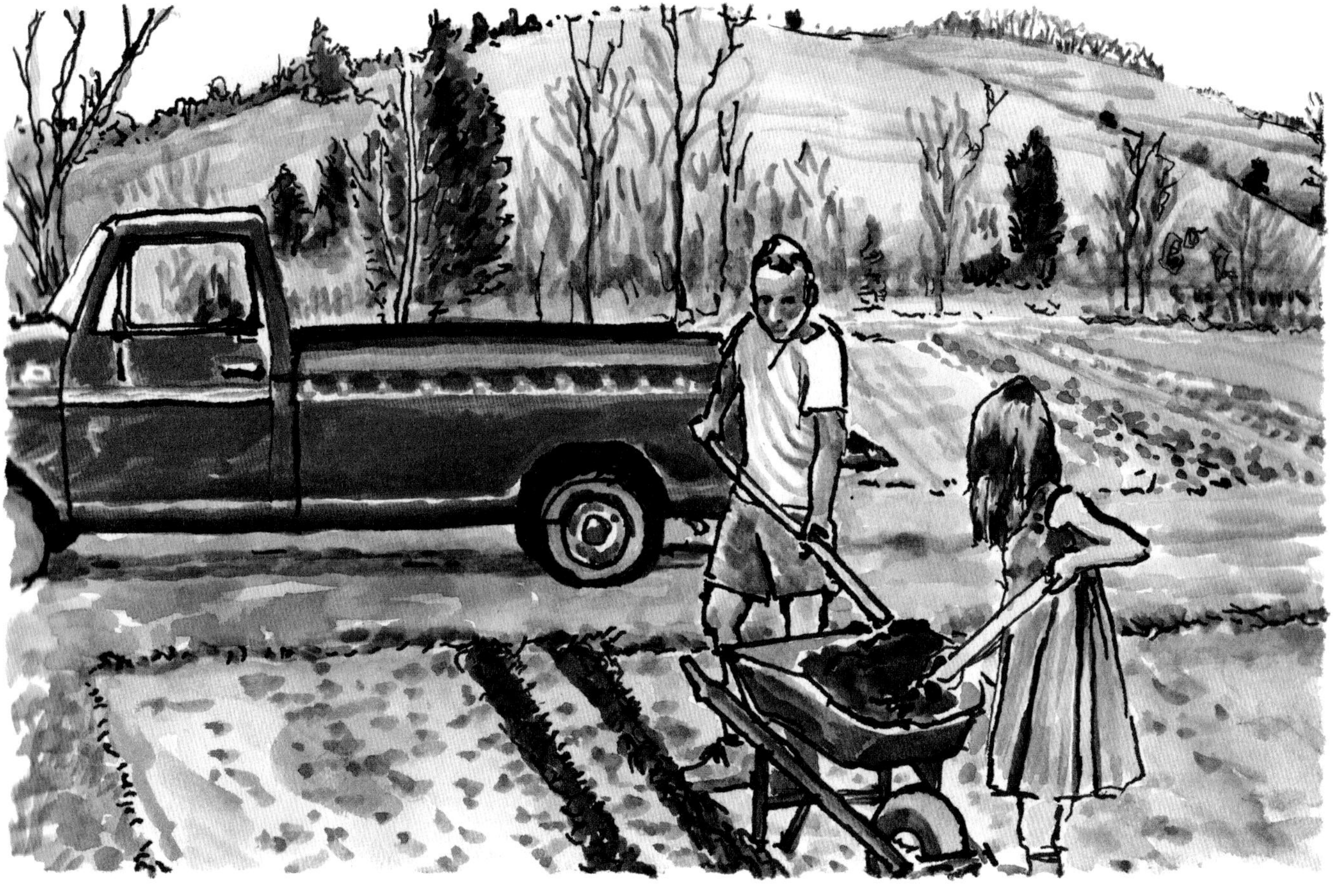

WEDNESDAY, APRIL 10

After we moved to the farm, we bought an Amish-built, hand-cranked washing machine. I thought this purchase was insane. It cost $500, not including wringer and rinse tubs. David thought it would make him fall in love with doing laundry. Washing the clothes, he said, would be his responsibility. If he'd been able to devote the time that the Amish machine required, he might actually have fallen in love with doing the laundry, but we will never know, because he soon discovered how much time farming takes: more than we will ever have.

We hand-cranked for about a year, and the work was divided more or less evenly between David and me, as I often reminded him. Then my grandmother bought us a washing machine. I appreciate the symbolism of this, because the automatic washing machine may be industrialism's greatest gift to women, as my grandmother would have known, having grown up in poverty as one of eight children. The Amish machine is now tucked in a corner of our barn. The two galvanized steel rinse tubs have seen years of use in cleaning vegetables after harvest.

We don't own a dryer. After a string of damp days, the sun shines again. I don't have enough clothespins.

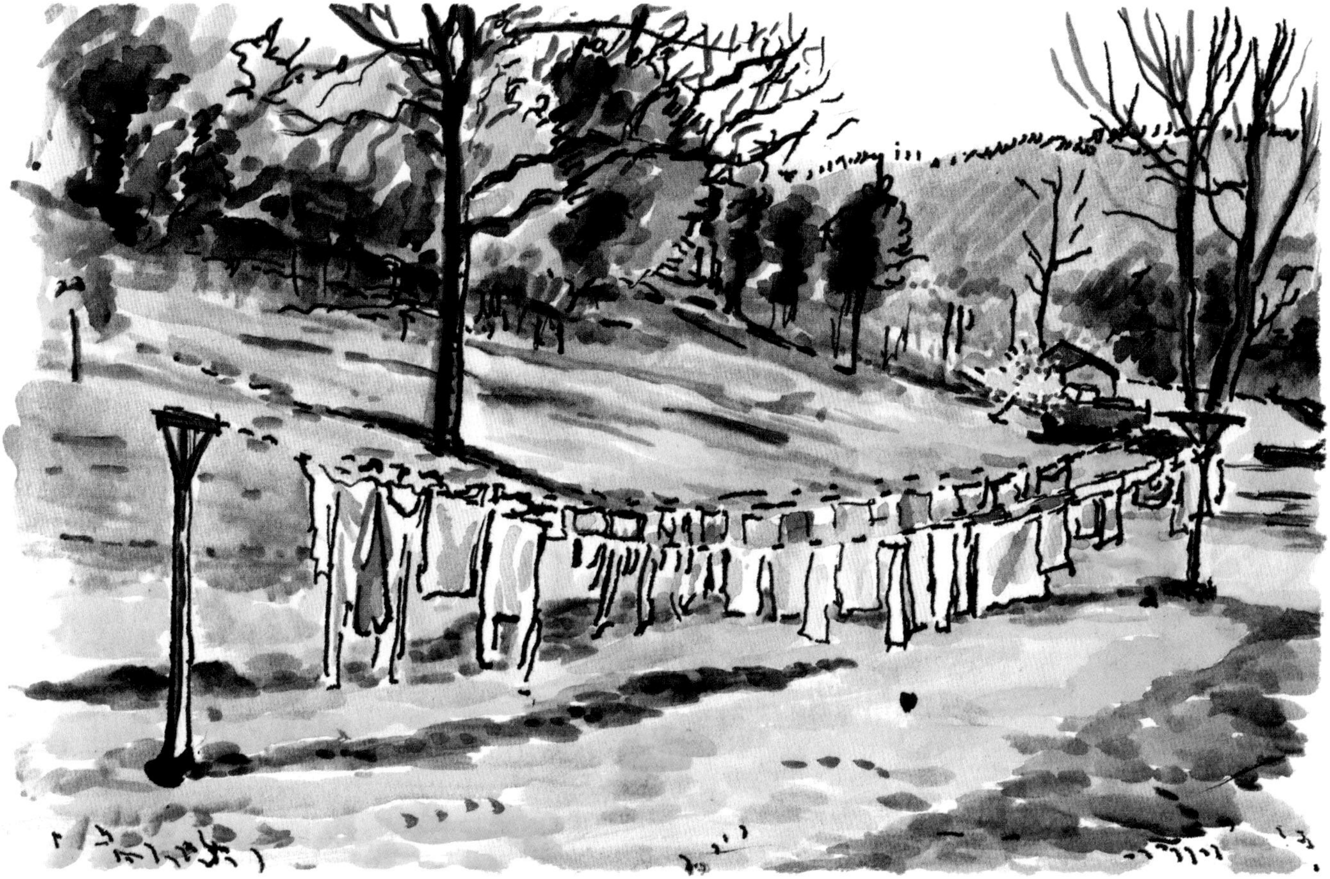

SATURDAY, APRIL 13

In early January, we sit by the hearth and pore through seed catalogues. By early February, we've sown flats of cold tolerant seeds in the greenhouse—lettuce, cabbage, broccoli, kale, onions, parsley—that sit on heated benches. By mid-March, we need the benches to warm the tender next round—tomatoes, eggplants, peppers, summer squash, zinnias—so the hardier seedlings move to the greenhouse floor. Soon they're set out the door, on a mild day, to acclimate to the vicissitudes of weather in the unsheltered world for a few days before being planted out in the field. We lay covers over them at night, nudge them toward independence, step in when they need a hand in a fight against a bullying weed. But if these plants begin their lives as our children, they will later become our mothers. They will know our bodies, in some ways, more intimately than we know each other's. They will move through our coiled innards, they will build our cells, we will burn them in the fire of our bellies, and yet they will return to give themselves to us, again and again.

There was a light frost this morning, after a few summer-like spring days. When the first warm day arrived, many plants burst into blossom, as if they'd been straining against a cold hand that suddenly released its grip.

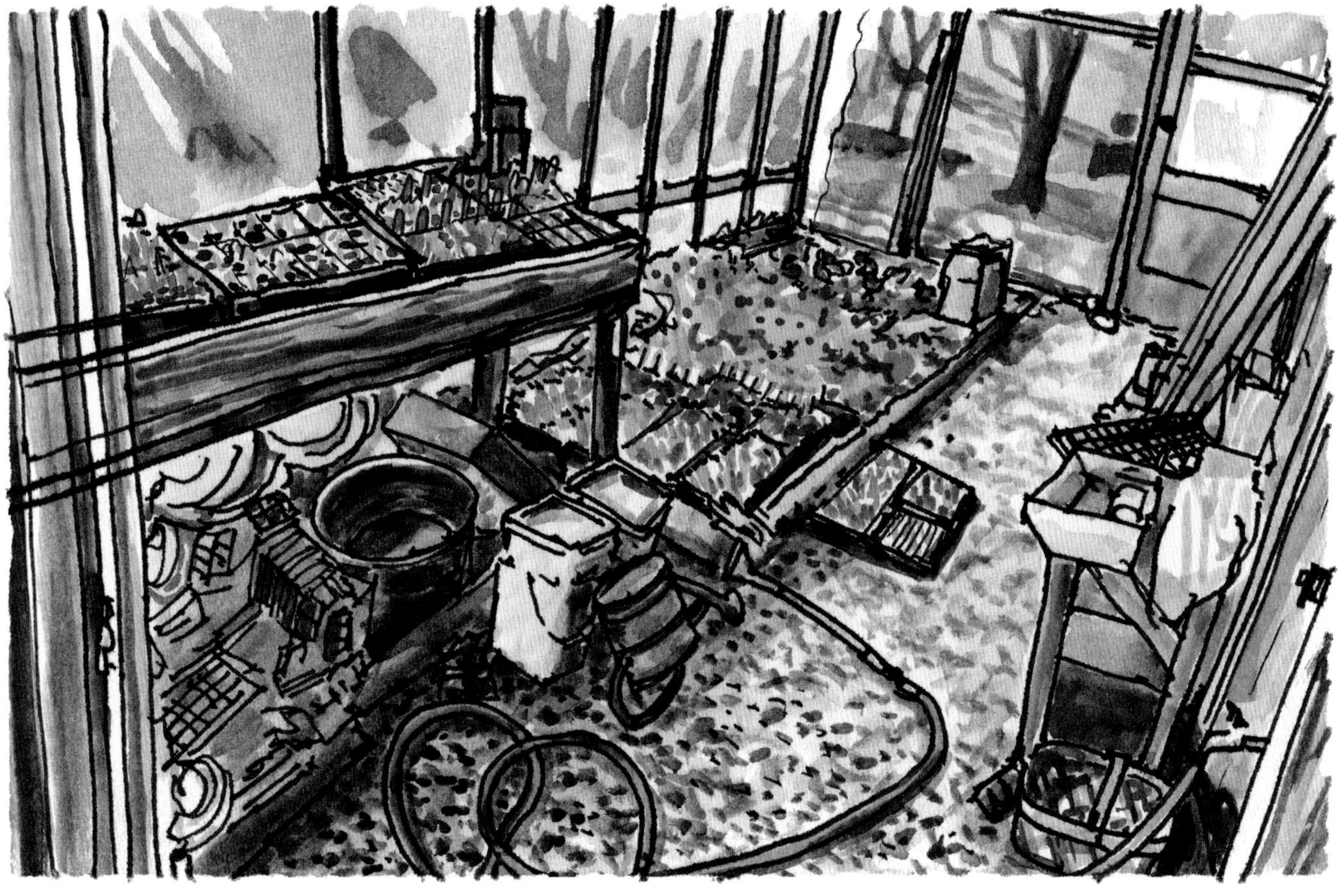

MONDAY, APRIL 15

When it comes to water, I am like a crow whose eye is caught by a shiny object: I want to capture and carry it with me. A small pool in the run—like this one by the barn, where we dip buckets for the cows' trough—is a bridge between earth and sky. To bend and see the tall tree-tips held beneath my face as if in the furrow of a palm, and then to warp it with my bucket, keeps me engaged as I walk back and forth, back and forth, from creek to barn, a trip of about a hundred steps, heavy and sloshing and uphill on the way there, light and bucket-swinging on the way back. Today, I only make five trips: enough for a good drink for the two cows, but not enough to fill their trough.

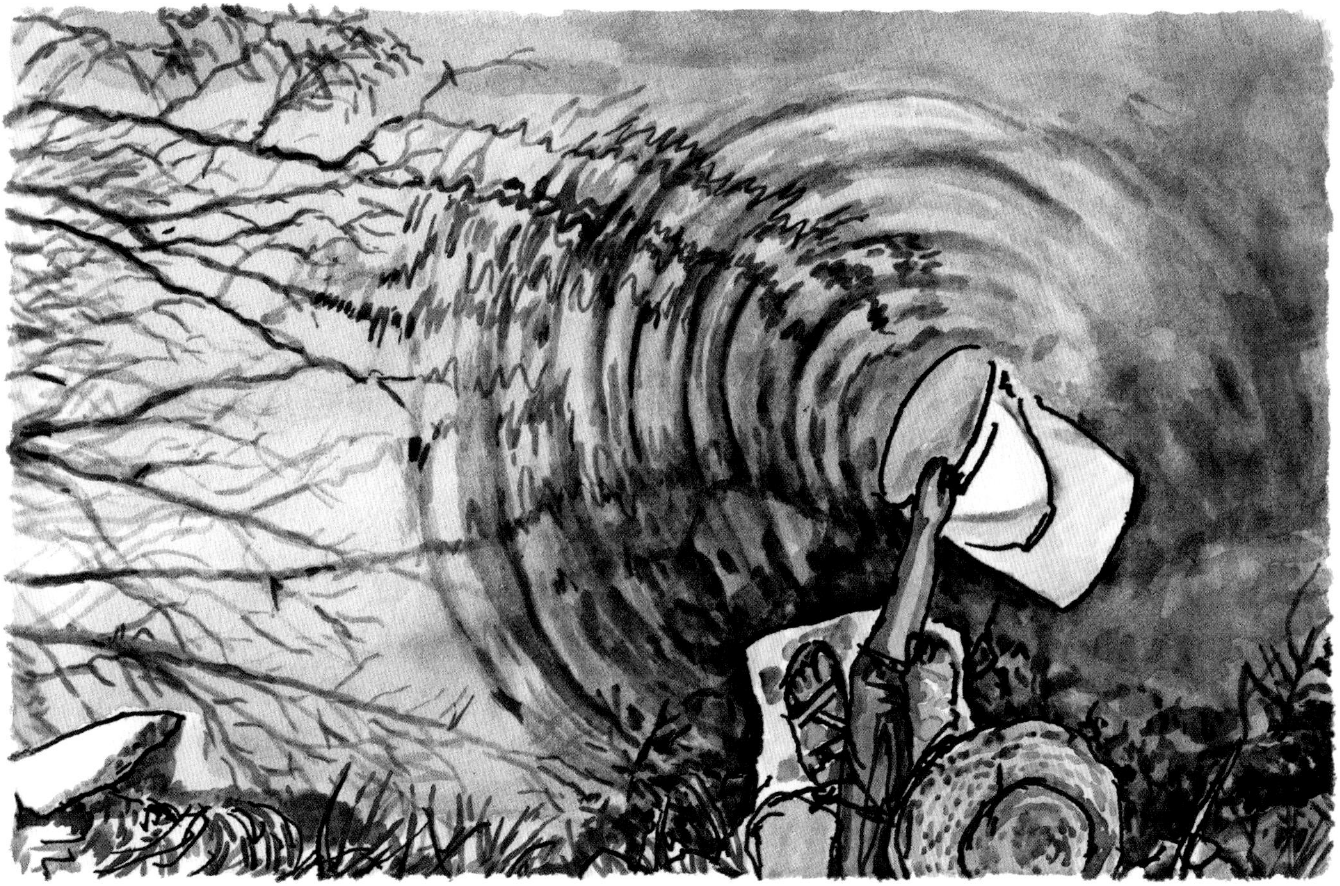

THURSDAY, APRIL 18

When I lived in cities, grass was easy to ignore, the vegetable equivalent of pavement. A lawn in town must be mowed, but if I happened to have one, it was scaled to my capacity: an hour a week would do. Grass seemed gentle: even the word 'blade' loses its threat when followed by 'of grass.' A blade of grass yields to the blade you wield against it, and yields a sweet smell when cut. It also yields to contemplation, as Whitman knew: "I lean and loaf at my ease observing a spear of summer grass."

But spring on the farm allows no leaning and loafing. Beginning around mid-April, Kentucky grass becomes a relentless force. The earth is a green-pelted animal with rank fur, in which we are embedded like ticks, hanging on for dear life.

Time is scarce. I mow and mow, cultivate and rake out beds in the herb garden, and plant parsley, cilantro, and dill. At day's end, I collapse on the couch. Phoebe is with her grandmother in Lexington, an hour away. We have stale popcorn and beer for dinner.

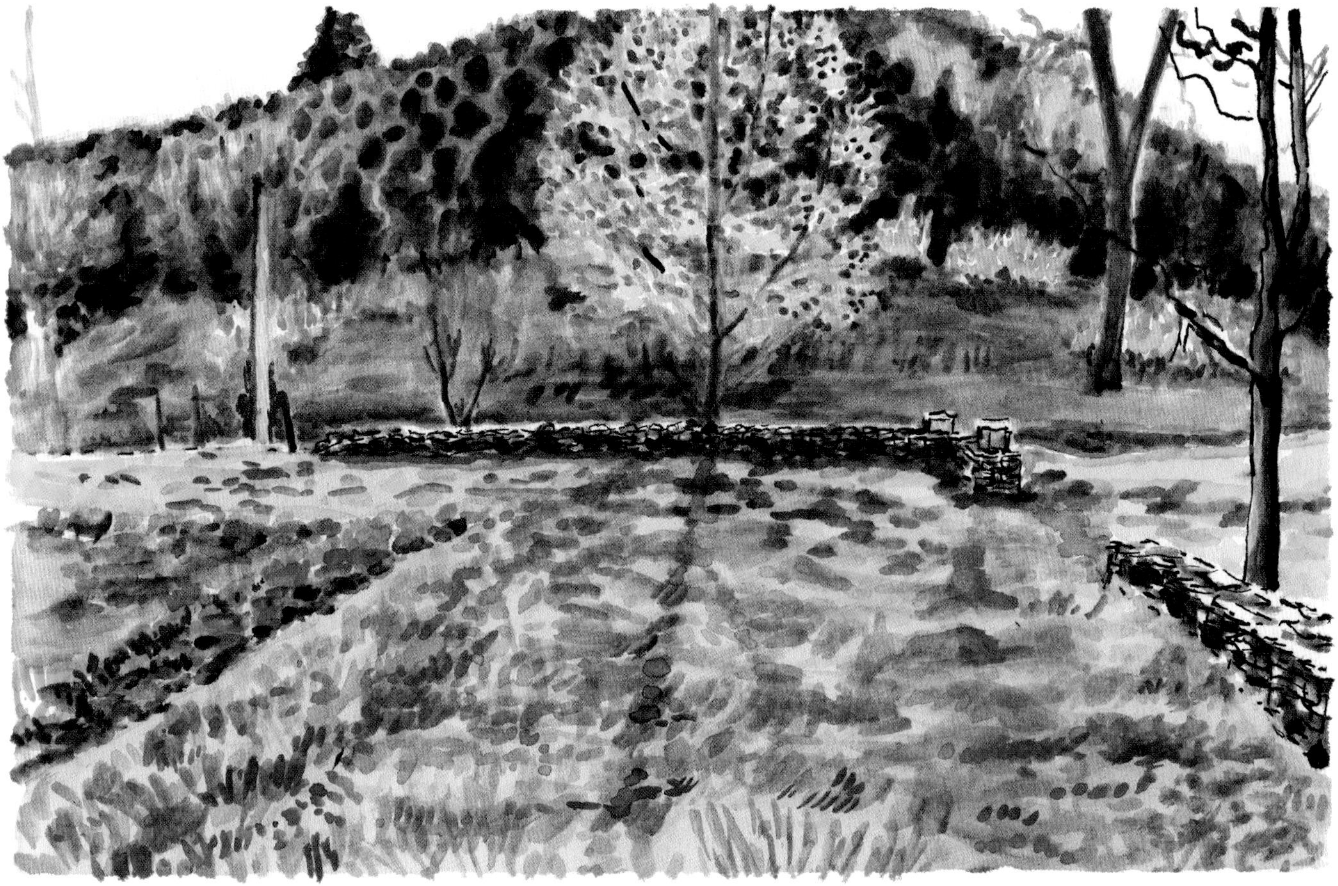

Saturday, April 20

We left out extra food for the animals yesterday, went to a gallery in Lexington for the reception of an exhibit in which I have a painting, and spent the night at my mother's house. Today, we did our grocery shopping, took a trip to the library, and returned home after dark. Frost is in the forecast. We pause in the lane and aim the headlights out to the fields to see that the row covers have shifted in the wind. I go out in the dark with a flashlight to straighten them so the greens won't get frostbitten. My wet shoes shine with moonlight: the grass is heavy with dew. Despite the cold air, I catch the scent of wild plum blossoms before going back in the house.

The world at this moment straddles the border between darkness and illumination. I've assaulted this paper with paint, layer upon layer, until it begins to disintegrate. The border between what's concealed and what's apparent disintegrates too.

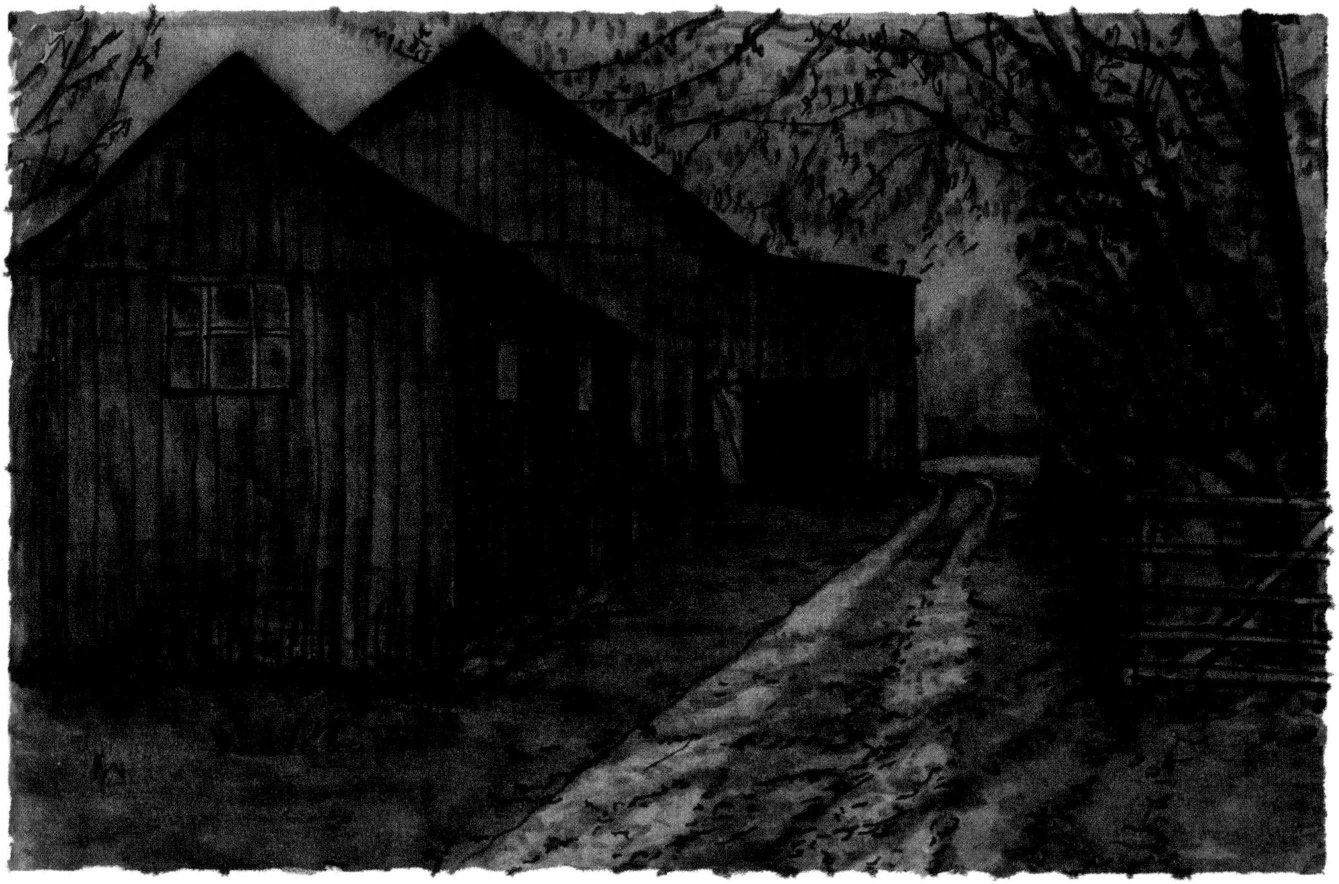

Monday, April 22

There is too much to do, so Phoebe and I run away into the woods. The land is swathed in color: redbud, yellow sneezewort, blue phlox, wild plum in white blossom, mayapple raising its glossy parasols, pale new leaves on the box elders by the creekside. These woods give me the gift of stepping into a space where I allow myself to believe that there is little to do. But look a little deeper, and see the garlic mustard, the Japanese honeysuckle: invasive species that proliferate as a result of human mistakes. We spend an hour or two before dark searching for morels and find only four. I allow Phoebe to drink a handful of water from a small tributary to Straight Run, which has its source near here. We get back to the house just as darkness falls. Dinner is late and the dishes don't get done, as usual.

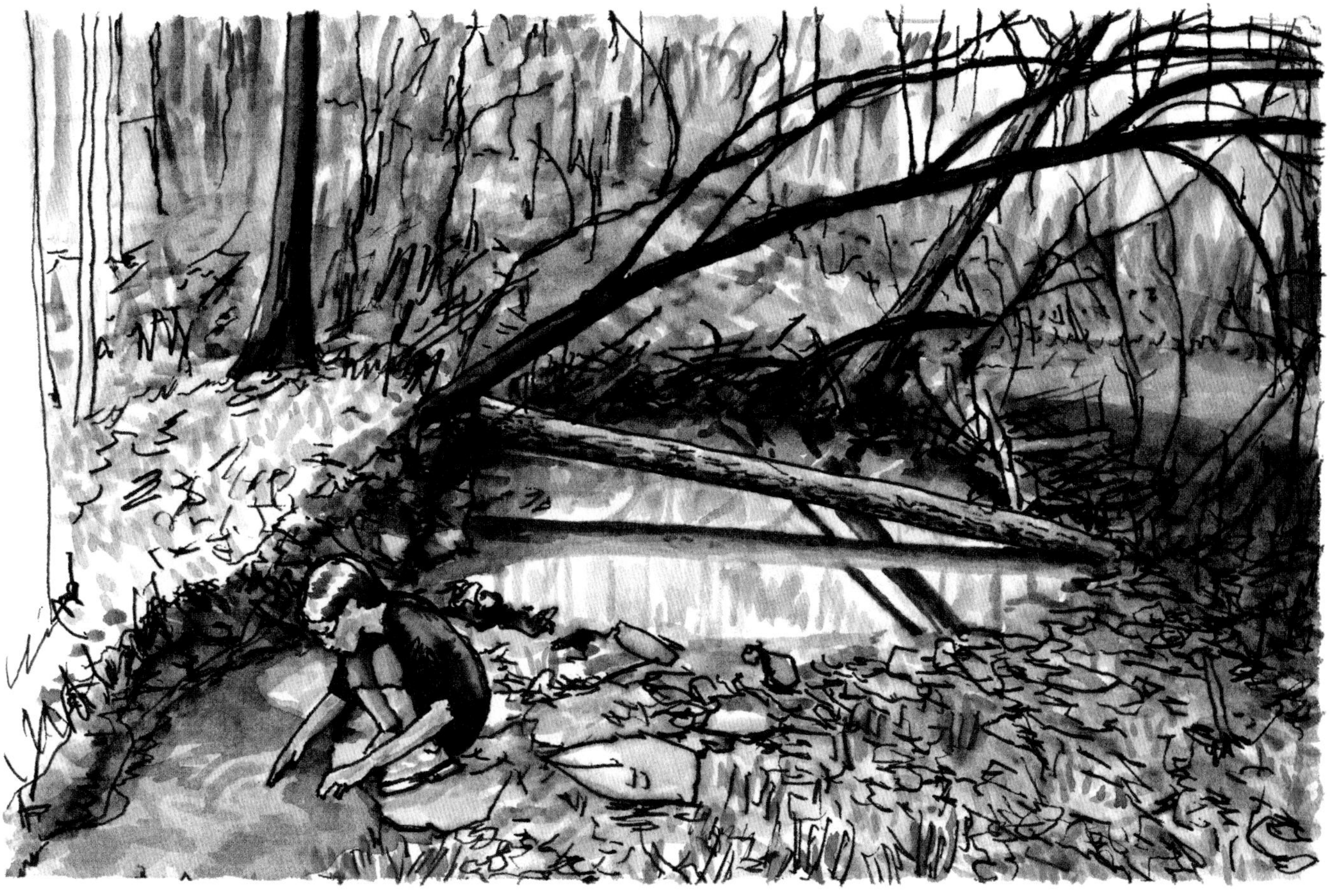

THURSDAY, APRIL 25

The front porch is littered with sodden clothes and boots after yesterday's rain-soaked harvest, our first CSA delivery of the season. There was no time to put anything away before we left—even our lunch things stayed on the kitchen table. We got home late and touched nothing before heading to bed, so we wake this morning to these tableaux of abandonment all around the house, inside and out.

We have fifty-four shareholders now, each of whom will receive a weekly half-bushel basket full of a variety of produce over the coming twenty-four weeks. We'll probably pick up a few more as the season progresses; we'll turn people away after we hit sixty. About half of the group has been our customers for many years. We delivered spinach, arugula, mizuna, spring onions, and French breakfast radishes. Our asparagus patch is in decline, and it will take a few years to re-establish, so on Tuesday, I drove to a farm in Cynthiana where a farmer I know who grows asparagus sells me all I can pick for two dollars a pound. I'm only able to glean eighteen pounds, though, so our shareholders must choose between asparagus and French breakfast radishes, which is not fair to latecomers—not that I have anything against radishes. Each customer also gets a couple of pounds of potatoes that have overwintered in our root cellar.

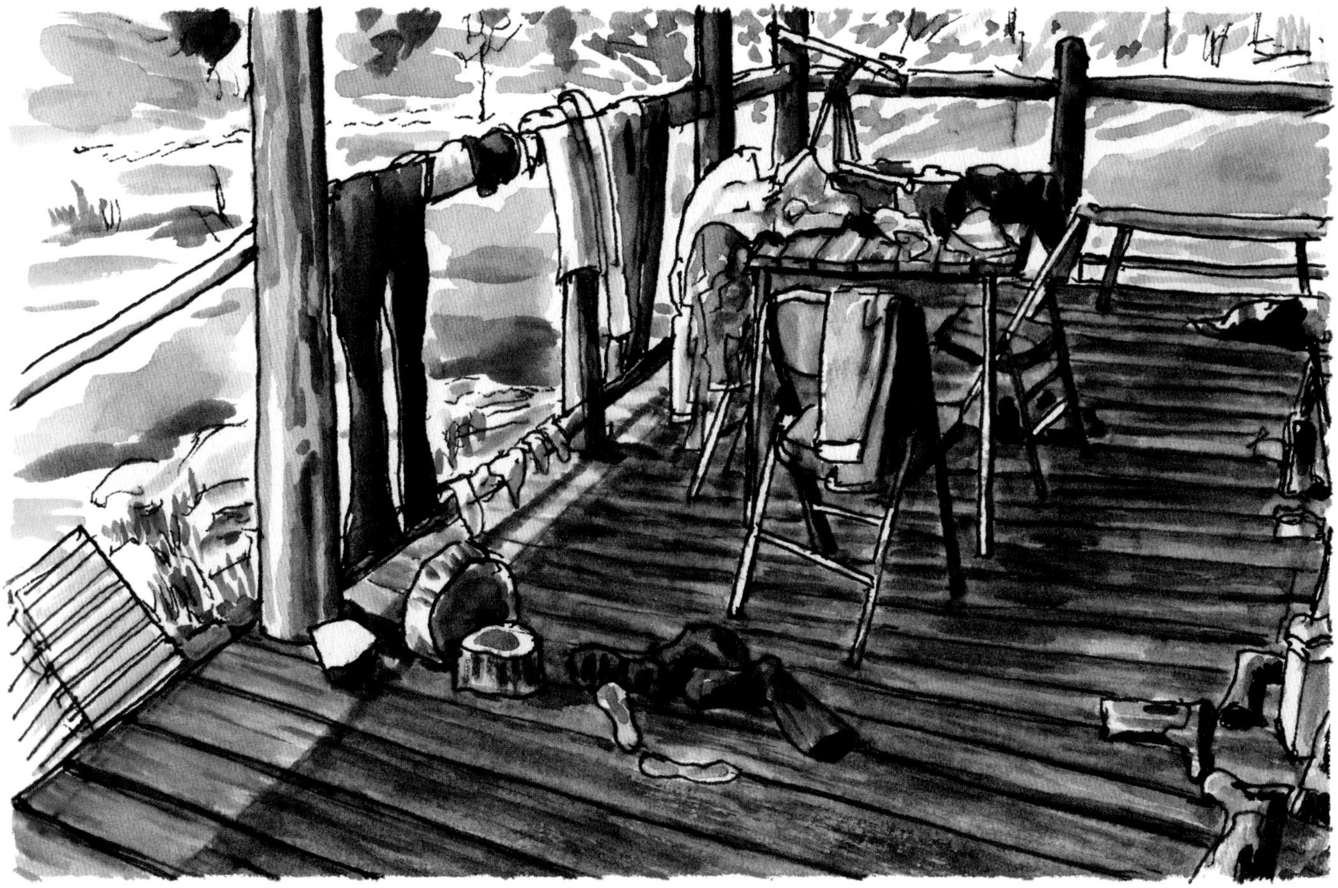

Saturday, April 27

The day after our first CSA delivery, Phoebe was silent and taciturn as we ate dinner, then excused herself and went to her room. A little later, I went to talk to her. "I miss Lou," she told me. Some of our customers were talking the day before about the delicious meat we'd recently delivered to those who placed an order. "I don't understand," Phoebe said, "why people have to be so *indelicate* about it."

We had a long talk, again, about the complex moral issues involved in what we eat. When I lived in the city, it was easier to believe that there was such a thing as clean, ethical eating, and that all I had to do was buy it. I was a vegetarian, as I still prefer to be, but I don't see my preference as superior to conscientious omnivory. Ruminants transform grass, our most abundant crop, into flesh, and a farm's economy, at its best, mirrors its ecosystem. Buying beans at the store grown hundreds or thousands of miles away—food provided courtesy of the fossil fuel burned to bring it to our plates—is that better? The more we talked, Phoebe said, the more confused she felt. Good, I thought. Confusion is underrated.

Tonight, after a day of fence-building, seed-sowing, tilling, cooking, playing, reading, eating, and dishwashing, father and daughter have fallen asleep together on the couch.

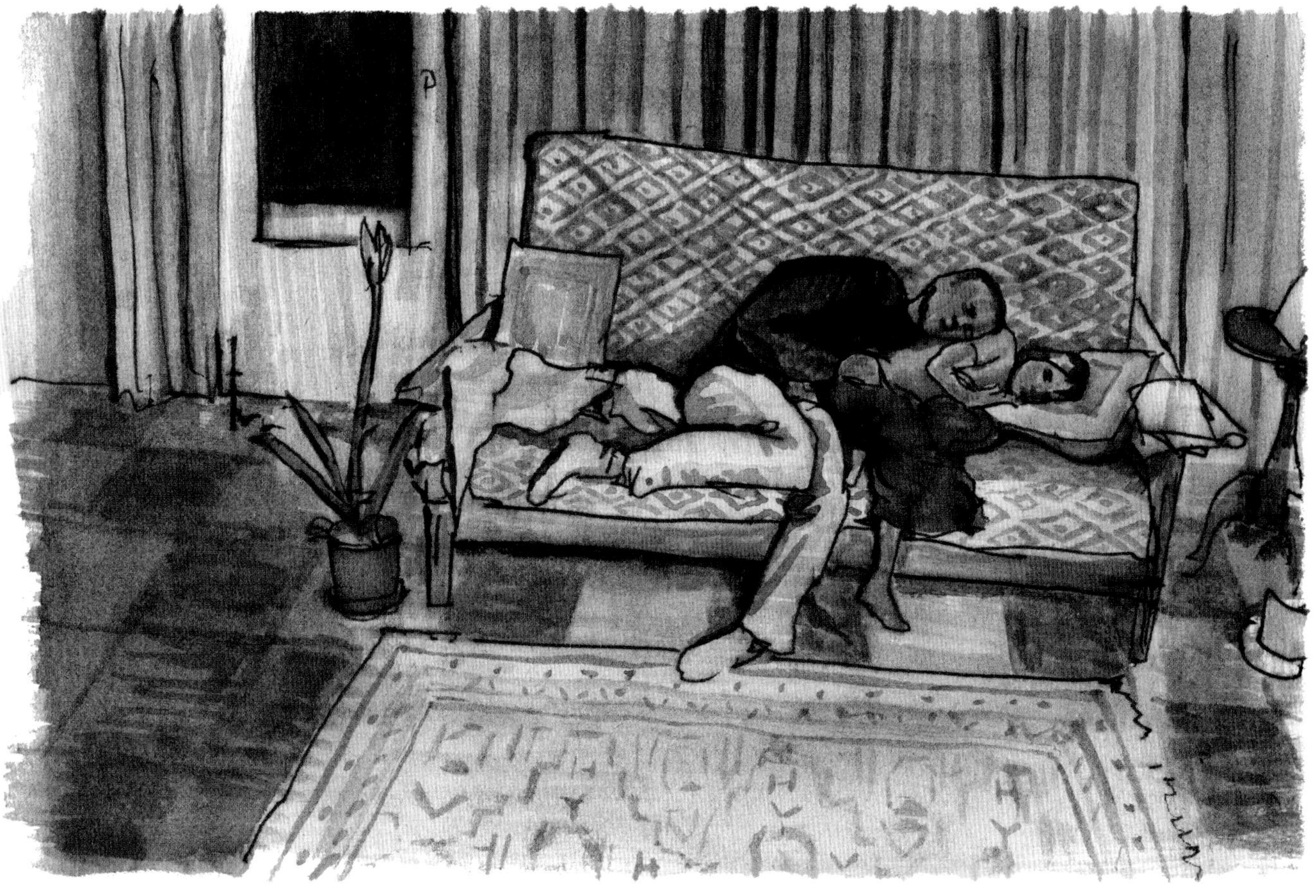

TUESDAY, APRIL 30

We are gathering wild garlic, *allium canadense*, on the banks of Crooked Creek, when we hear the flute-like song of the Baltimore oriole for the first time this spring. Each year, a pair of orioles nests in the shagbark hickory a hundred feet from our front porch. And each year, the male sings the first eight notes of the Spring Concerto from *The Four Seasons*. I wondered if Vivaldi had plagiarized an oriole until I learned how much their song varies by region. I heard an oriole once in Bourbon County, thirty miles from here, singing a completely different tune.

I've read that an oriole may return each spring to a particular tree to raise young. Those young fly south in fall, thousands of miles, then return to this tree the next spring. This can continue for generations. Here and in their winter homes, orioles choose places that resemble one another: fields dotted with trees. In other words, they like small farms like ours. Maybe there's a woman on a farm in El Salvador or Mexico who hears this same song. The oriole carries a long shining thread that stitches us together. Some might call our farm a backwater, but the vast world is present here. The fences and walls we erect and protect mean nothing to a songbird. This farm's population is largely a migrant one, and that population is always in flux.

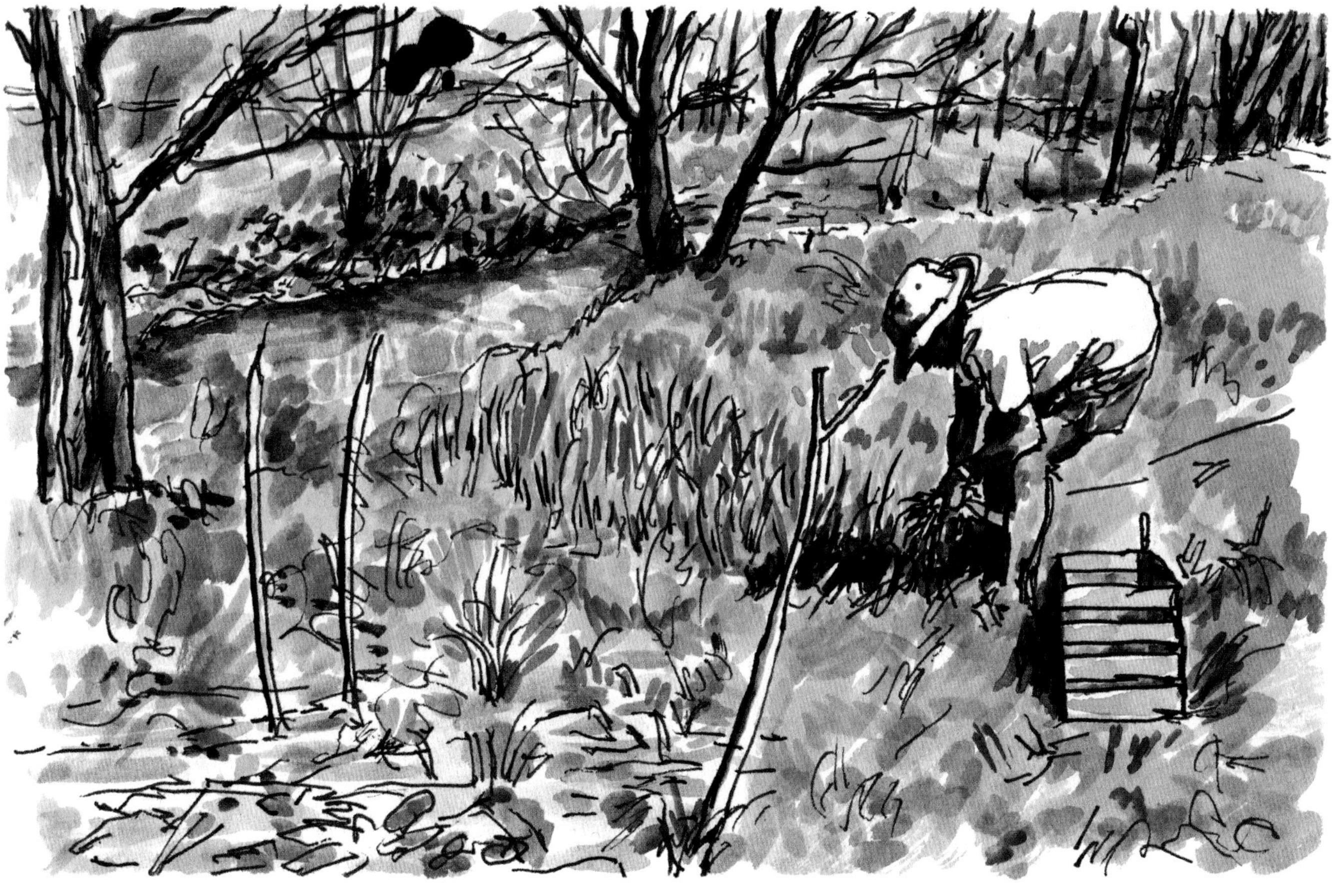

FRIDAY, MAY 3

David has been building a bent willow fence around Phoebe's garden. It's almost complete, ready for her to plant whatever she'd like to grow here. This fence is decorative, but many tall posts have been set for a deer fence we're building around the circumference of this cluster of garden beds, which lies just to the south of our house. Here are our strawberries; new plantings of blueberries, gooseberries, currants, raspberries, and blackberries; and our herb garden.

This morning, David and I went together to the Cynthiana farm to pick asparagus. We got seventy-five pounds: enough to give our customers a pound each, plus have more than a dozen pounds left over for the swap basket. If anyone cares to, they may swap out another item from their basket for an additional share of asparagus.

I spent the afternoon weeding the precious strawberries. A temporary fence has kept the deer out of the patch, just beyond Phoebe's garden, and we hope to have a good crop this year.

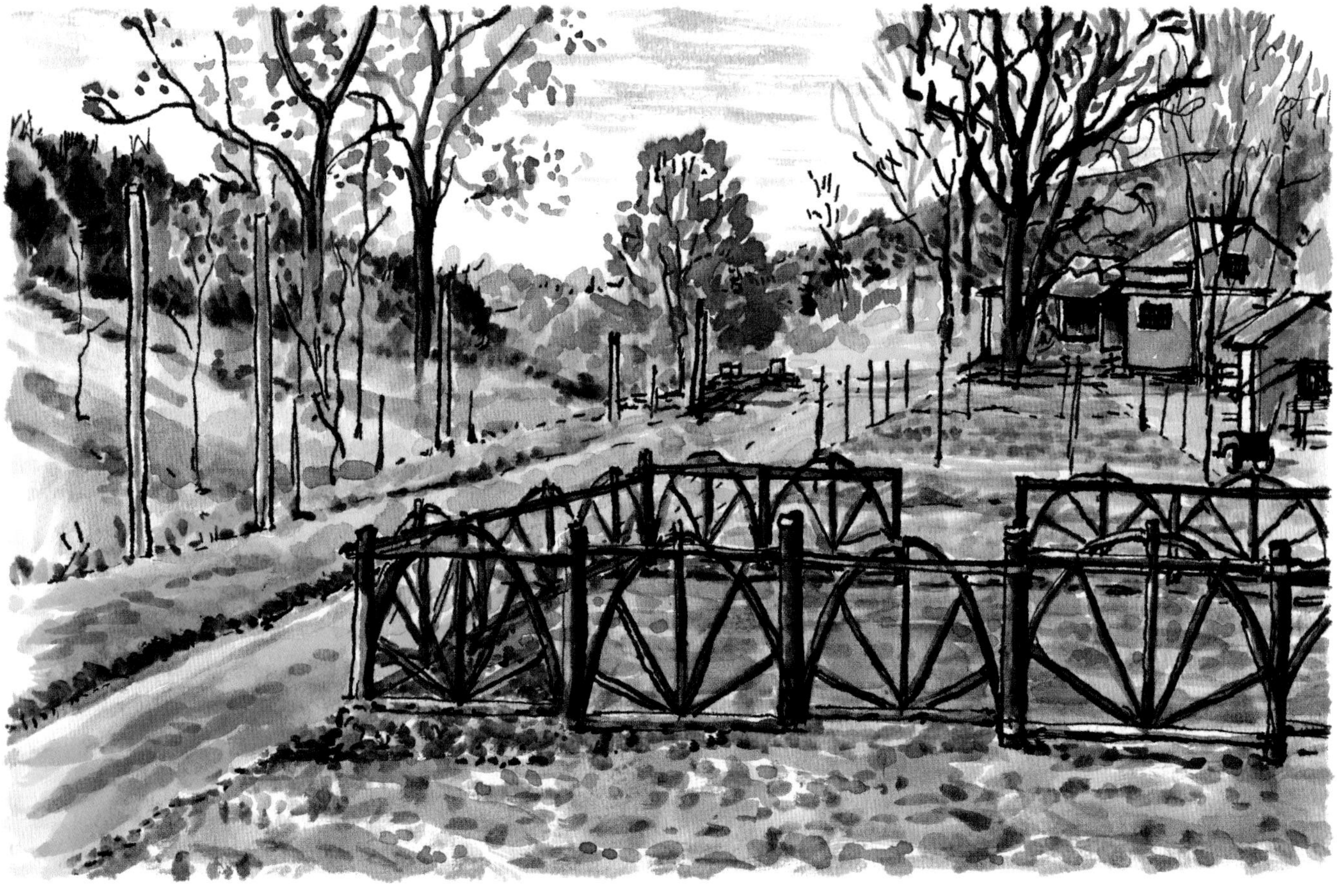

THURSDAY, MAY 9

Kentucky has long been home to a vibrant community of writers and artists for whom land and language are closely interwoven. From time to time, I seek out conversations with them, conversations that are like soil cultivation: they bring oxygen to the roots of my life.

Today, I go to Lexington to visit the poet Nikky Finney. Growing up, she spent summers on her grandparents' South Carolina farm, where her grandmother, Beulah Lenora Butler Davenport—Ma Bea—lived to be 99 years old, and was a farming woman all of her life. Nikky hungered for her grandmother's family stories, despite how much pain that history carried: her ancestors were born into slavery. For Ma Bea, some things were better left unsaid. She only told Nikky about what happened after Emancipation, when her ancestors bought as much land as they could afford, vowing that they would never have to work for another white man. "Land meant freedom," Nikky tells me, "land meant you always had a place to go, and you didn't sell it, you did everything to defend it."

Nikky lives in a house that was once owned by the writer Guy Davenport. She shows me some floorboards on which his name is written in pencil. She took up the floorboards when she replaced her writing studio floor with tiles.

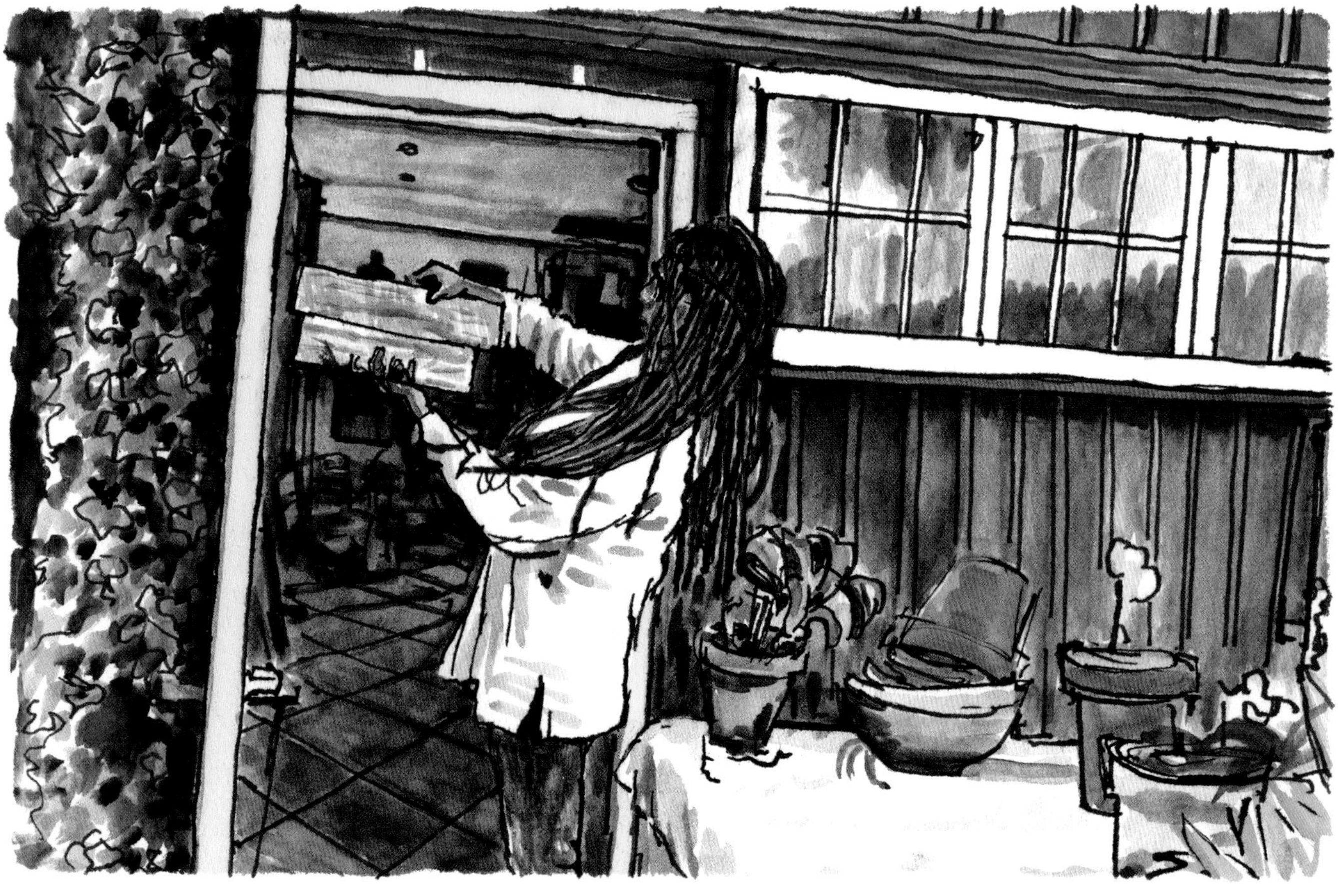

SUNDAY, MAY 12

Every week during harvest season, there's a wild dance of trying to store, eat, and preserve surplus produce, and then the moment of surrender, when we bring the remains to the compost heap. After a Mother's Day nap, I gather up the compost, including a backlog of eggs laid by the hens before we had a steady market. David helps by digging a hole, an egg-well, deep enough so dogs or raccoons won't dig them up again.

We're free for an evening walk in the woods. The sky is gray, grasses thick and tall. "Well well, so it is," the wood thrush trills. On the ridge, as a chilly darkness falls, the trees look pleased in their new green coats. A chuck-wills-widow calls from somewhere to the north. Usually I hear them in the woods to the south. On a night in May, the locust blossoms can reflect enough moonlight to allow us to walk the ridge without a flashlight, but tonight they are past their prime, and the sky is too muted to show them up well. At the creek crossing near the meadow, where the branch meets Straight Run, it's nearly dark, and the water sings like bells over the stones. Then the rain comes, light enough to be little more than a sound, more heard than felt, a blurring of the clarity.

We walk past the house to the barn and close the chickens in. The pasture hill is lit with the first fireflies of the year.

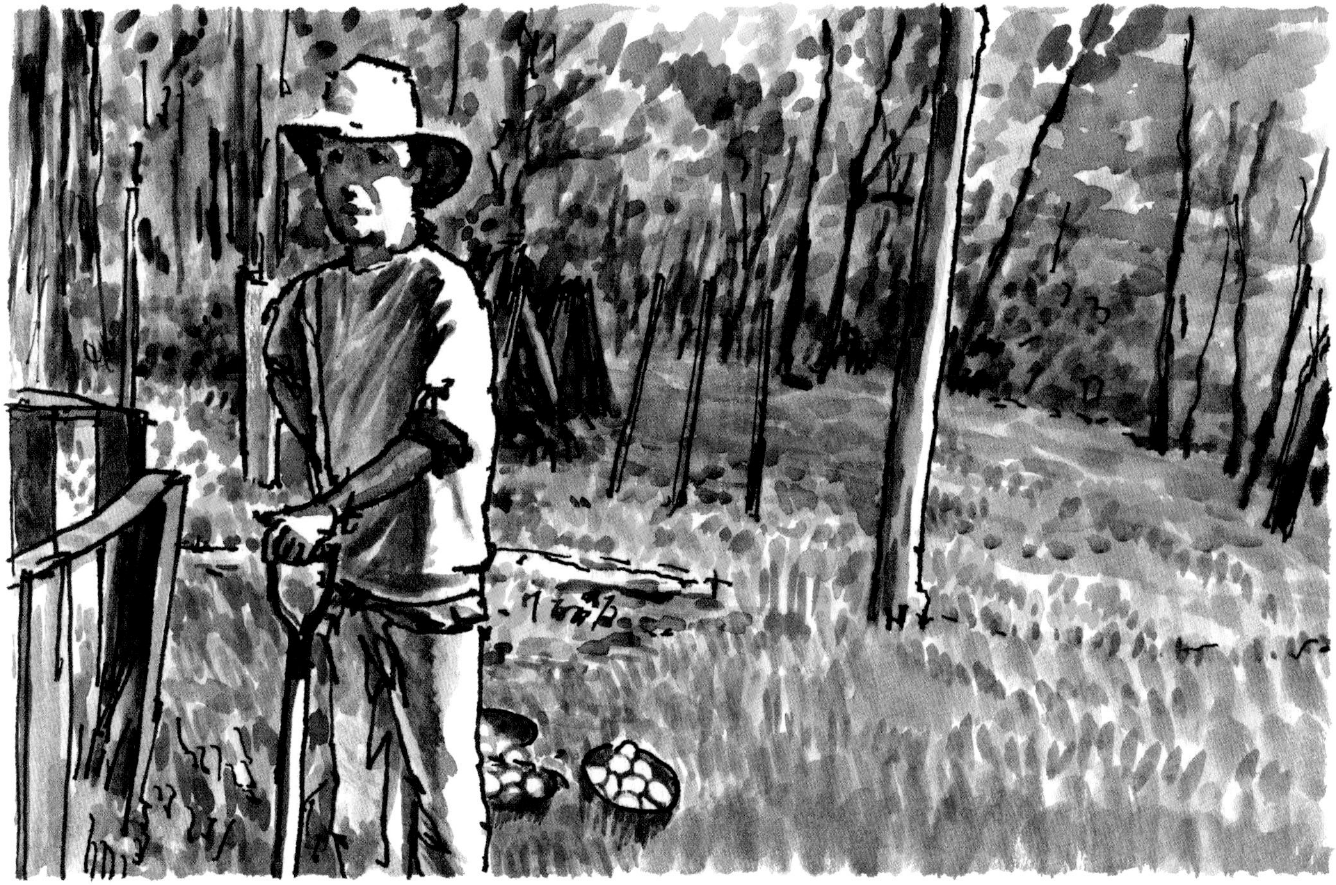

MONDAY, MAY 13

Light frost last night might have killed the sweet potatoes we plant today, had we planted them yesterday. The slips arrive in the mail at a time of year when their planting must compete with many other time-sensitive tasks. We often plant them later than we should, and the slips suffer. I know we can start our own by sprouting them from last year's potatoes, but I haven't tried that yet. This year, determined to have a good crop, we plant the slips soon after their arrival. They're wrapped in wet paper towels, then separated and pushed into the earth with a repurposed pestle.

I feel a kinship with these near-rootless stems. They're not newborns, like seedlings; they're outgrowths of a mature tuber, so they have an air of experience about them, a touch of worldliness. Yet their real work still lies ahead. Their name, *slip*, is evasive, non-committal. When you give someone the slip, you give that person your absence. But now we give the soil the slip, and with luck, we'll receive roots in return.

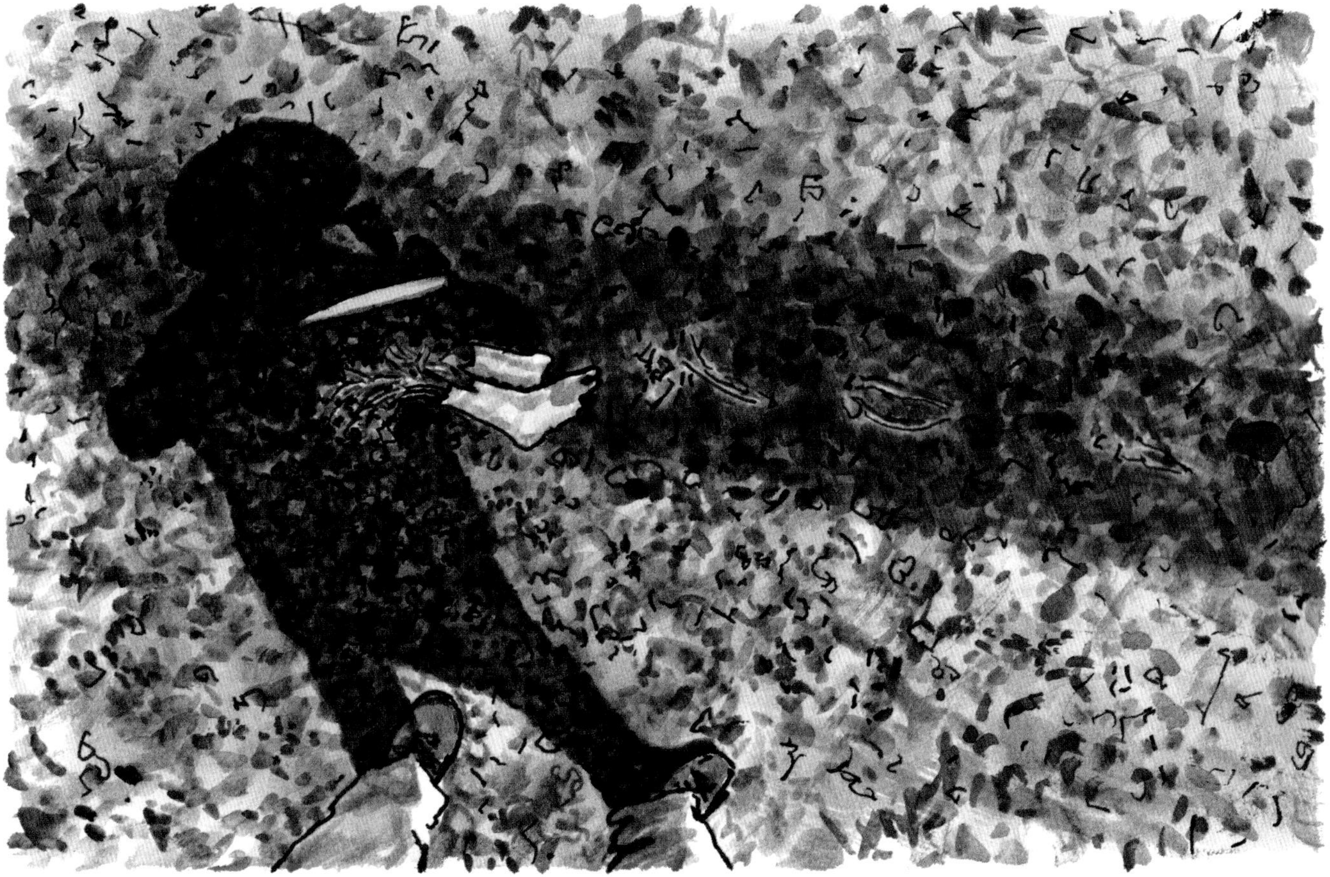

THURSDAY, MAY 16

David checks in on the new colony of bees, from a swarm just caught on Tuesday: A swarm in May is worth a load of hay! They had clustered in a wrist-thick low branch of a sycamore near the swimming hole. We set a sheet and an empty hive box under the branch, and David sawed it off the tree with one pole saw while I held the branch steady with another, hoping to lower the branch gently once it was cut. Swarming bees are not territorial and so are less likely to sting than those that have an established home, but these bees did not seem to know that. I was stung a few times but managed not to drop my end of the branch.

The hives we wrapped in an old tarp in January to protect them from the cold were unwrapped once the worst of the frigid weather passed. One night a few weeks later, a heavy wind blew off the hive box covers, and a cold rain followed. It was more than the bees could withstand. Our more established hive also didn't survive the winter. Until this week, we were bee-less for the first time since we started keeping bees about a dozen years ago.

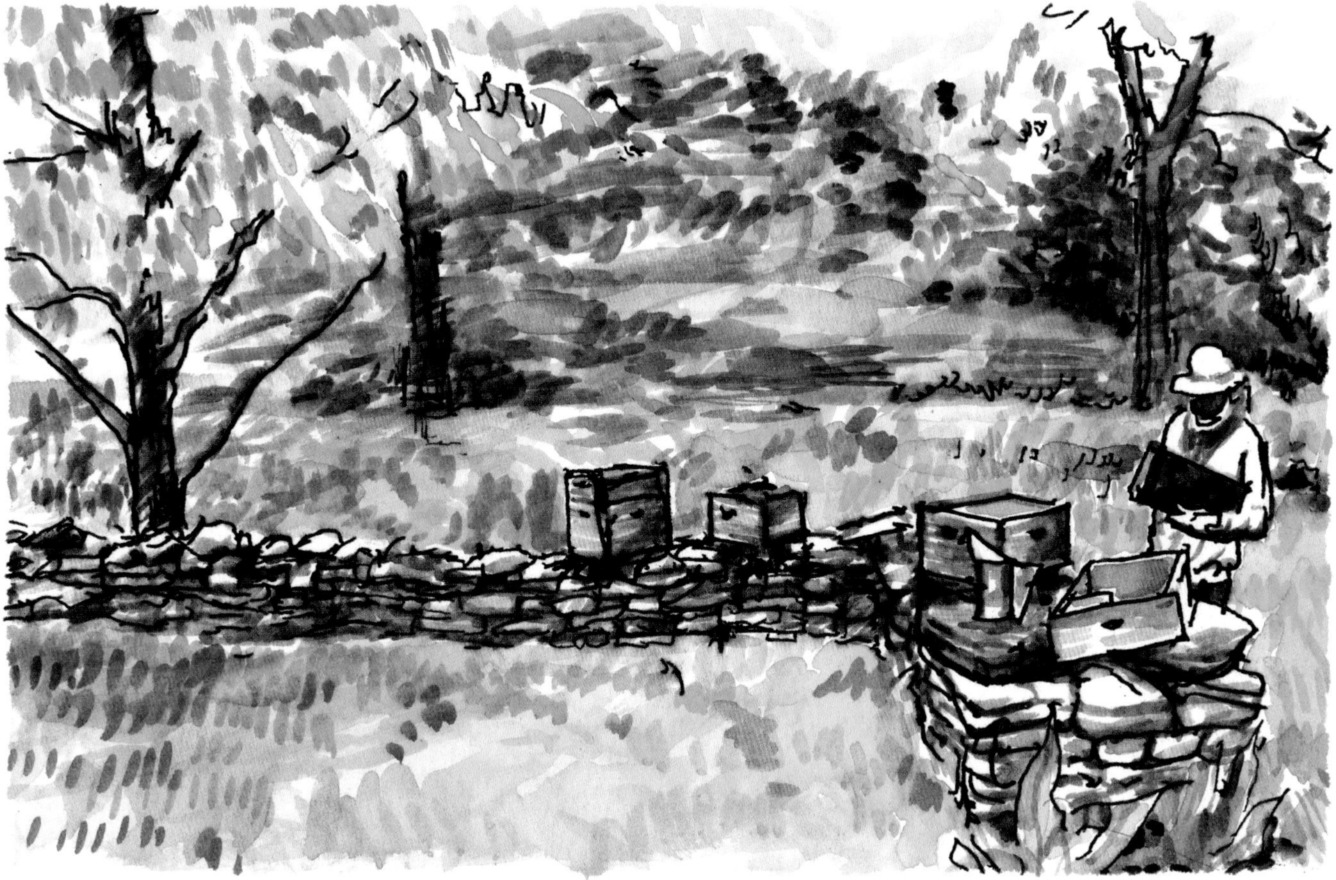

SATURDAY, MAY 18

After planting and weeding in the herb garden, while putting tools away in the shed, I hear a loud rattle right behind my head. I turn and find myself eye to eye with a large Eastern milk snake, sometimes called a cowsucker, as it's falsely rumored to drink directly from the udder. It's not venomous, but the rattling tail and ready-to-strike pose has just the effect on me that the snake intended: I scream and run away.

Big, non-venomous gray rat snakes and black kingsnakes seem to like our house and find inventive and mysterious ways to get in. One recent evening, while I sat reading in the living room, I heard a delicate clinking coming from the kitchen, as if someone were gently reorganizing the plates. I went into the kitchen and looked around: some pottery was off-kilter, and the door to the fuse box in the corner of the kitchen was open, but I didn't see whatever had caused it. I walked back into the living room and found a kingsnake, as long as myself, using Art Spiegelman's *Maus* as a stair-step to reach toward an open nook on our bookshelves, into which it curled itself.

I spent that evening alone in the house with a bookish snake. It was gone by morning, and as far as I know I never saw it again.

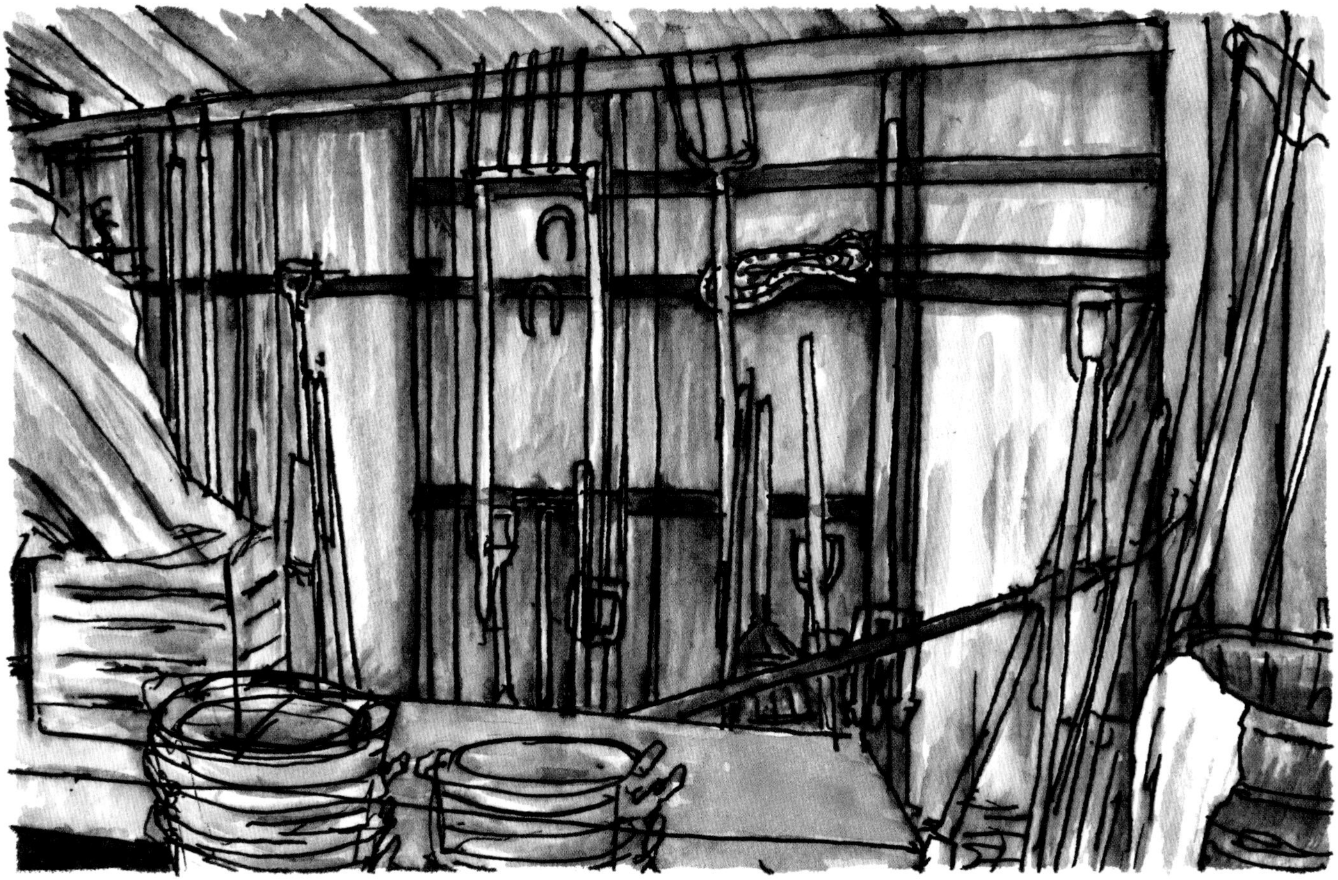

THURSDAY, MAY 23

The first strawberries ripen, and the first catbirds and thrashers find them. We drive to the barn for the roll of bird netting, which weighs a few hundred pounds. Phoebe, just home from her last day of school, hops on for the ride. She's excited for summer: it's a time when she can immerse herself in creative endeavors. Turning around, I see her through Big Red's back window; facing forward, I see her in the rearview mirror.

In winter, there were lines, hard black shapes. Now everything is softening, and I miss the stark structure, the bones of this landscape laid bare. I'm fighting with the ink: it's too strong for the flush of spring, but I don't want to let it go.

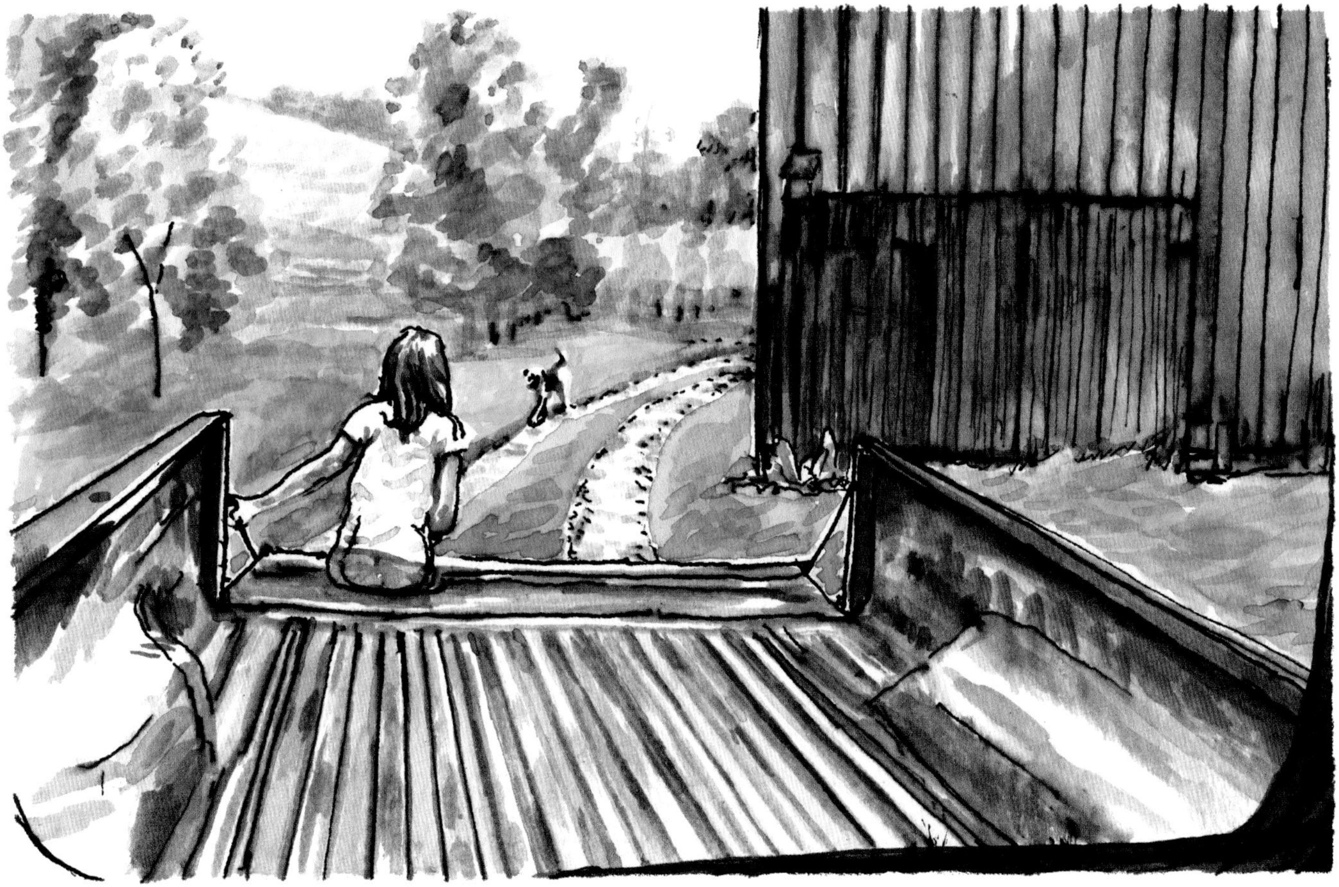

FRIDAY, MAY 24

When grass was scarce, we walked down the lane, and Lily would come running, hollering for hay or a scoop of grain feed. Now the grass is so good that she won't even look up when we pass. Something similar happens to us during the first flush of lettuce season. No, I can't go to Lexington today to work; I have to stay home and eat salad.

Our shareholders each received two heads of lettuce on Wednesday. We've devoured six heads since then, plus four endives, a bag of mizuna, a couple of dozen radishes and spring onions, a pound or so of asparagus. We have possibly consumed more salad over these days than we did all winter long.

It may dip below freezing tonight, so it's back to the barn to gather covers I braided up weeks ago and put away for the season. There's more to protect now: strawberries, sweet potatoes, zinnias and other flowers, beans, summer squash. Luckily, our tomatoes, eggplants, and peppers are still in the greenhouse. Hurrah for being behind schedule!

The row covers look like giant loaves of unbaked challah. I chose to draw this because the barn's interior is well-suited to ink lines, unlike the soft, blowsy greens outside. I can cling here to a bygone time.

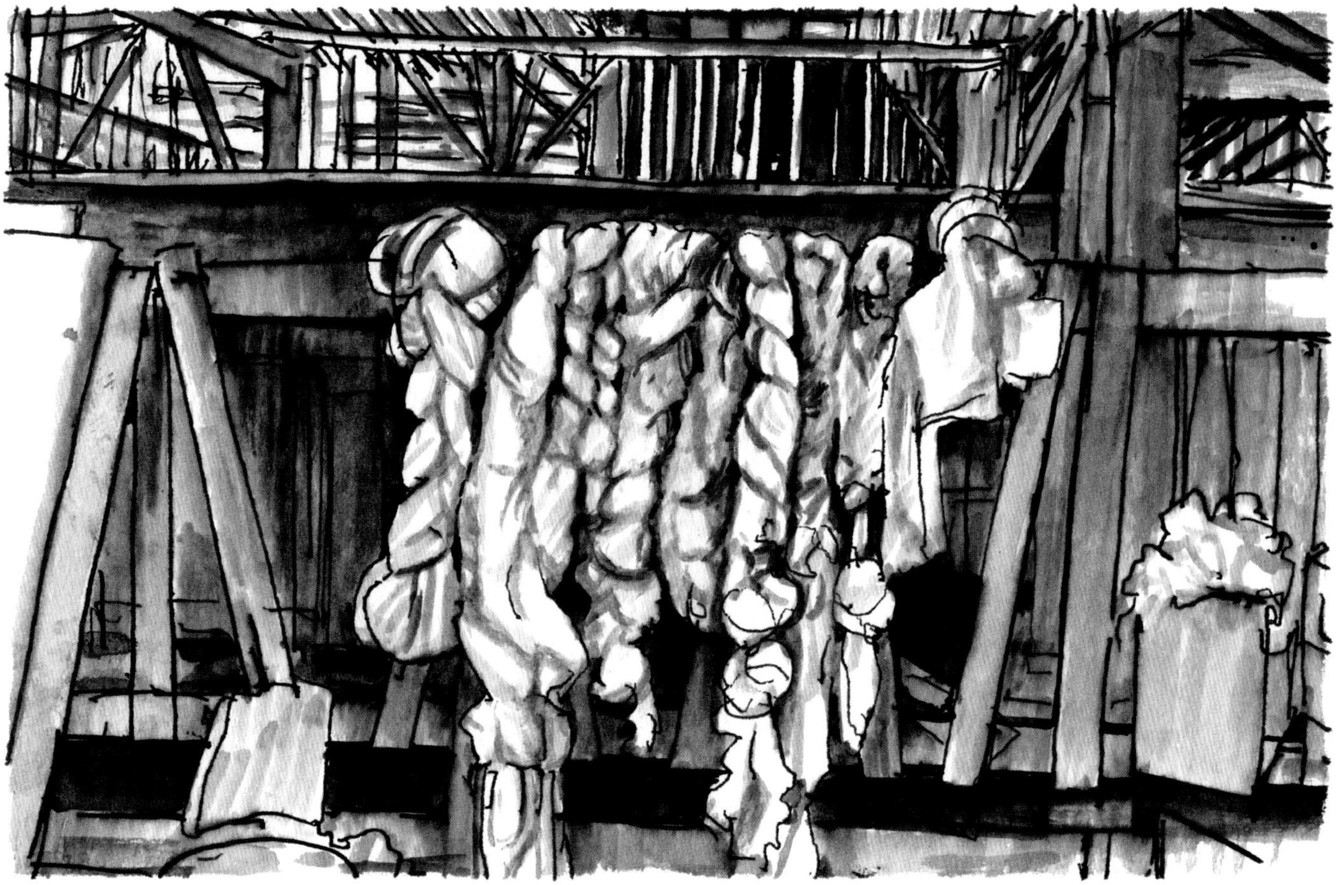

SATURDAY, MAY 25

Tomatoes, peppers, and eggplants harden off outside the greenhouse, beside the drying laundry. This is the first picture I've made for this journal without laying down ink first, then adding watercolors. It felt like trying to tailor a suit for a jellyfish.

After planting in the flower garden, I go into the toolshed for a rake and find a perfect snakeskin draped over the tines of a pitchfork, where I saw the snake last week. Phoebe and her friend Amelia hold up the skin to show how long the snake was. I fixed them a salad earlier, which Amelia ate with intense focus. "What kind of lettuce is this?" she asked. "I've never tasted anything like it." It's red bibb: delicate, crisp, perfect, and too tender to survive long-distance travel. Bibbs found in the store under plastic domes that weigh as much as the lettuces do are someone's terrible idea of trying to defy this reality. Part of the pleasure of this lettuce is its seasonal evanescence, and plastic is about as remote from evanescent as you can get.

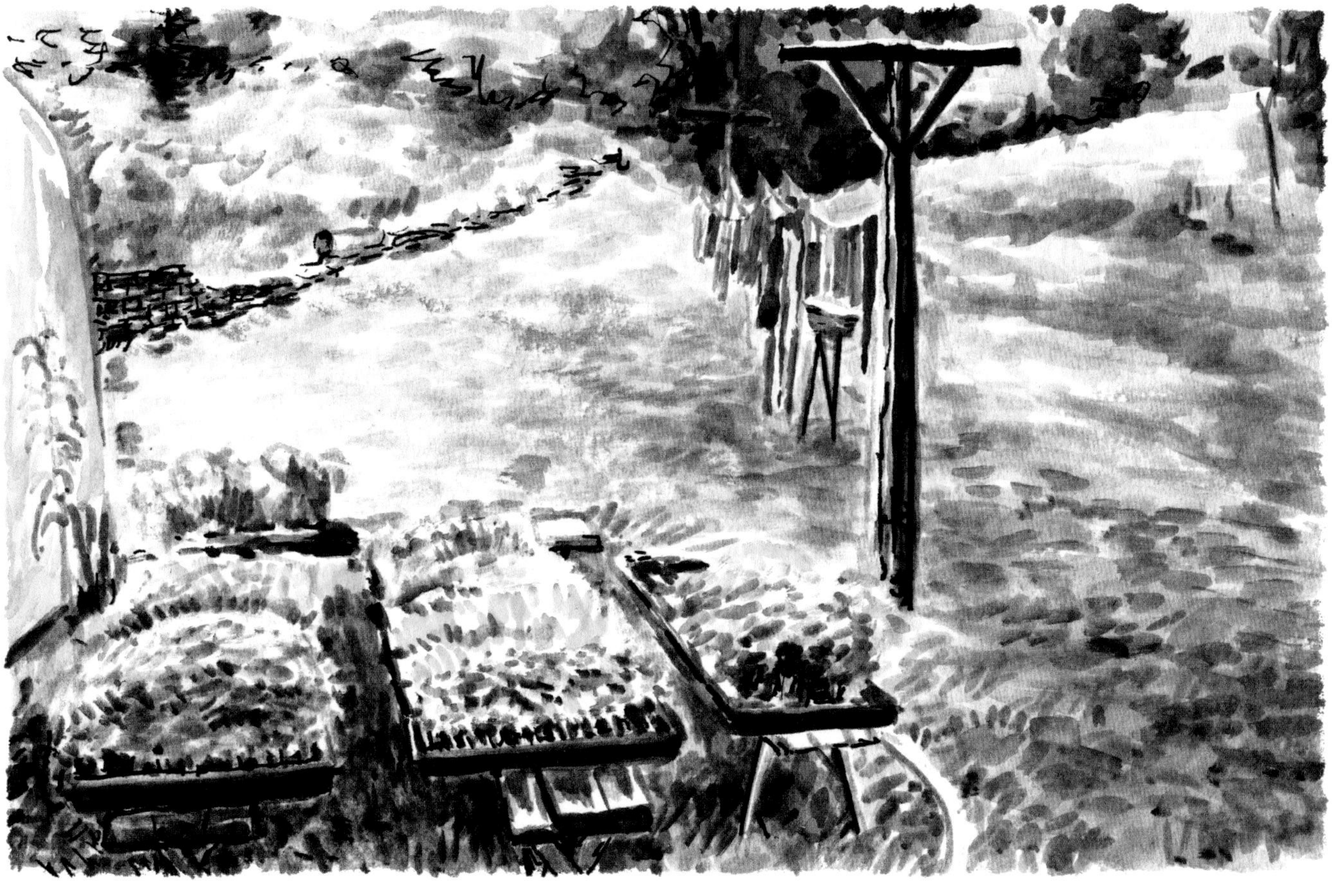

TUESDAY, MAY 28

Years ago, a neighbor stopped by while I was cooking a batch of strawberry jam. "You can get a big jar of jam at Walmart for three dollars," she said. "Why would you make your own?" Our agricultural past sometimes seems like a phantom limb. We aim to exercise it, but the so-called efficiencies of global industrialism have rendered it useless. Frank keeps draft horses that have rarely pulled a plow. Charlie raises a crop of beets that his wife Helen throws away, because cooking them is too much work. Jay milks his goats each day, but dumps it in the dirt, because his family won't drink it. I weed, pick, clean, hull, and preserve strawberries, when I could buy jam at Walmart for three dollars. Yet in that Walmart jar are debts we have yet to pay. And I love to watch the tiny green buttons swell, turn white, then pink, then red. I love to taste the sun in the fruit. I love to eat of the soil of this place, to know that my flesh and this patch of earth are stitched together. What good is an economy that disregards love?

I picked strawberries last night until it was too dark to see, and I didn't get the bird netting back in place, so this morning David and I bring our coffee out to the toolshed, beside the berry patch, to keep the birds away until we've woken up enough to cover the patch again. We're groggy scarecrows.

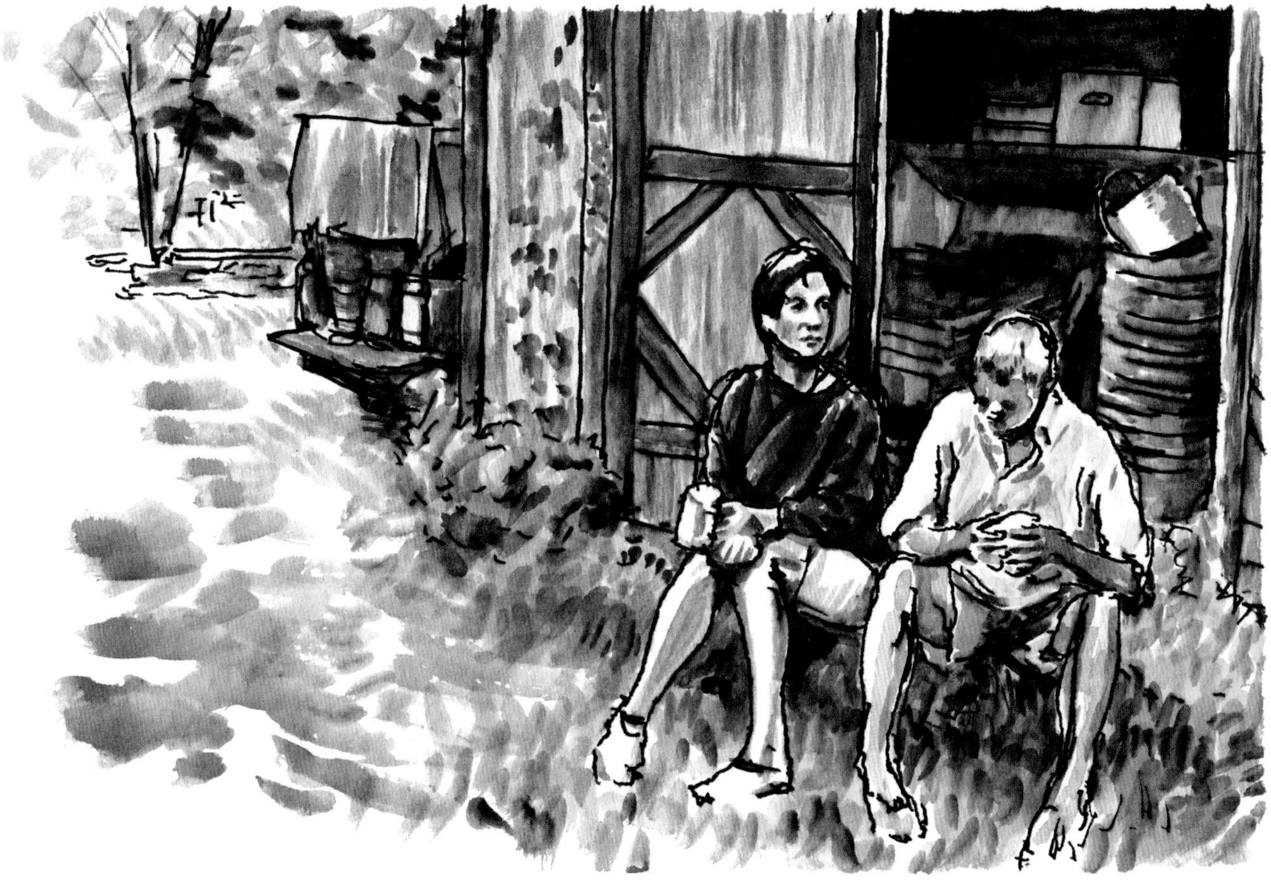

SATURDAY, JUNE 1

The year after Phoebe was born, we planted hundreds of strawberry crowns in a bed that had been in sod for decades. The soil there was a wonder of fertility, and we had a new deer fence. Deer particularly love strawberry plants, and we had never before experienced a harvest that was not decimated by their incursions.

The following year, for a few weeks in late May and early June, we woke to strawberries and ate strawberries before going to bed. Mornings, I hulled and packed them into the freezer. Afternoons, I made jam. Evenings, we picked more. Phoebe sat in the patch while we harvested and grazed as if she were a bear cub. Her cloth diapers were stained pink that year—as were most of our clothes—and peppered, even after laundering, with strawberry achenes, the seedlike specks on a strawberry's skin. We had strawberry vinaigrette on our salads, strawberry ice cream for dessert. We delivered the berries to our customers and invited friends and family out to pick their own. Still, the patch was never more than half-picked.

Our patch has since been relocated to the garden near the house. It's smaller, but provides enough for us. Today, we harvest thirty-four quarts of berries, our biggest haul since that year. Phoebe helps hull them, slicing off their green hats with a teaspoon.

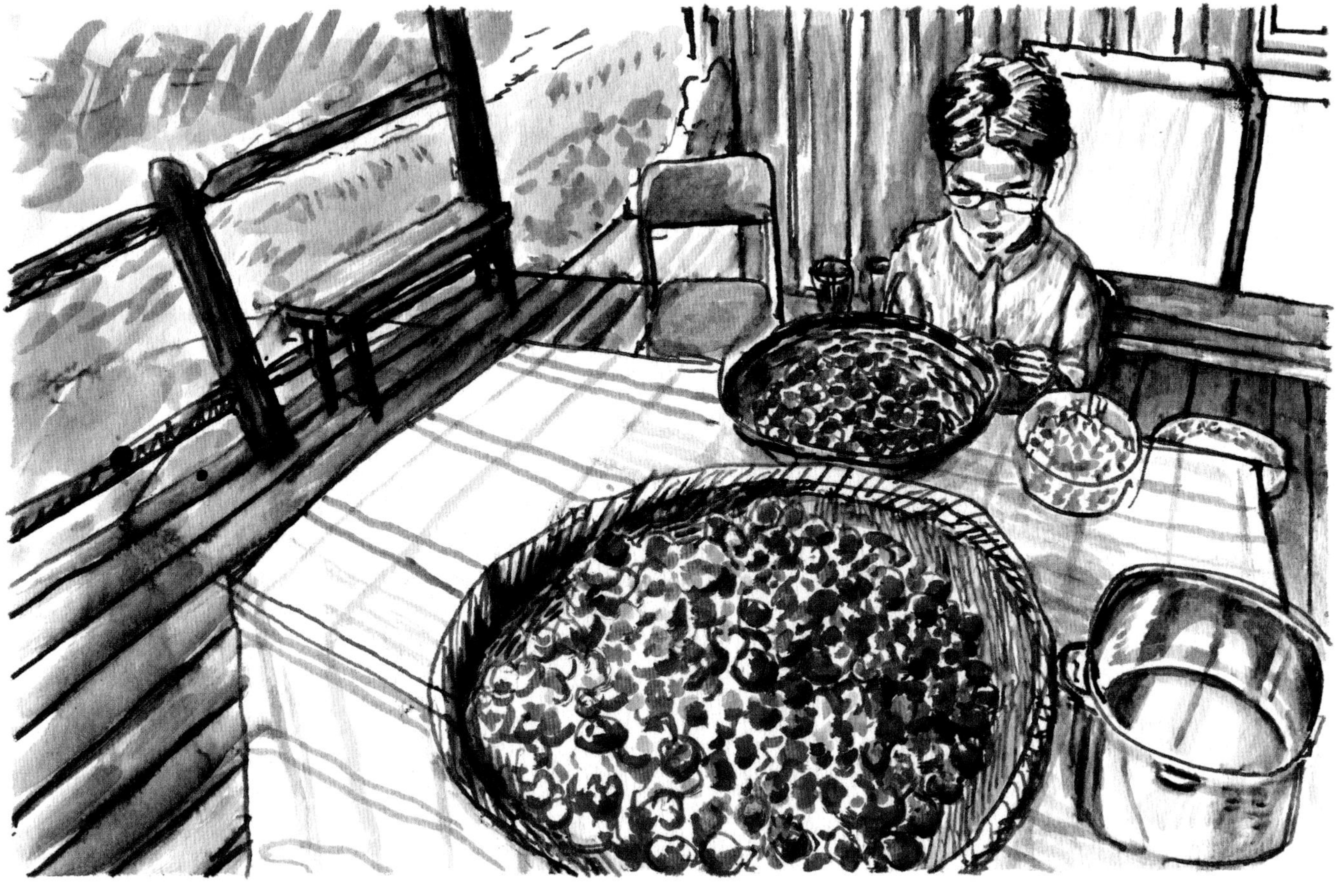

Sunday, June 2

On Sundays, we go to the soccer field in Carlisle. Phoebe plays on the orange team; David coaches the gray team. A herd of cattle graze on the hill behind the field. I like seeing the farmers here, like the man in his suspenders and camo cap. It's good haying and planting weather, and he likely didn't grow up playing soccer himself, but he's here, cheering on his grandkids, I guess. The green team coach wears the team's turquoise tee with Wranglers, Red Wing boots, and a John Deere cap perched on top of his head. Phoebe's league, age seven to ten, consists of five teams. There are only two teams in the older league, age eleven to fifteen, and they play each other every week. Once you turn sixteen, you're out of luck if you want to play soccer in Nicholas County.

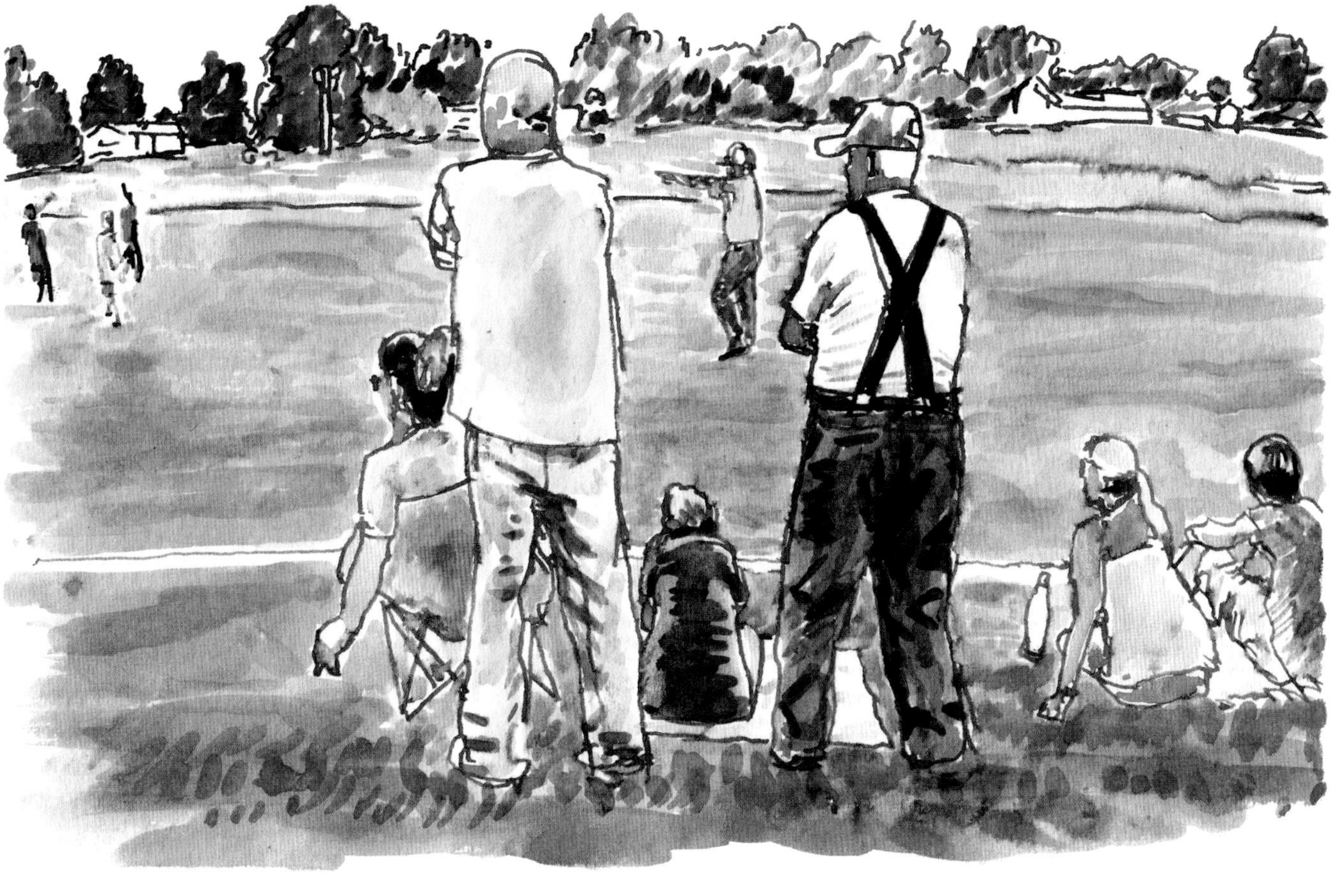

TUESDAY, JUNE 4

David has cut hay from a small field near the banks of Straight Run that we've left fallow this year and raked it into windrows. We head out in Big Red and fork the hay into the truck bed, stomping it down now and then, until it drapes down the sides and back of the truck like a thick head of shaggy brown hair. The poison hemlock is in blossom, so the air smells like plumber's glue. The neighbors call it *stinkweed*.

Haying can be a perilous task in the Crooked Creek valley. Most everyone has a herd of cattle, and therefore most everyone has a need for hay during the winter months. That need can press people to mow hillsides that are just steep enough to roll a tractor. A neighbor was haying a few years ago when his tractor rolled. His head was sliced open to the skull, and he was evacuated by helicopter. He survived, thank goodness. David does our mowing with a walk-behind tractor. If he starts to lose control, he can simply let go of the handlebars and watch it roll off without him.

We drive the truck to the barn and fork the hay we've gathered into the loft. Lily looks on, chewing at her fresh grass cud.

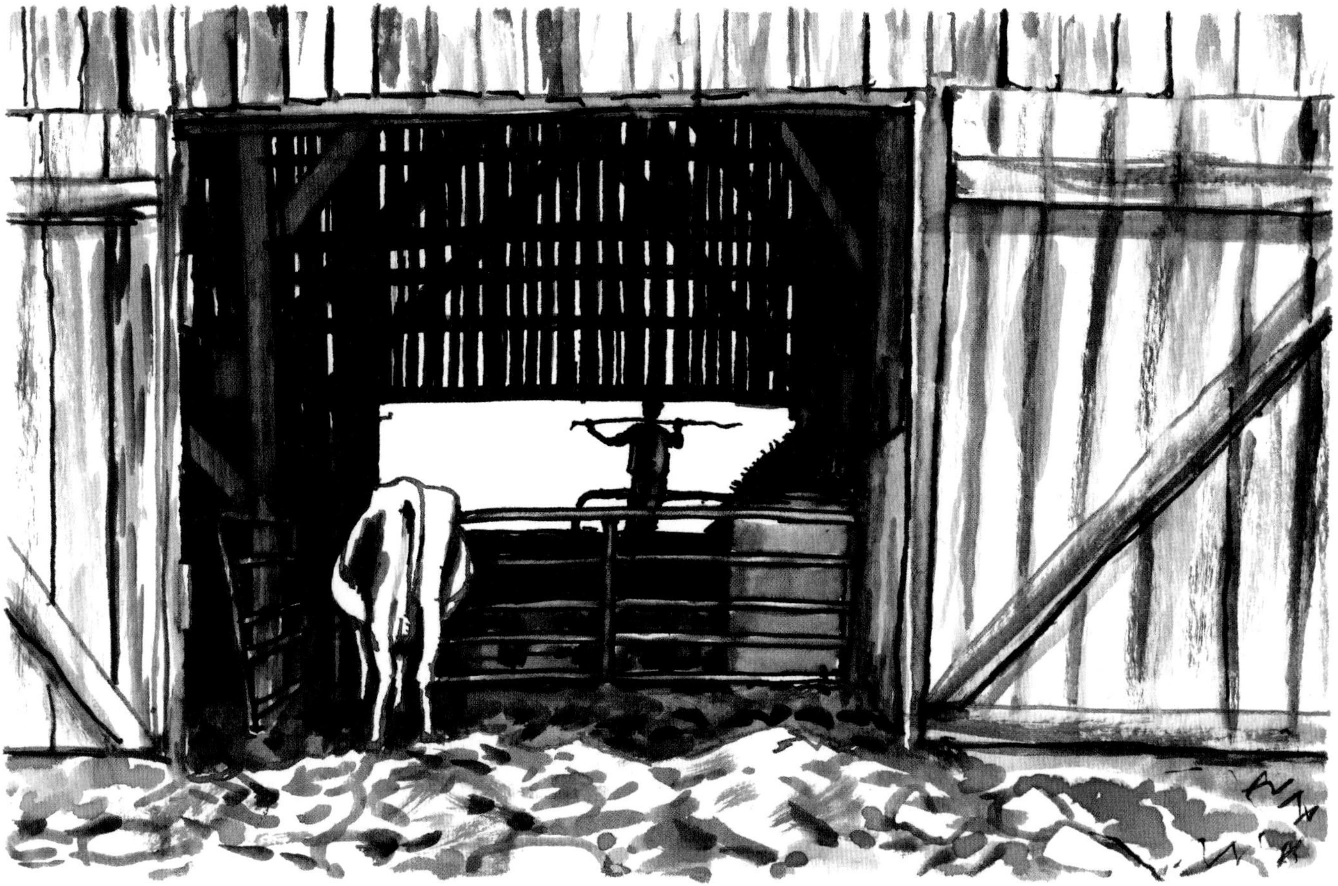

MONDAY, JUNE 10

Hard rain falls for most of the night. As the shaggy gusts pour down, I lay in bed and listen to the shifting forms of water: heavy drops striking the tin roof; those that skim, thin and slanting, like combing fingers; the roaring creek and pouring gutters; the ominous drum of another gust moving in. Thunder shakes me out of bed. On the porch, I watch lightning flash-freeze the land, then, just as suddenly, all melts back to darkness.

By morning, all is calm. I am giving Phoebe drawing lessons this week. I strike minute-long poses, and she makes gesture drawings to capture the sense of my body's movement: an exercise we often did during my first semester of art school. Afterwards, as we walk together along the newly-puddled lane, she pauses here and there to gather lemony wood sorrel: "I'll make something for you and Dad with this." She's put on a vintage dress, blue and white, belted, with a high lacy collar: something she would not have worn to school.

Walking back toward the house, a gentle rain begins to fall. We step into Straight Run near the barn and watch the drops make widening white circles in the green water, then fade away, like moon-bows appearing and disappearing.

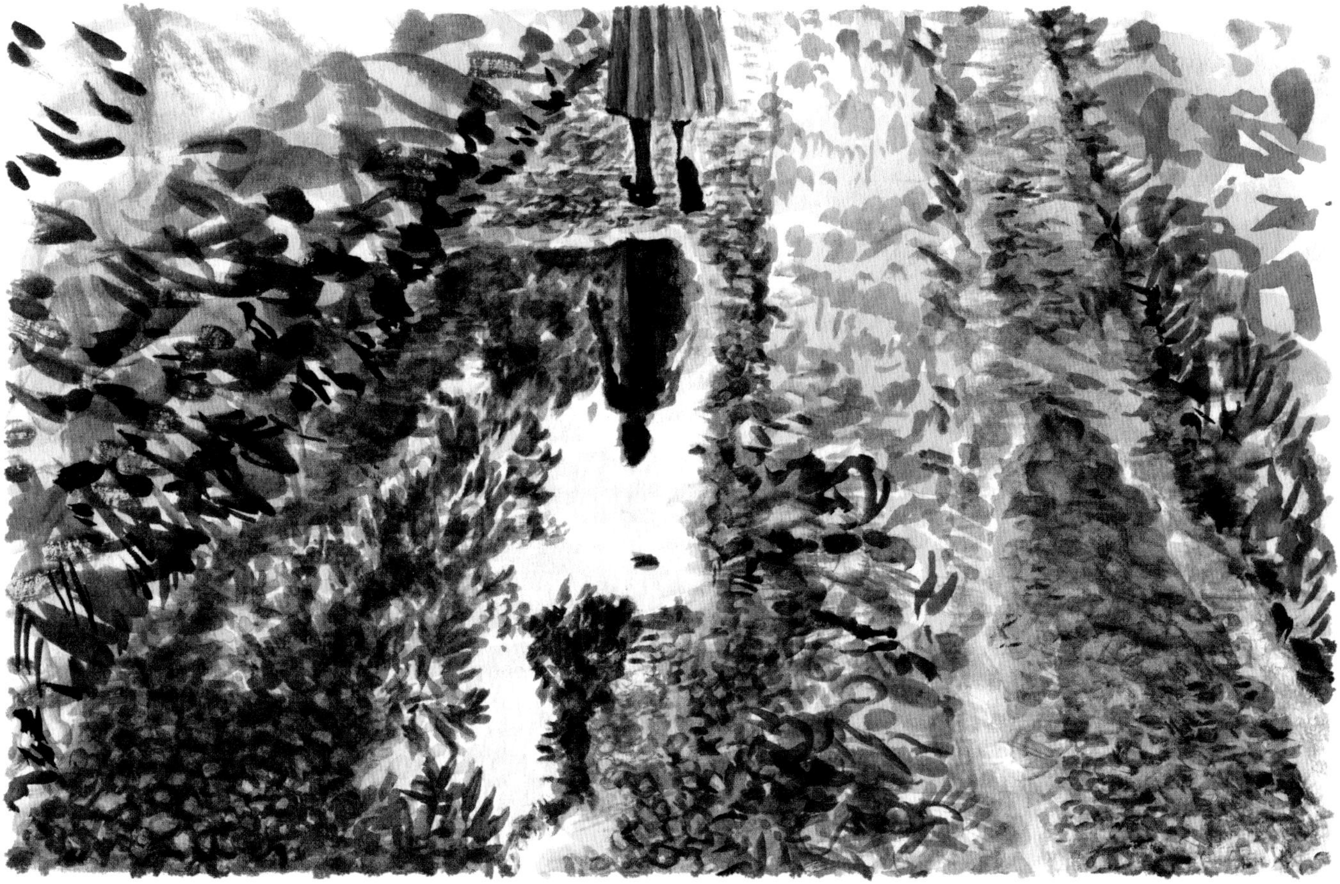

TUESDAY, JUNE 11

First pea harvest: fifty-five pounds, from the patch we sowed on Easter Sunday, the day we listened to the frogs' spring concert. We will distribute them to our customers tomorrow, along with an admonition that they should shell and eat them as soon as possible. The sugars will soon be converted to starch. Get a child to help you, we will tell them, and your child will eat them all up, and it will make you happy to see her eat all those peas. But our shareholders are busy people, whose lives are not built around shelling peas, as ours sometimes are. As a post-harvest treat, Phoebe shells us each a saucer of peas, and garnishes each dish with wood sorrel.

In the evening, I head to the hills to make bouquets of wildflowers. Bright orange butterfly weed spreads over the west-facing slopes, and oxeye daisies thrive wherever there's sun in the afternoon. I also see Philadelphia fleabane, yarrow, cinquefoil, St. John's Wort, Deptford pink, Carolina rose, and milkweed. I keep making a picture of myself in my mind's eye: Look at me! I'm doing something so *pretty*! But it takes a few hours to make sixty bouquets, and I never seem to work fast enough. There's still much to do to be ready for tomorrow's harvest and delivery. It will be another late night.

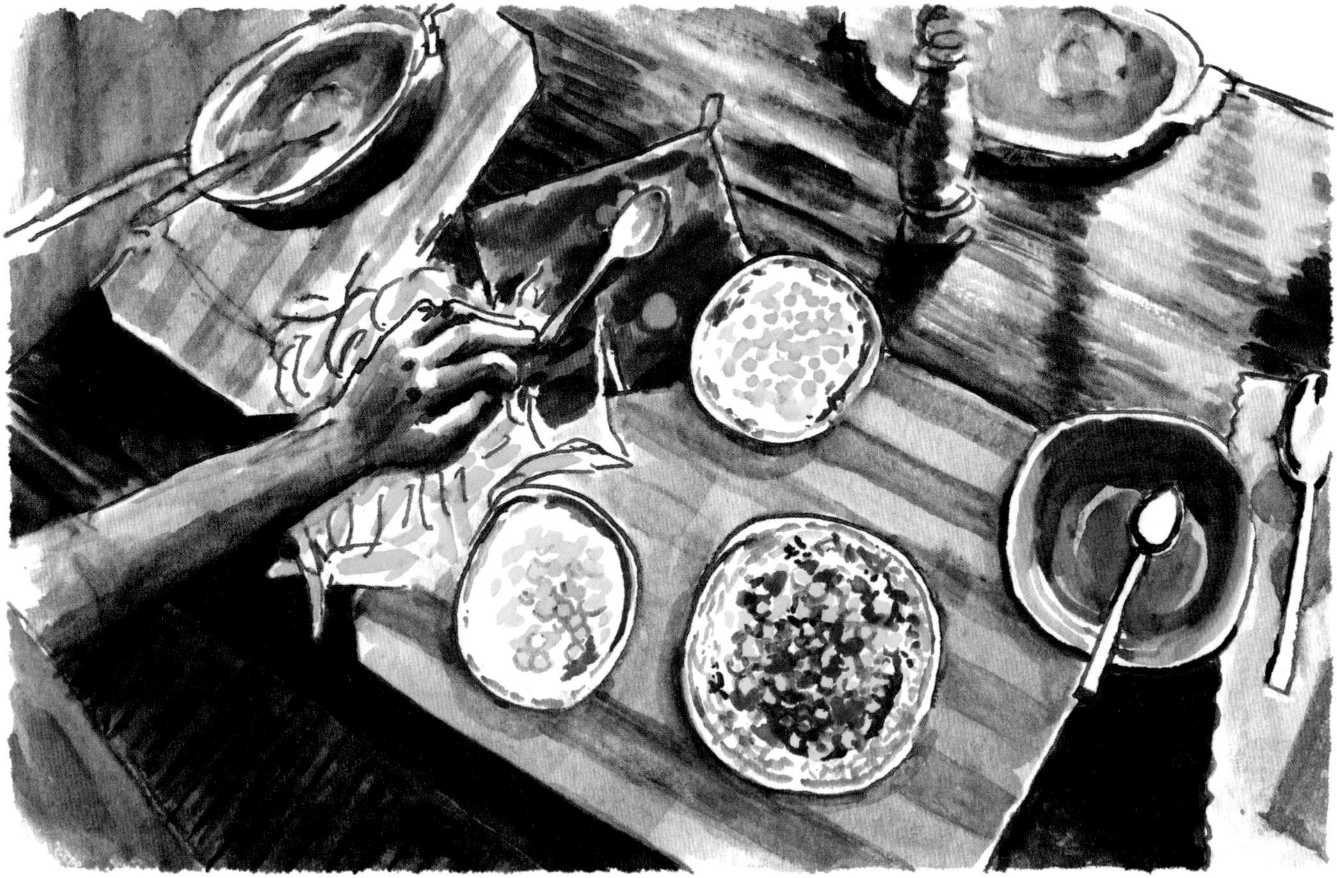

SUNDAY, JUNE 16

The chicks have grown up enough to be moved out of their greenhouse pen and into the chicken house, where the hen matriarchs live. Phoebe has named each of the twenty-two surviving pullets and hand-feeds them every day. She'll miss having them so near. The dog's crate is on our garden cart: we've hauled two groups already, and the last is on its way. As we pull the cart toward the barn, the lane is full of robins walking toward the barn too, as if in solidarity with their chicken kin. We all march along together in this humble, earthbound avian migration.

We've made a wire pen inside of the chicken house for the pullets to stay in for a week or so. If they went straight in, unprotected, the hens might kill the pullets. Soon, they'll be big and strong enough to hold their own. David and I will start to have trouble telling the difference between the old hens and the new, but Phoebe will probably always know who is who.

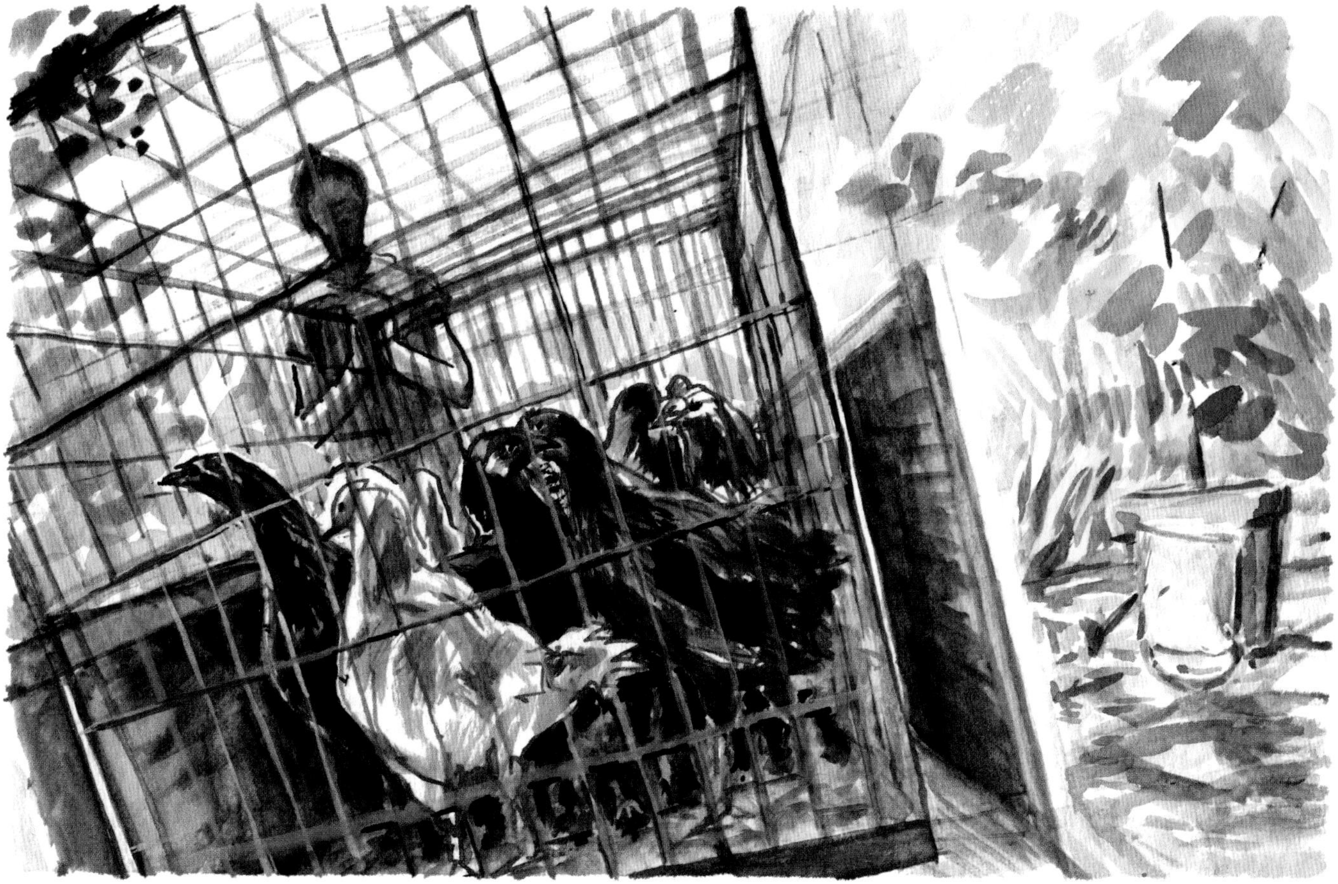

MONDAY, JUNE 17

Tomato cages, pulled from the field last fall, were set aside behind the pear trees. Now, they are tightly tied to the deer fence by bindweed and to the ground by tall grasses and poison hemlock. David cultivates around the tomato plants while I pull and set cages.

I'm hot, sticky, chigger bitten, showered with the pollen of the towering stinkweed. Working in the summer fields, I've sometimes been stunned by the volume of my own sweat, as if I'd stood out in the rain. Sweat that streams into and stings my eyes, finds its way into the corners of my mouth and feeds me my own salt. I measure the heat of summer this way: two-shirt days, three-shirt days. Last week's harvest was the year's first two-shirt day.

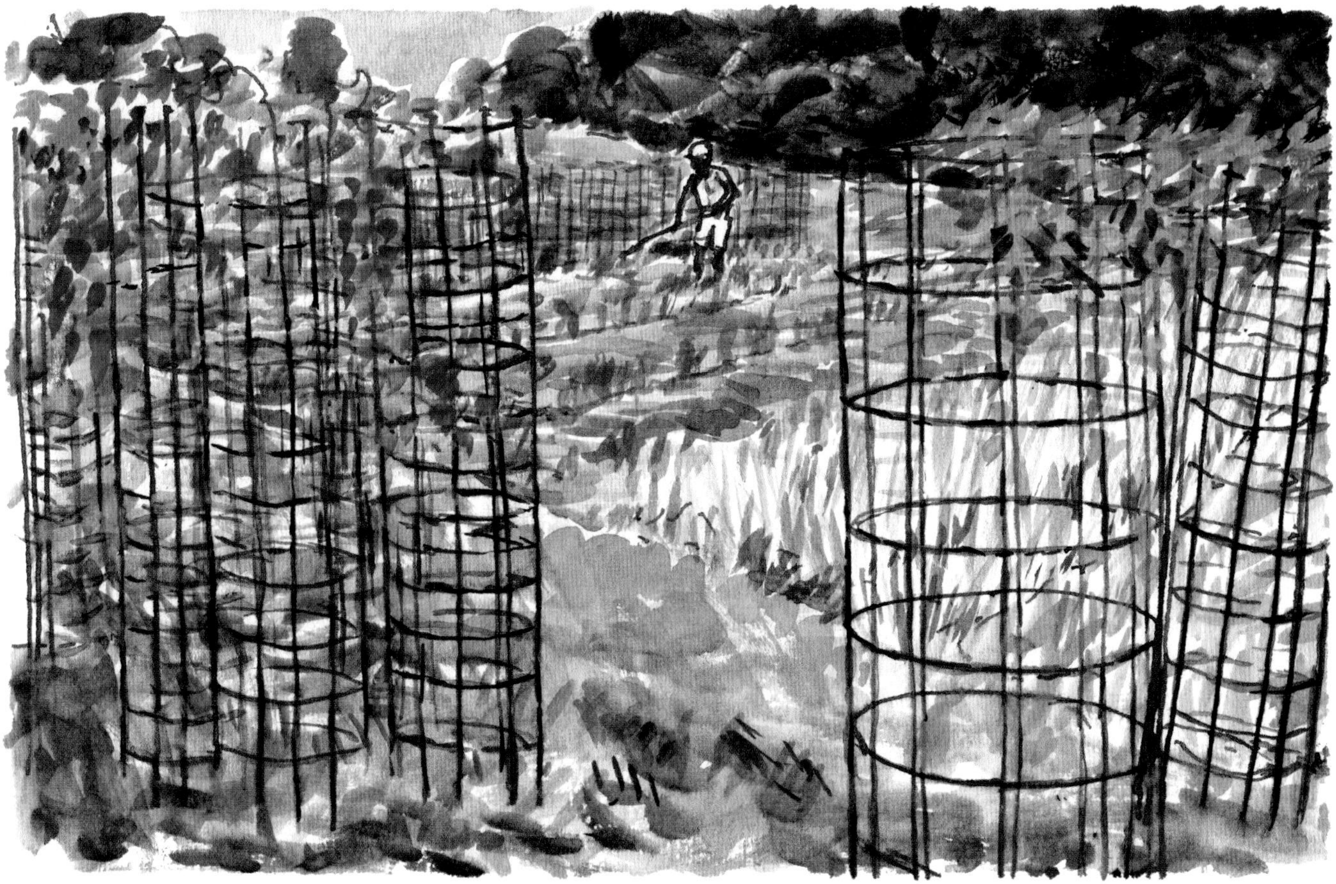

Thursday, June 20

Four weeks after we covered the strawberry patch with netting, the berries are finished, and the netting is stitched to the ground around the edges by strawberry runners and by a stunning abundance of weeds: shaggy soldier, mostly, but also curly dock, mallow, dandelion, and ground ivy.

It's also been almost four weeks since the last frost, yet the white row covers we used to protect the berry patch still lie twisted in the grass. At first, uncertainty about whether another frost would strike kept me from picking up the covers and putting them away, and then it was the willful blindness that keeps me from seeing all that needs to be done, because I don't want to.

I shake the covers out, spread them to dry the dew, and braid them up again. The air smells like hot, fermenting strawberry jam. The diminutive last berries of the season are in a basket on the kitchen counter. Some have dull, even-toned skins, and you expect them to taste a little off, but those are the most intoxicatingly sweet of all.

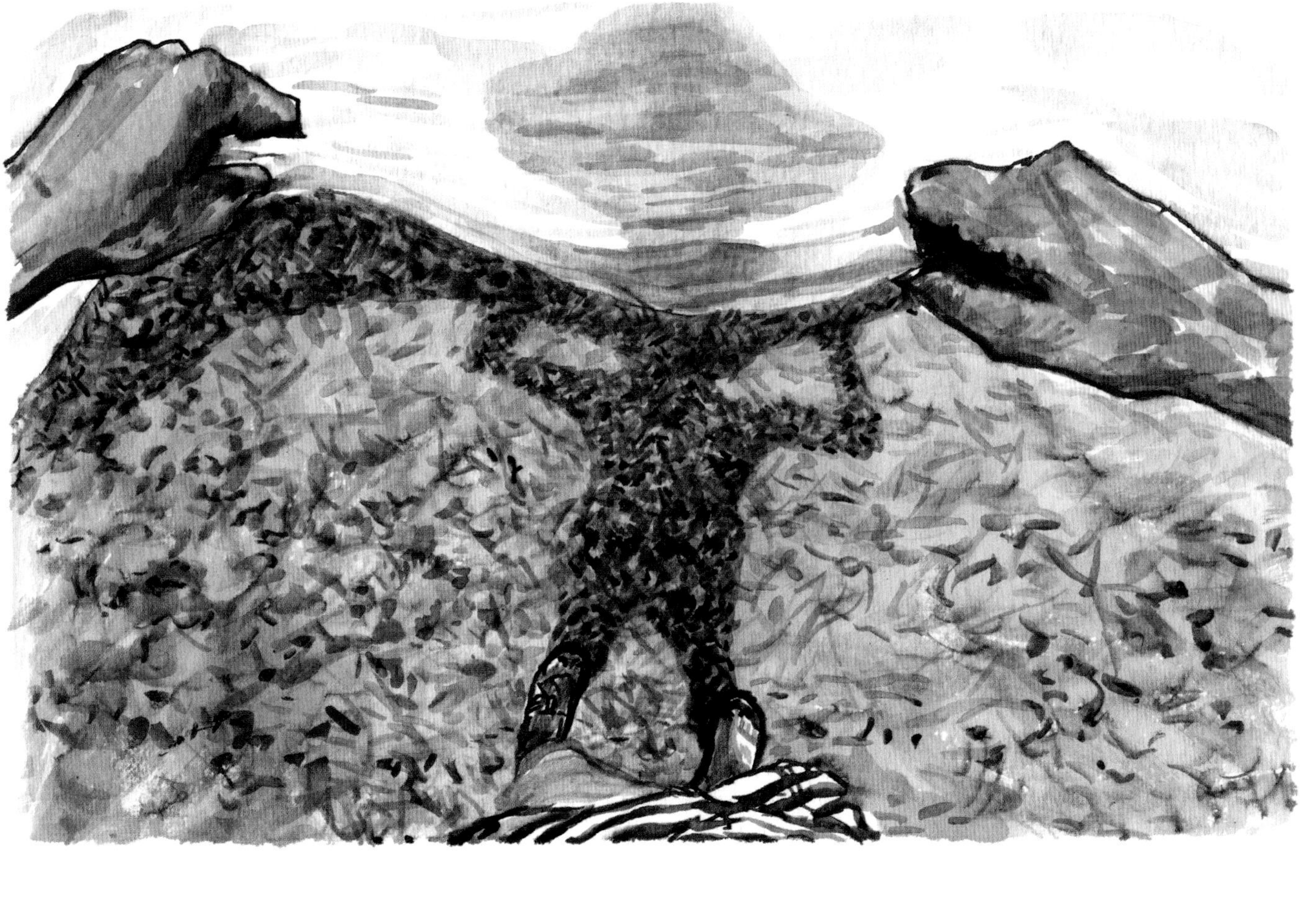

Saturday, June 22

With the heat comes a sense of being mired. The lettuces shoot the moon, the kale goes buggy and bitter, weeds swallow whole sections of the garden. Mold blooms in the house, which gives off a dank, stale scent, like a giant fly-attracting flower that opens fully when summer sets in. I clean all the surfaces with vinegar diluted in water, which will keep the bloom at bay for a week or two.

David and Phoebe leave for music camp on Monday, and Phoebe is with her grandmother in Lexington today. David and I work hard to get to the point where I can care for the farm on my own for the week.

A good meal will hearten us and give us strength. We have an early dinner of a summer squash frittata with onions and marjoram, steamed beets and snap peas with fresh dill, green salad, and fresh-baked bread (from our machine) with butter and raspberry jam. The jam is laced with elderflower blossoms that Phoebe and I gathered from the bush near the swimming hole. We waded through thigh-deep water skimmed with fallen blossoms to gather them. It paints a pretty picture, but the jam just tastes like raspberry jam.

David and I take a short nap at the table before getting back to work. "Toil, misery, and *great food*," he says after we eat, just before his head goes down.

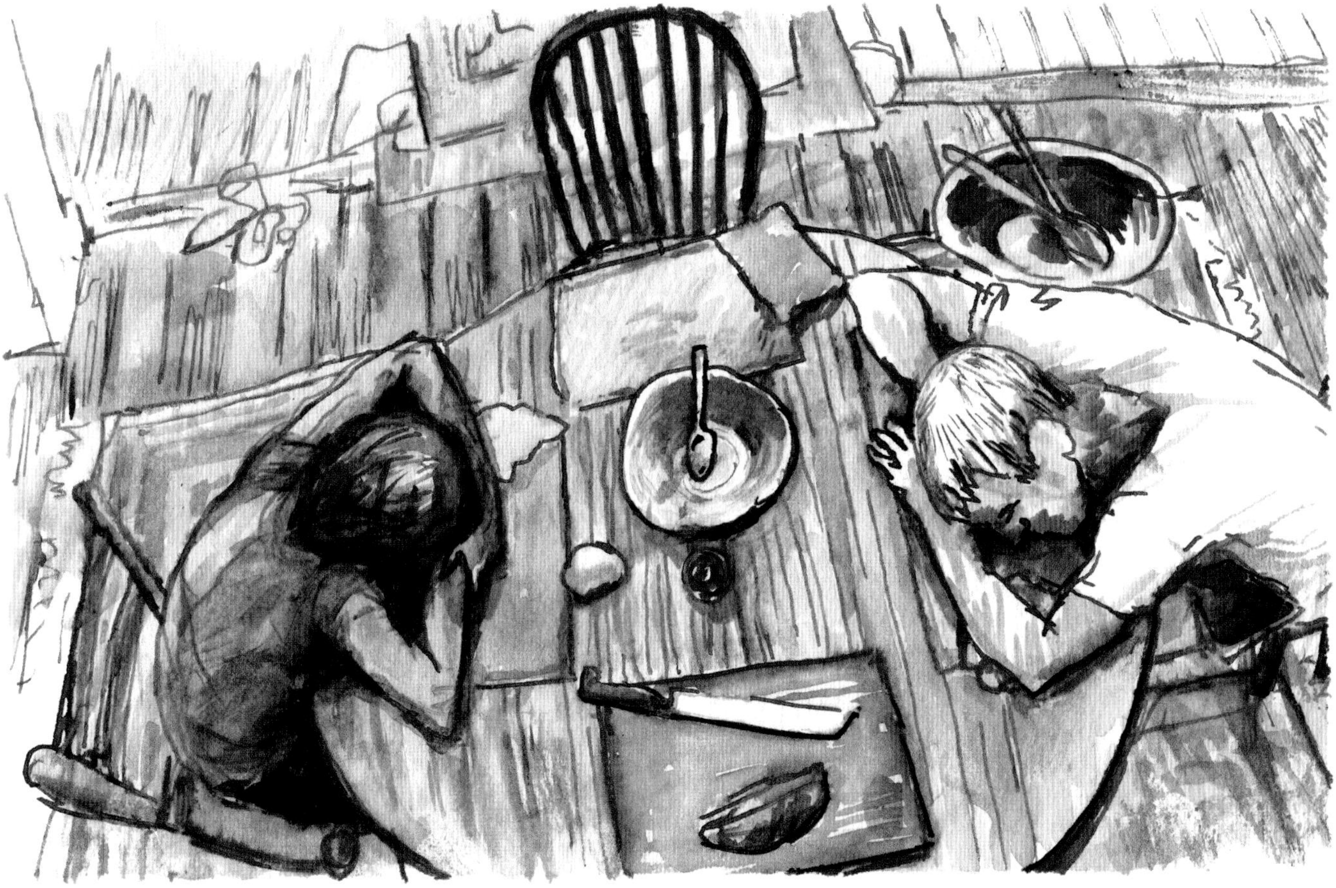

SUNDAY, JUNE 23

David and Phoebe head off to Cowan Creek Mountain Music School in Whitesburg for a week each summer. The car is full of camping supplies, musical instruments, and lots and lots of lettuce: David brings enough salad for all the participants' lunch each day, about three-hundred servings. We need room to hold the greens in the refrigerator until they leave tomorrow morning, so I take out ten pounds or so of kohlrabi left over from last week's delivery and make a big batch of kimchi, with carrots, radishes, lots of ginger, garlic, green onions, and chiles. I've never used kohlrabi in kimchi before—it's usually made with napa cabbage—but kohlrabi and cabbage are in the same family, so why not?

There's still another big bag of kohlrabi in the fridge. Every week, we harvest extra items and put them at the end of the line in a swap basket, so our customers have a chance to trade out if they find something in the swap basket they'd rather have. Lately, by the end of the delivery, the swap basket is full of kohlrabi. I must find ways to keep it from landing in the compost heap. The kimchi will ferment in a stoneware crock on the counter for a week or so, after which I'll move it into the refrigerator, and hopefully, we'll like it enough to eat it for months to come.

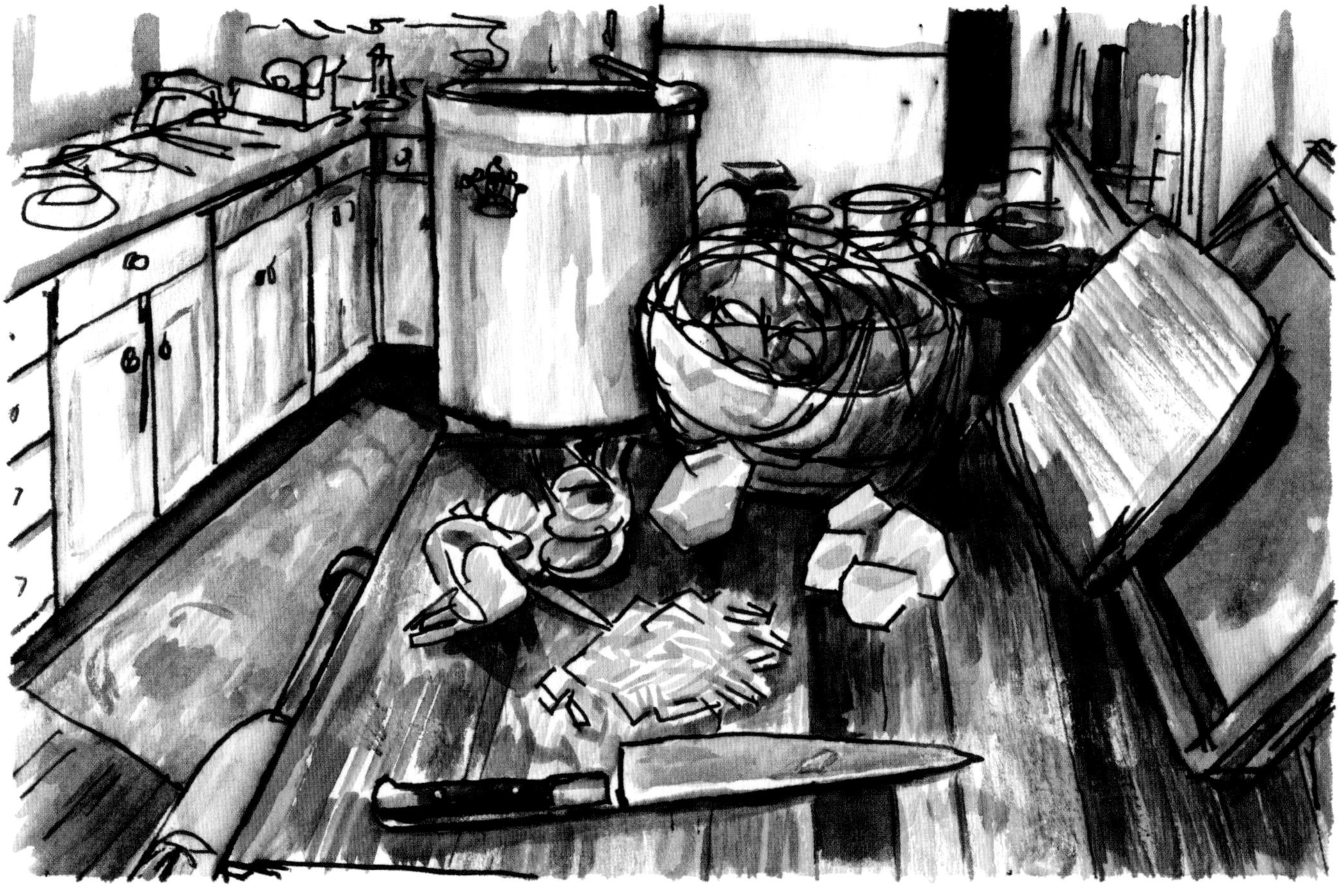

WEDNESDAY, JUNE 26

For the first time, I attempt the harvest and delivery not only without David but also without the help of a team of farm interns. A couple of friends come out, though, and we pull together enough produce to fill sixty beautiful half-bushel baskets: carrots, beets (both red and gold), leeks, big shiny bunches of swiss chard, dill and cilantro, kohlrabi, summer squash, and spinach. We meet our customers in the parking lot of a synagogue in Lexington. There, we set up crates of produce in a line, with a tag stapled to each that tells people how much to put in their basket. At the end of the line, the swap basket starts out with lettuce, cabbage, kale, broccoli, rhubarb, and green beans. Of course, it ends up mostly with kohlrabi. We also sell eggs: right now, with our flock depleted, we only have a few dozen to sell each week, and they disappear quickly.

Ten minutes before we leave, the sky darkens. Rain soon pours down. My mother has arrived, and we're loading crates onto the truck when David's sister Analisa appears. She's just gotten off of work and is in her business suit and heels, but she hops out of her car and helps. Rain comes down in sheets, and the three of us are drenched to the skin. Mom loans me dry clothes and takes me out for dinner. I can't rouse myself for the drive home, so I crash at her house.

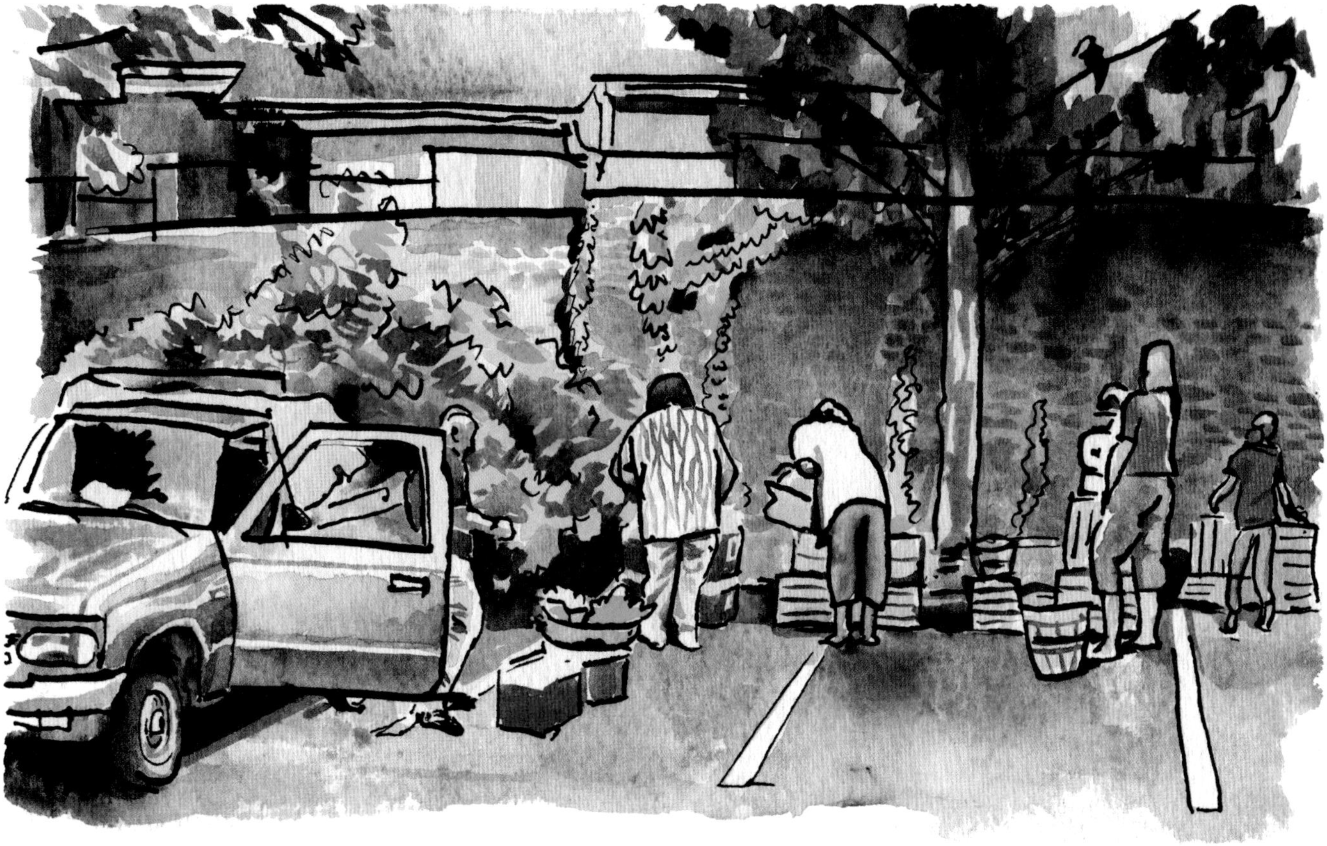

THURSDAY, JUNE 27

I arrive home this morning to find a large dead tree spanning the bridge, its three trunks packed with sticks, muck, and trash. I can't budge the thing, so I park the truck by the road and wheel the garden cart out to haul the leftover vegetables back to the house. Then I do barn chores.

Four and a half inches of rain in the gauge.

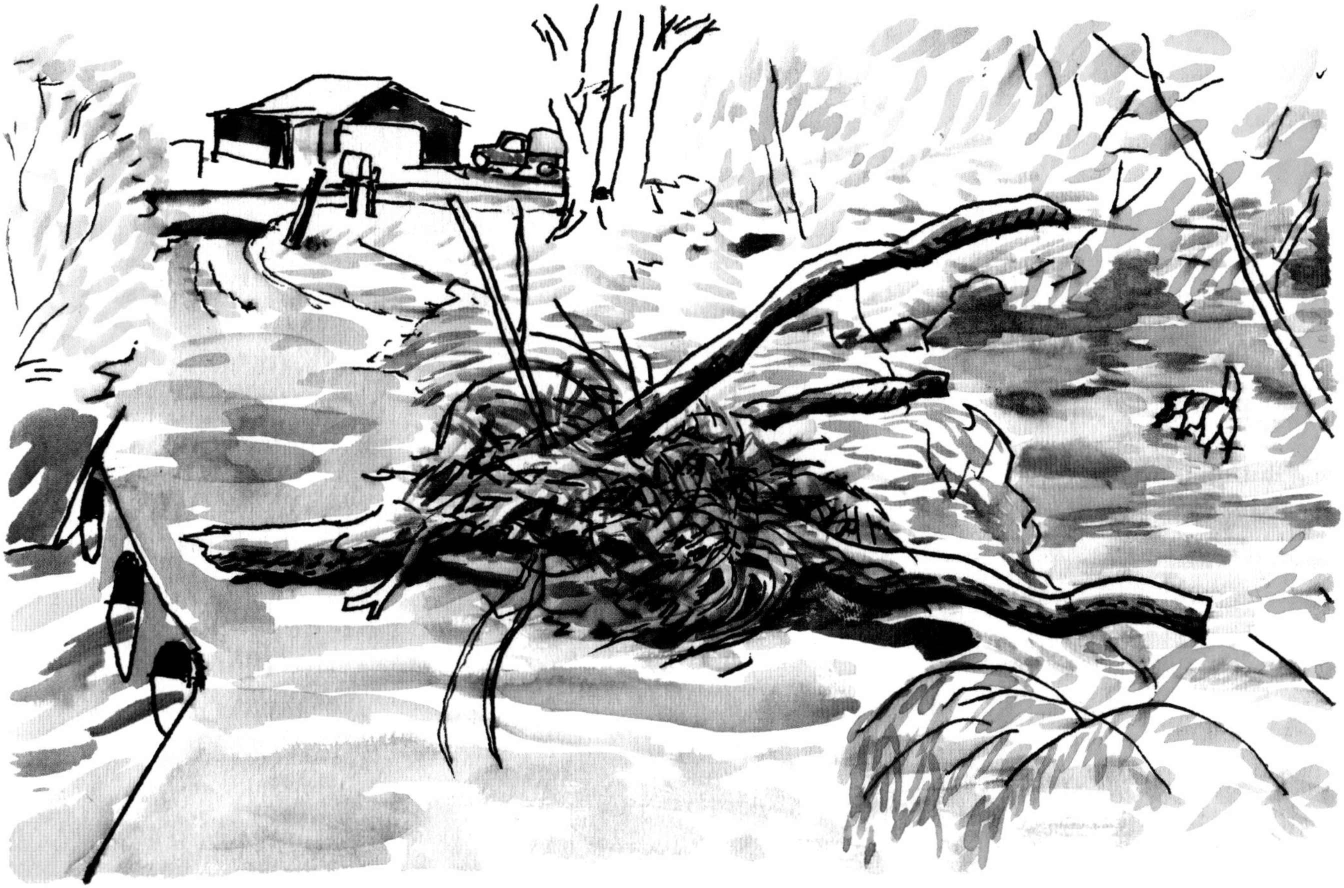

FRIDAY, JUNE 28

After breakfast, I read the last bit of a memoir by a New York chef, after which I feel prickly enough that I head outside to pick over the squash patch, which has just reached full production. Squash-picking is a prickly job, so I'm in my element. The squash are shiny under their broad, sandpapery leaves. As I snip them from their stems, I think about the gooseberries that need to be picked, the blueberries that need to be covered with bird netting. I'm puzzling over the chef's contempt for "self-righteous" farmers at the New York markets, and her affection for the toothless Italian ones whose flies are unzipped and whose trousers are held up with twine. It takes distance to celebrate the poverty of the latter and disdain the small, hard-won successes of the former. Farmers in the U.S. work hard for little pay and little understanding. We are yoked to our small patches of earth, like oxen to a plow, and in return for our service, we are sustained, if we're lucky. It seems to me we've earned some self-righteousness.

David and Phoebe are coming back home tonight. I pull the cart back to the bridge, with various saws and pruners, and clear the way. Now, I can also get the three big bags of squash I just picked over to the fridge at the Green Bean, the trailer across the road.

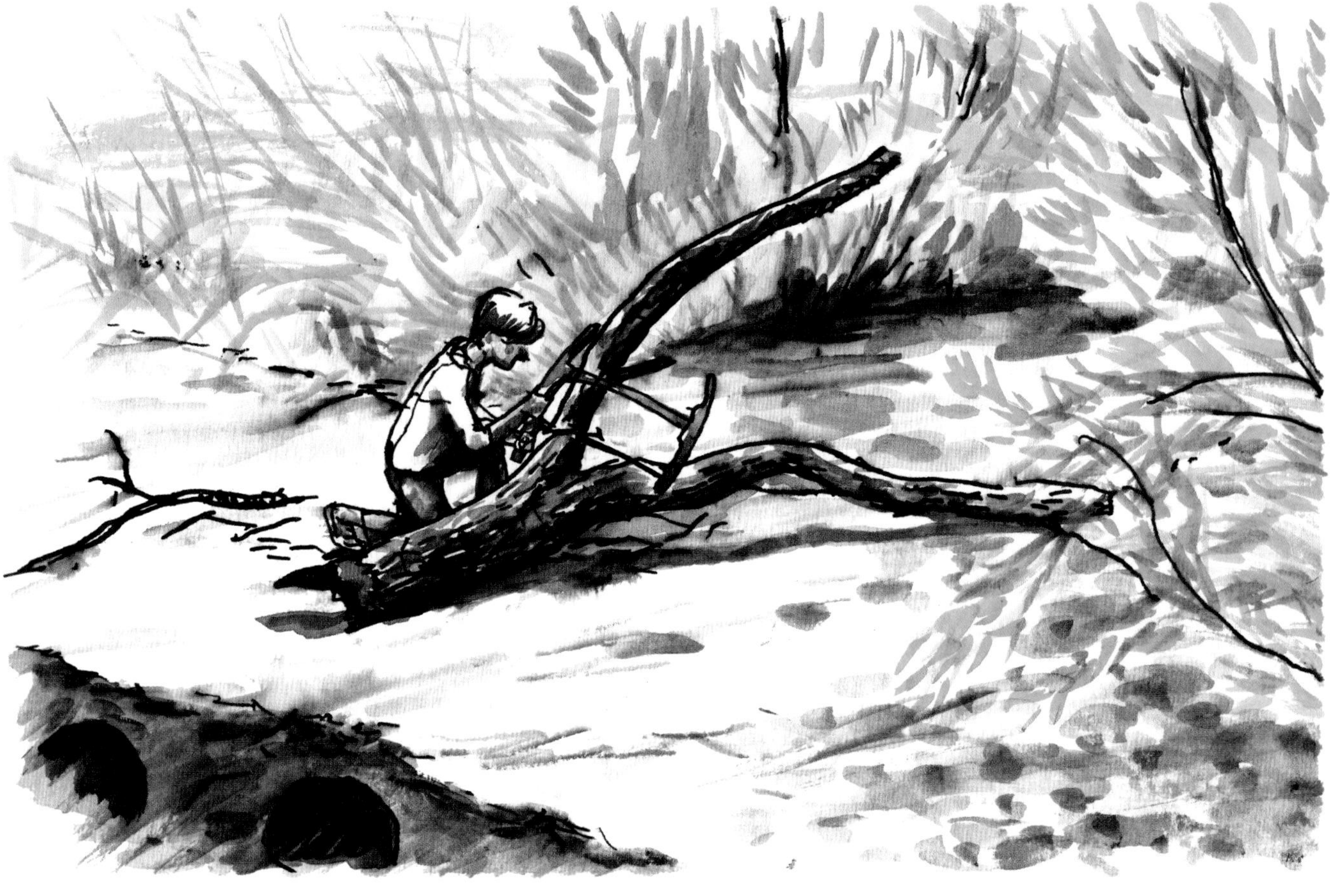

TUESDAY, JULY 2

This countryside is dotted with root cellars. They are often grassy-roofed mounds with small doors, as if each farmstead hosts its own household of hobbits. Few of them are used anymore, though. David's great-great-great-grandparents once lived less than a mile from our farmhouse, near the source of Straight Run. A stone chimney still stands there, deep in the woods. Iris and daffodil have naturalized around the house's low stone foundation. A large flat rock keeps wanderers from falling into the well. The generous size of their root cellar, slumping into the hill, testifies to what must have been an ample garden.

Luther Hollar, who once lived here, built our root cellar. I think he said that was in the 1940s. His brother, Lovell, bulldozed the cellar when its ceiling began to collapse. About ten years ago, we excavated and rebuilt it. The round concrete floor was solid, and the foot of the mortared rock wall was sound. We store our potatoes and other roots here through the winter. We store green tomatoes, wrapped in newspaper, which can be unpacked and eaten in December.

Today, David totes the crates of beets, greens, and tiny carrots we just washed into the cellar, to stay cool until delivery tomorrow.

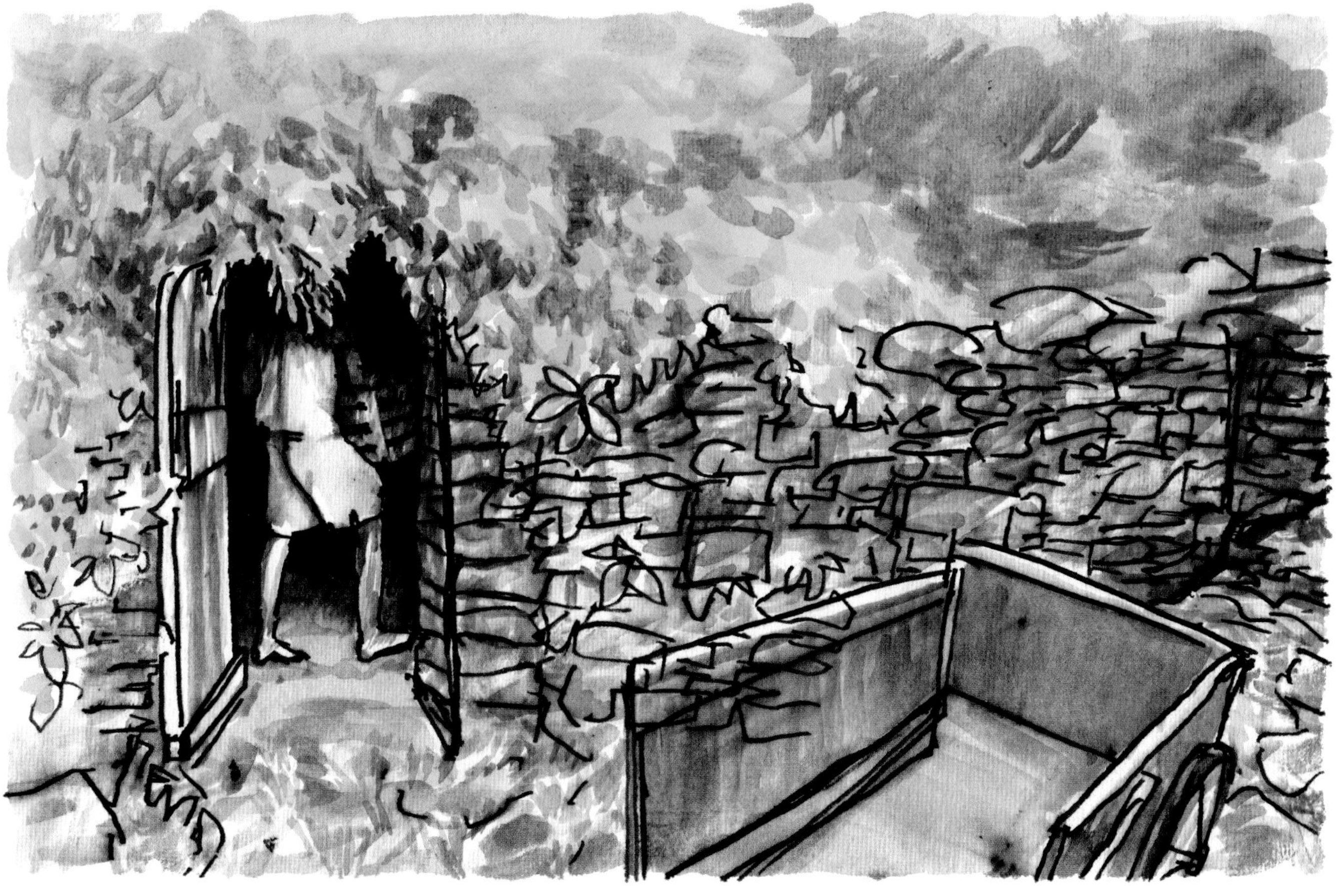

Thursday, July 4

Despite being covered by netting, the gooseberries have been entirely taken by birds. I counted seven of them under the netting several days ago: thrashers and catbirds, mostly. We work to secure the edges, but they're expert at finding a way in. So I give up on the gooseberries and use that netting to reinforce the blueberries, beginning to ripen now.

I am thankful the netting keeps some berries from the birds for us, but I hate it for torturing and murdering snakes. Enticed by trapped birds, they poke their narrow heads through a square of the net's grid and begin their slide, only to find that their trunks are too wide to fit through. So they try to work their way out, poking their needle-heads through another square, until their bodies are macabre knots.

I pick in the drizzle, hunched under the low-draped netting, which is magnetically attracted to entanglements with buttons.

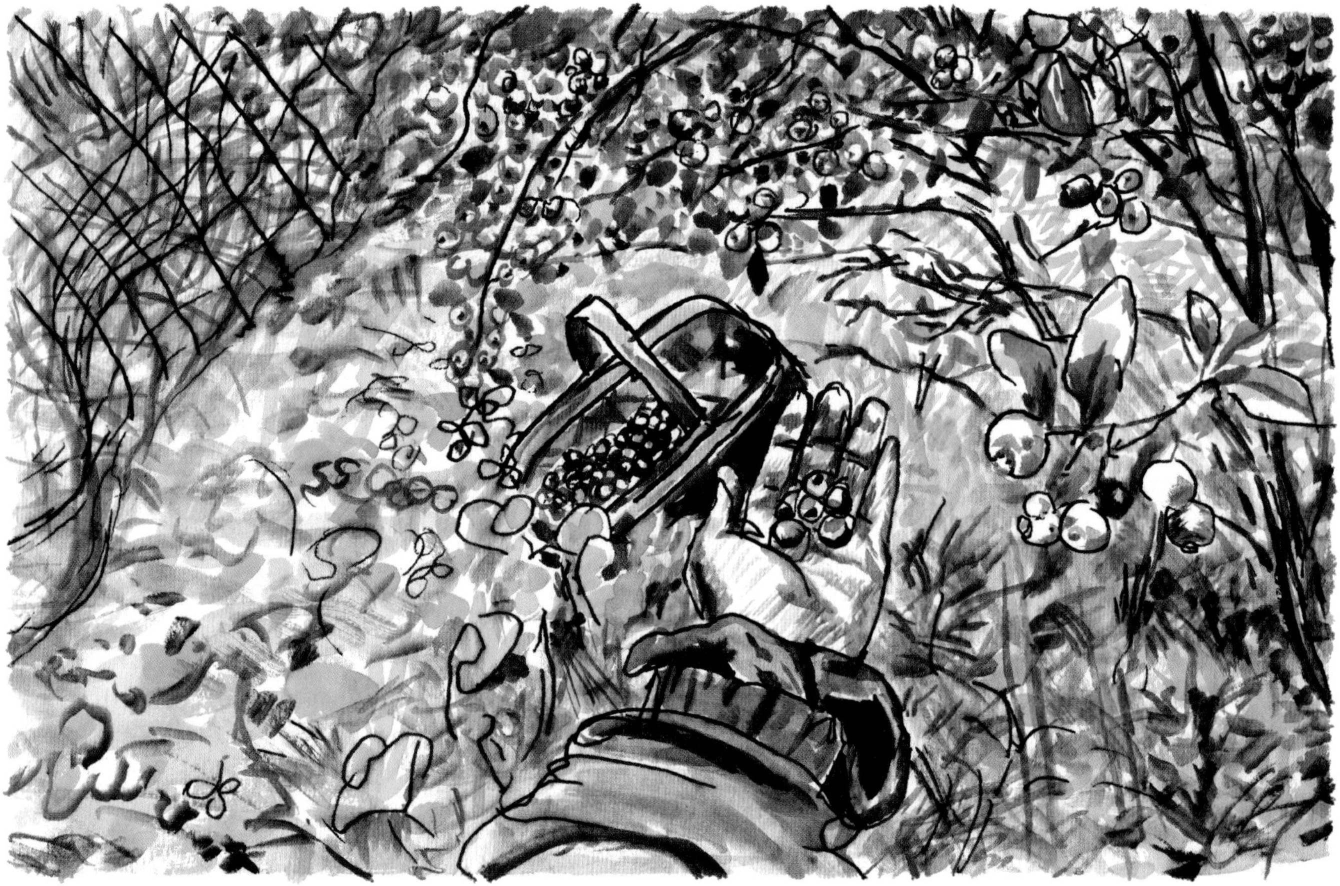

FRIDAY, JULY 12

These flowerbeds are a constantly shifting patchwork of wildness and domesticity, of the intentional and accidental. We start zinnias, marigolds, gomphrena, celosia, ageratum, and cosmos each year in the spring greenhouse and sow sunflowers directly in the soil once it's warm. We cut them for our customers but are the beneficiaries of their beauty. Black—eyed susans, dame's rocket, cleome, nicotiana, and mullein re—seed themselves readily. I keep an eye out for them in spring and give them room. Baptisia, irises, hydrangea, and sedum are long—term residents. Weeds are too, some familiar and some new to me. Sometimes, I let them grow to see what they turn into, forget to pull them out before they go to seed, and soon I have a new problem. Milkweed, beloved by monarch butterflies, is common along the creek banks and low lying areas of the farm, and likes our flower beds very well. I like it, too, and have allowed it to take over one of the beds.

We have eighteen aunts and cousins coming from Atlanta, Birmingham, and Lexington on Saturday, so I do a blitz weeding of the flower garden. A well—kept flower garden creates the illusion of leisurely living, of a life in which beauty is a priority. I toil in order to live in that illusion for a day or two.

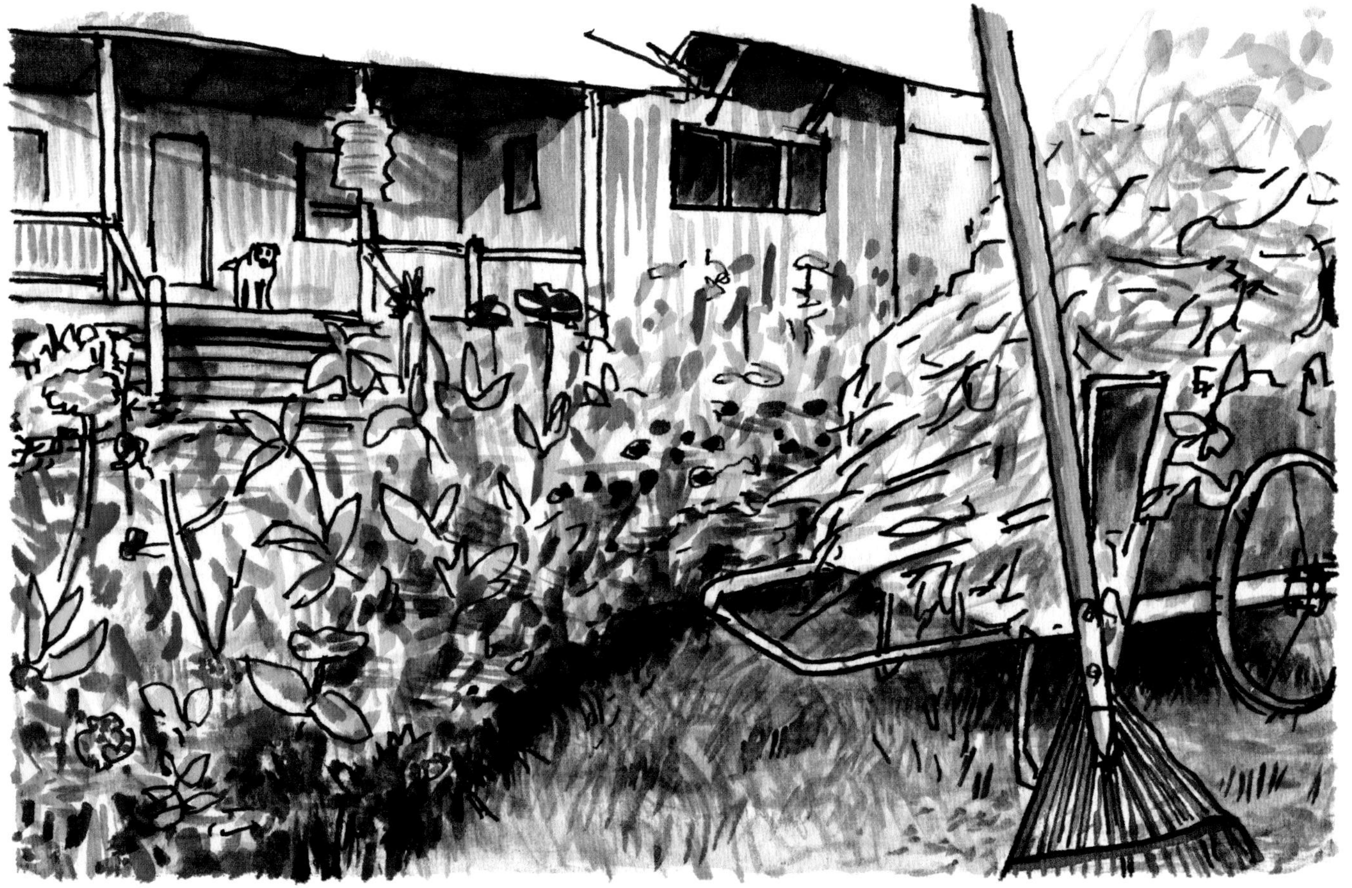

SATURDAY, JULY 13

Before the sun goes down, after aunts and cousins leave, we head to the squash patch. It was entirely under water a few days ago, after three and a half inches of rain. Many of the fruits are shriveled and moldy, but the plants seem to be recovering.

When we first moved here, we thought water would stay in the creeks, runs, and draws; they would rise and fall, but those fissures were drawn by rain and, we figured, would keep it contained. Since then, floods have strafed our newly planted fields, carried off our topsoil, gouged our gravel lane, and swept away David's tent and sleeping bag (before our first deer fence was built, he sometimes slept in the fields to keep deer away).

We live in a rain economy, in which wealth is dependent on the persistence of a sweet spot that lies between too much and too little. Money, it seems to me, is the same way: too much leads to profligacy; too little leads to starvation. Before we moved here, my pleasure in rain was in its atmospheric properties, its ability to create a mood. Yet our waterways, fed by rain, set down the lines of our lives.

David heads to the truck, a basket of squash in each hand. He'll drive them and the two baskets I'm carrying to the fridge at the Green Bean.

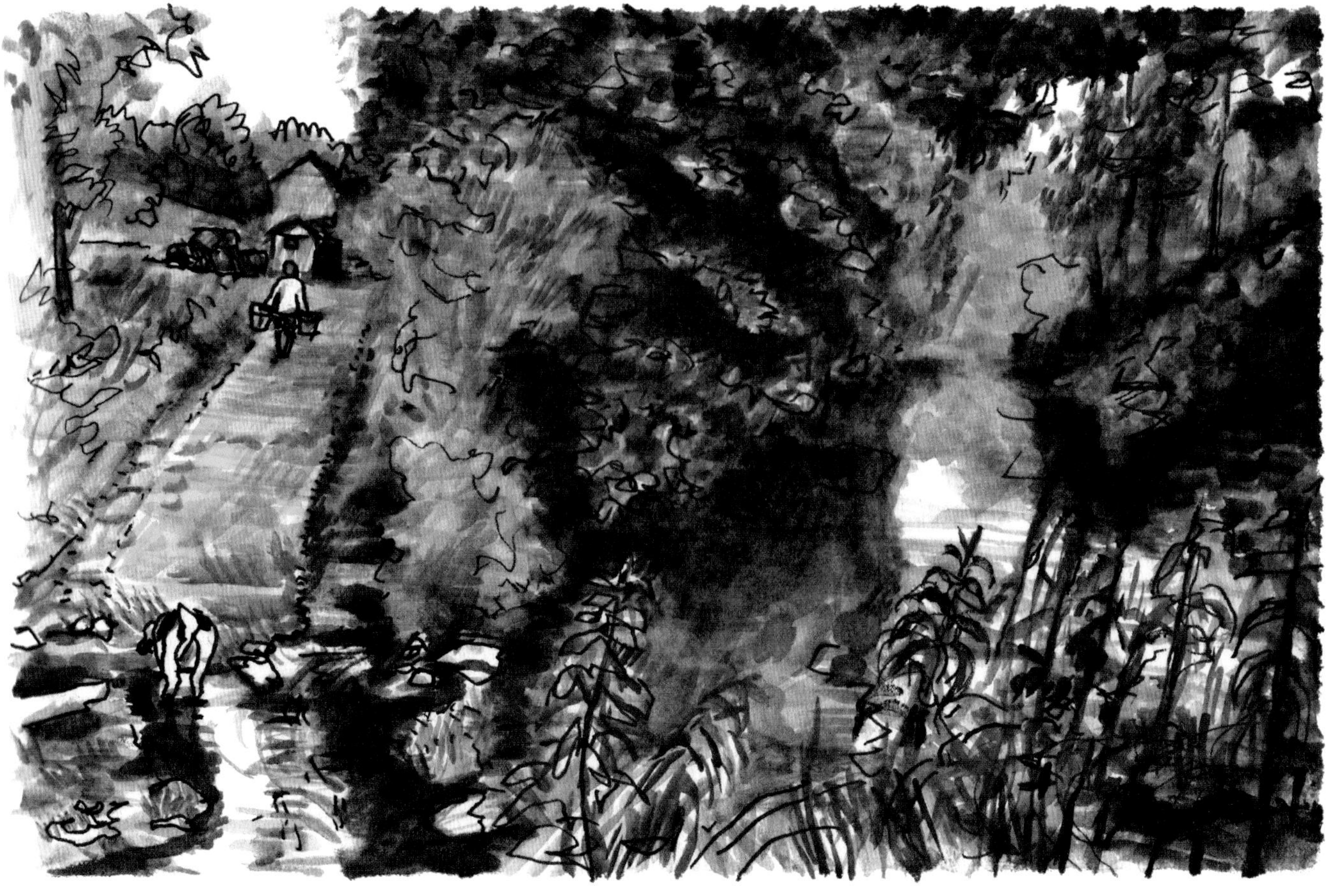

TUESDAY, JULY 16

July is always tough. It's too hot to enjoy laboring in the fields. The tomatoes, eggplants, and peppers are slow to ripen, and we scramble to have enough produce, as the greens wither in the heat. Weeds threaten to swallow us whole.

I harvest the most pathetic garlic crop I've ever seen. My only comfort is in thinking that some people pay good money to sweat this much for their workout. An earned sense of self-righteousness may be one of the perks of this line of work, but I guess it's not earned if we have to buy our garlic from someone else.

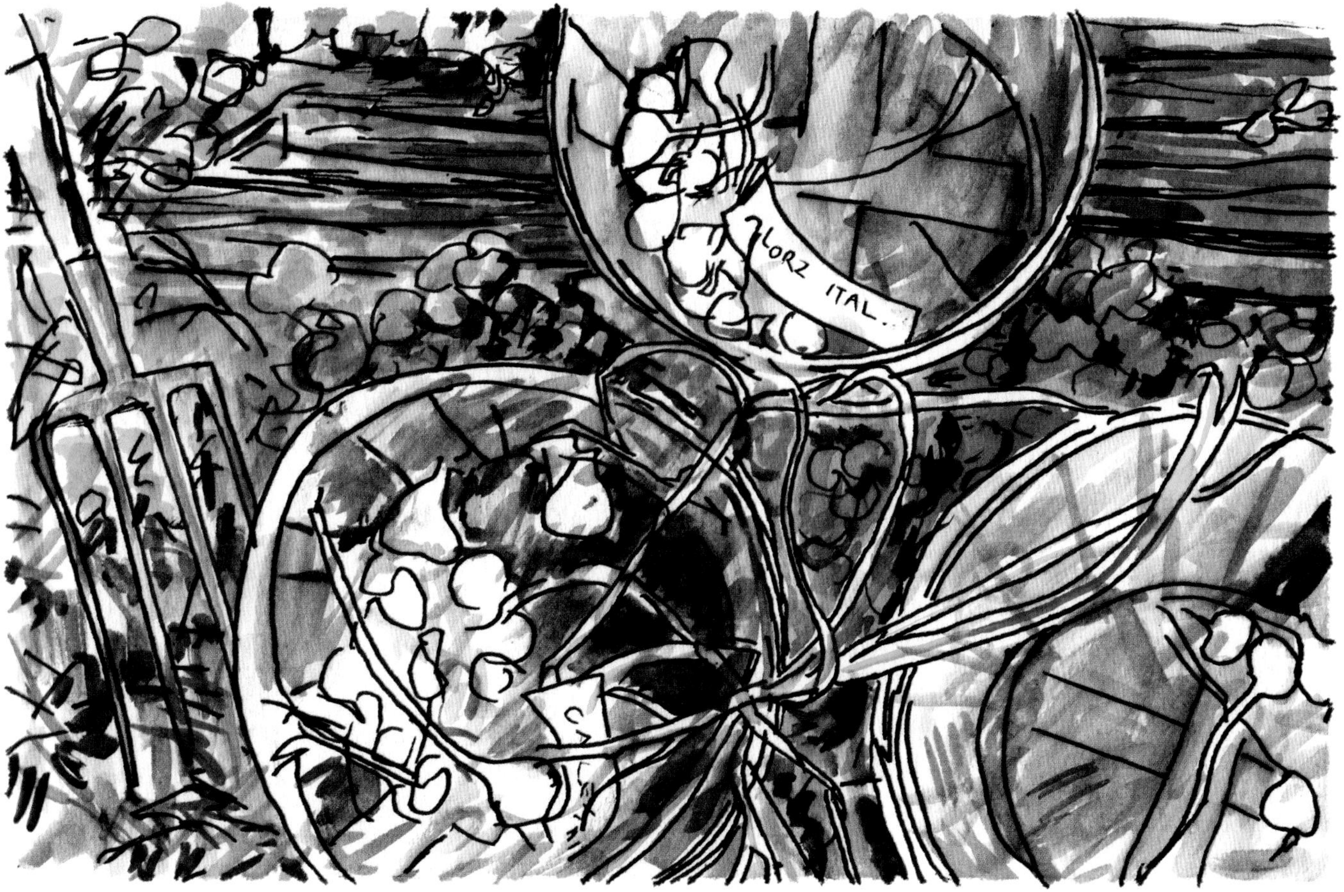
LORZ ITAL.

WEDNESDAY, JULY 17

Harvest day. Up at 4:30 and in the fields by first light. By 9:00, we're soaked with sweat. Two and a half hours later, we've finished harvesting and are ready to start cleaning, sorting, and packing. First, though, we need a dip. We park the truck, grab two towels, shed our sodden clothes, and drape them over the porch rail to dry. Naked but for sandals and sun hats, we head to the swimming hole. It's a cold, spring-fed spot in Straight Run, thigh-deep at best, but our daughter managed to learn to swim here, and a dip once or twice on a scorching day helps us to not miss having an air conditioner.

One advantage of all the rain: the water is fresh and clear. Tiny brazen fish occasionally peck at our skin. The top of my head bakes while the rest of my body is deliciously cool. Just above the surface, and only here, the air smells of both cold water and leafy, flowery growth—as if the pool is a platter holding those scents up for my pleasure. I help myself, breathing in.

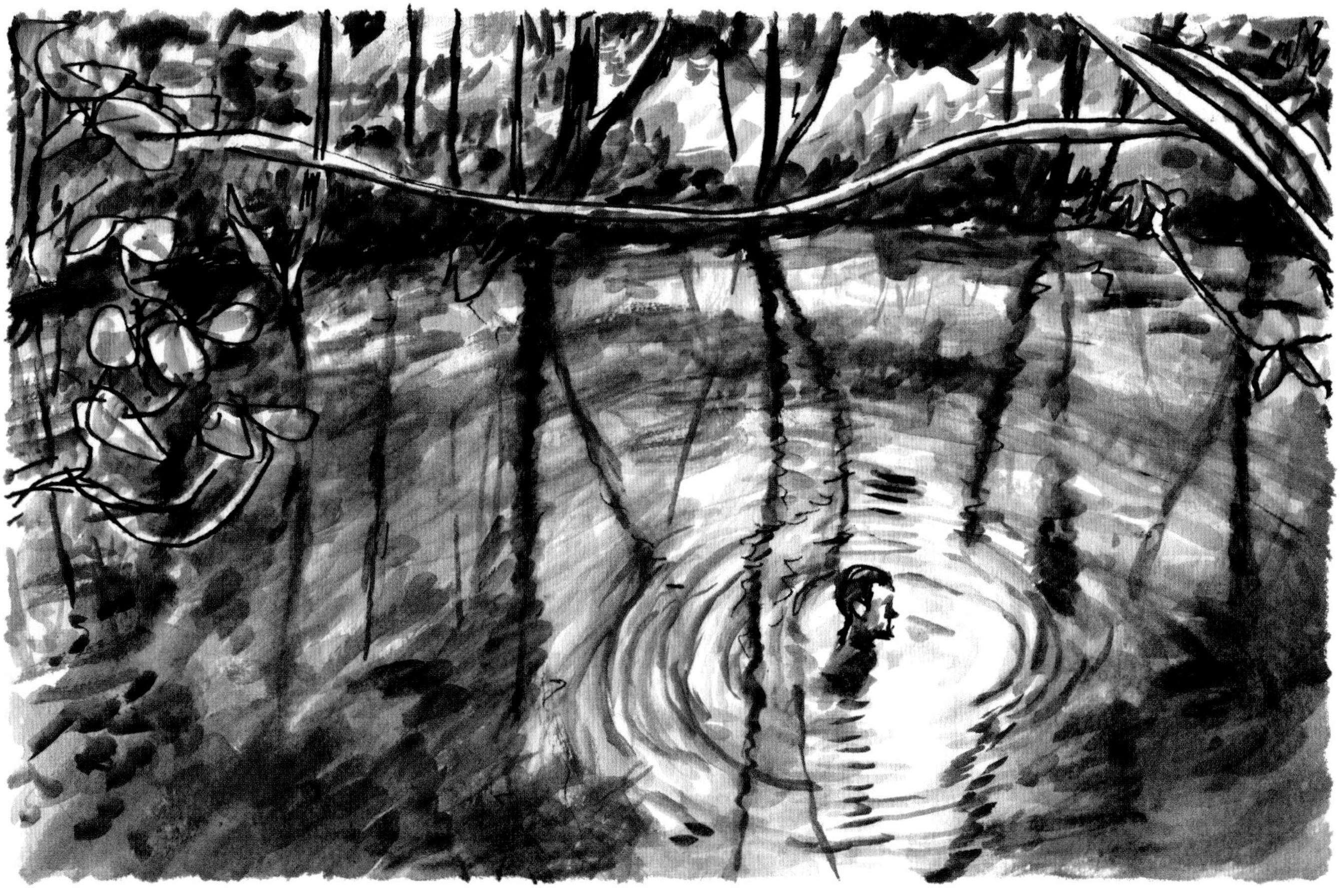

FRIDAY, JULY 19

We harvest the mature onions the three of us planted on March 10. That day, we celebrated blue sky. Today, we'd appreciate some cloud cover. The tomatoes still haven't been completely trellised. They are planted where the claytonia, minutina, and mache grew in March. It's hard to find all the onions: this has become, primarily, a bed of knotweed, prickly amaranth, and fescue.

Many of the onions are rotten. Some rot from the outside in, some from the inside out. The inside-out ones are insidious: we can't always tell when we're giving our customers sound bulbs. We've read that you just can't grow onions in Kentucky, which clearly isn't true. You must simply accept a lower yield than you'd get in Texas, and a few slimy surprises.

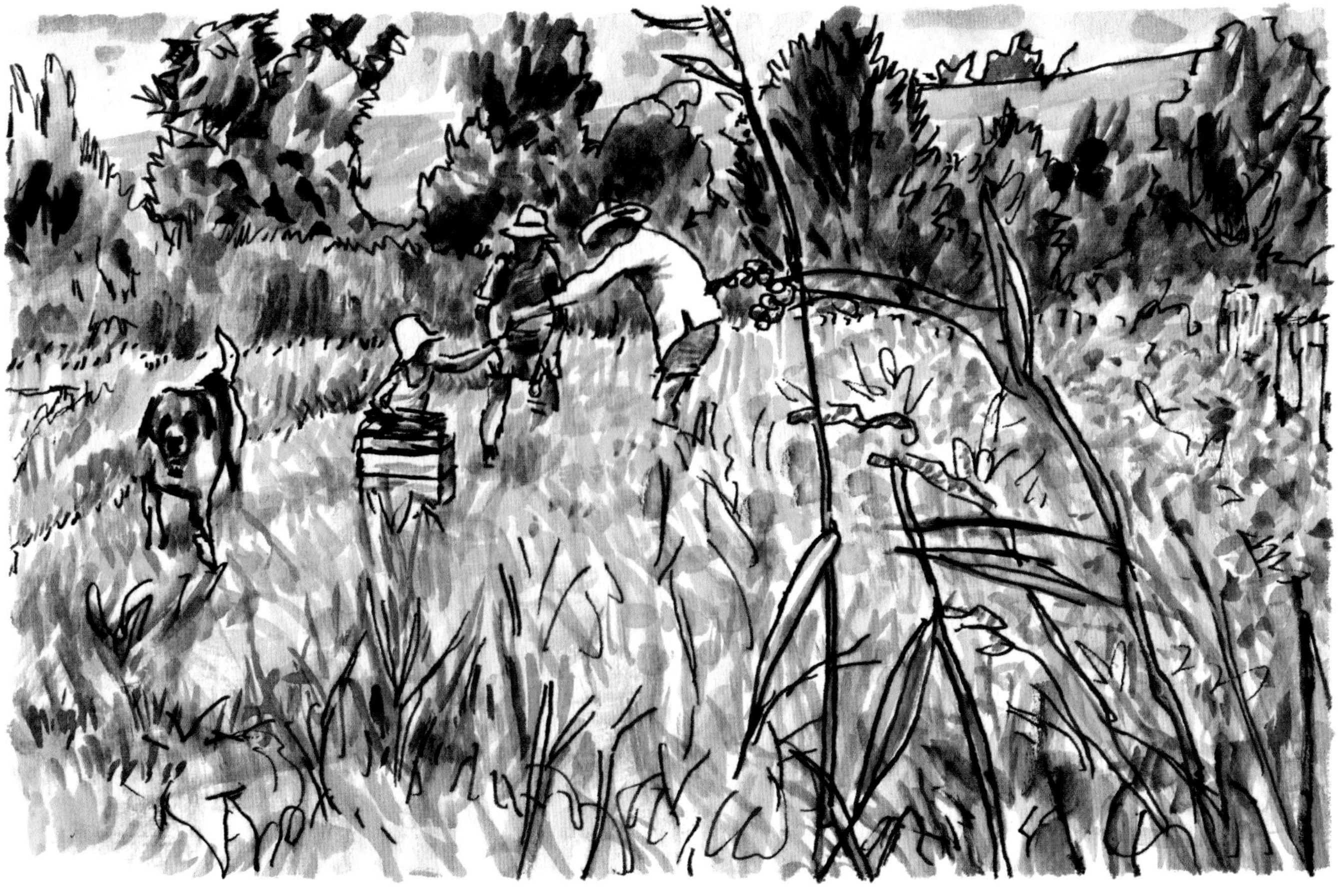

SATURDAY, JULY 20

I'm taking down laundry when I hear heavy steps in the thicket. Lily and Cassie have escaped from their fenced pasture and are headed up towards the woods. Unlike goats, these cows won't return to the barn at night. If they wander deep into the woods, how will we get them back? How will we even find them? In my shorts, sandals, and tank top, I pick my way through brambly thickets of blackberry, wild rose, and poison ivy until I am uphill of the cows, pretending to be calm. If I move quickly, they may bolt, so I exercise a subtle cowgirl art, grazing on wild blackberries as they grab mouthfuls of grass, keeping my body between them and the woods, nudging them down toward the house and the lane, which will funnel them back to the barn.

They peel off and make me run, and I'm scratched and winded, but eventually, I herd them into their paddock. I get the bucket of fencing tools, David arrives in the truck from his work at the hoop house, and we spend the rest of the evening fixing the section of fence that the cows trampled. I'm sitting with a bucket of tools, reattaching wires to posts, when Lily and Cassie amble up the hill, hoping to get out again. Cows seem to be genetically incapable of not sniffing at a sitting human, and Lily puts her snout right to my nose.

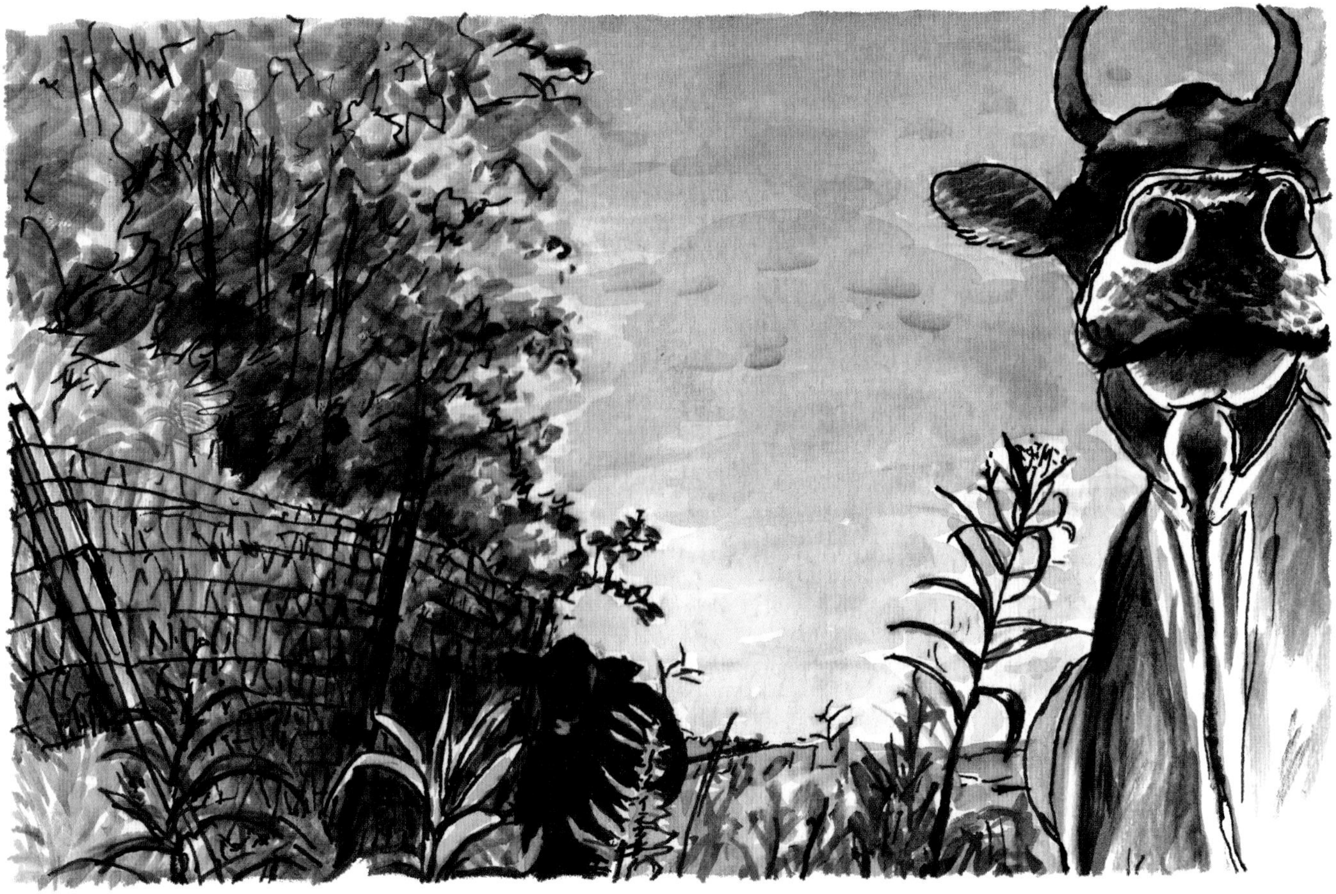

Sunday, July 21

The silver skeleton of our new hoop house lies on the ground David has prepared at the Green Bean. We don't have flat land available in our farm fields. These are the bones of a federal craft: we've acquired the hoop house through a Department of Agriculture cost-sharing program, which encourages local food production by extending growing seasons. Our neighbors see us working and come over to help. Ms. Helen and I race Mr. Charlie and Tyler, their great-grandson, to get the frames set in their posts. It's close, but the women win. I worry about Mr. Charlie's heart in this heat—he's almost 80, and has had some heart trouble—but he insists on helping.

Mr. Charlie was born with the help of a "Granny-woman" and doesn't have a birth certificate, so he's not sure how old he is. He was one of fifteen children. His father abandoned his family for long drunken binges, and his mother kept the family alive on a shoestring. Her sons hunted rabbits and squirrels, which she cleaned and cooked. She took her grandchildren fishing and tucked the catch in the deep pockets of her apron, over which she layered wild greens she found on the walk home. Charlie and his brother once brought home a few crows they'd managed to kill. His mother plucked and prepared them as if they were chickens. "And they were *good*," Charlie says.

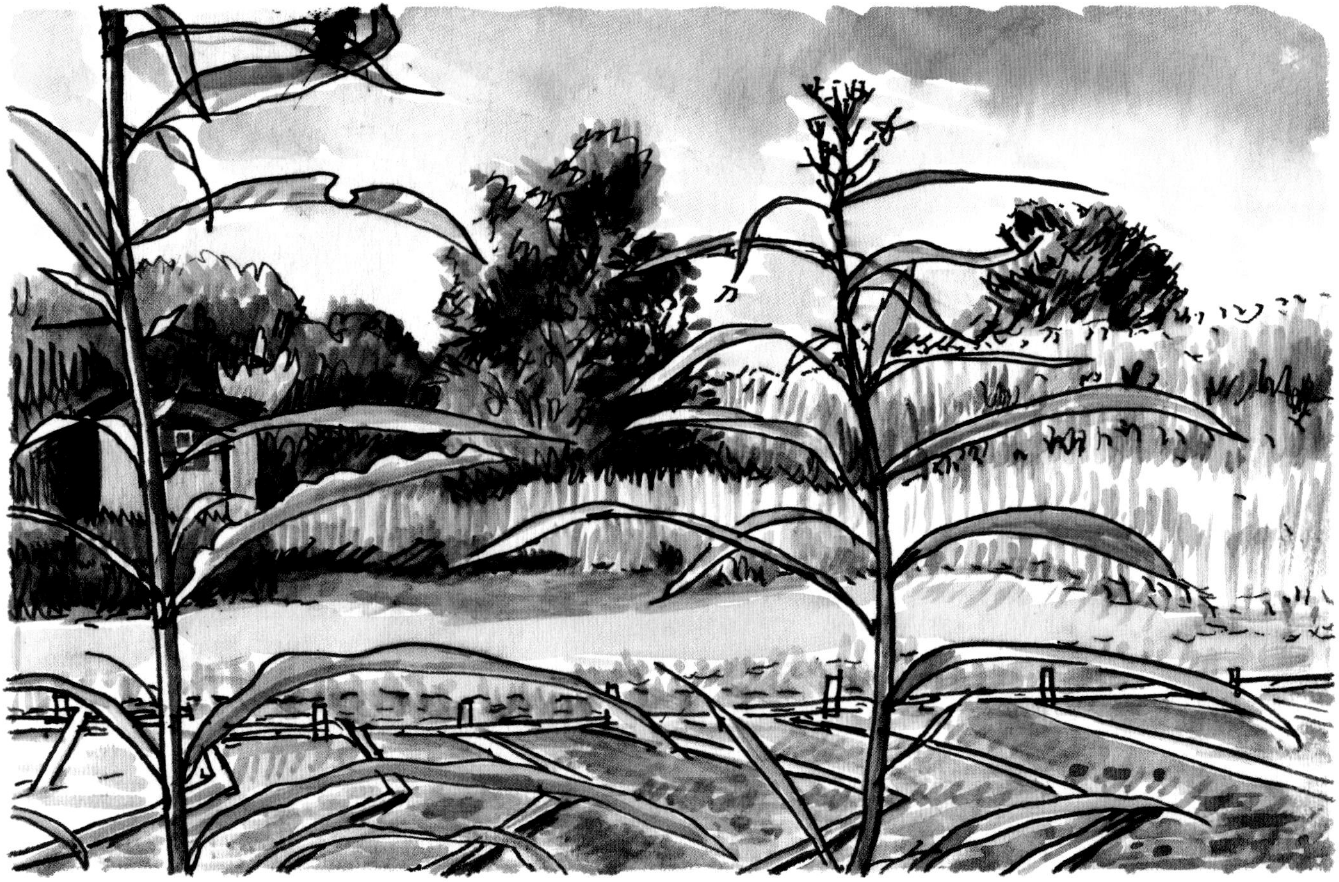

WEDNESDAY, JULY 24

Our harvest day rinse-and-pack setup has been virtually the same for fifteen years. The galvanized steel wash tubs David bought when he believed he could hand-wash all of our laundry have been repurposed for washing greens. We fill the tubs with a hose that draws water directly from our well. A window screen set on a couple of sawhorses holds the produce once it's been washed. From there, we pack it into crates and onto the delivery truck.

We would like to graduate from this makeshift arrangement but have not yet found the money or the time to make it happen. Last year, we applied for a state grant of $5,000 to half-fund a packing and rinsing shed. The grant was designed to help small-scale organic growers add value to their products. We figured we had a good shot at it—after all, we had a demonstrated track record after more than a dozen years of farming, and ours was one of the first CSA farms in the entire state. We were denied the funds, though: there was nothing in our plan, we were told, that proved we wouldn't use the packing shed as a garage. Proving such a thing would have necessitated a commitment to investing more money in plumbing and other architectural infrastructure. That's money we don't have right now, so we'll continue to make do.

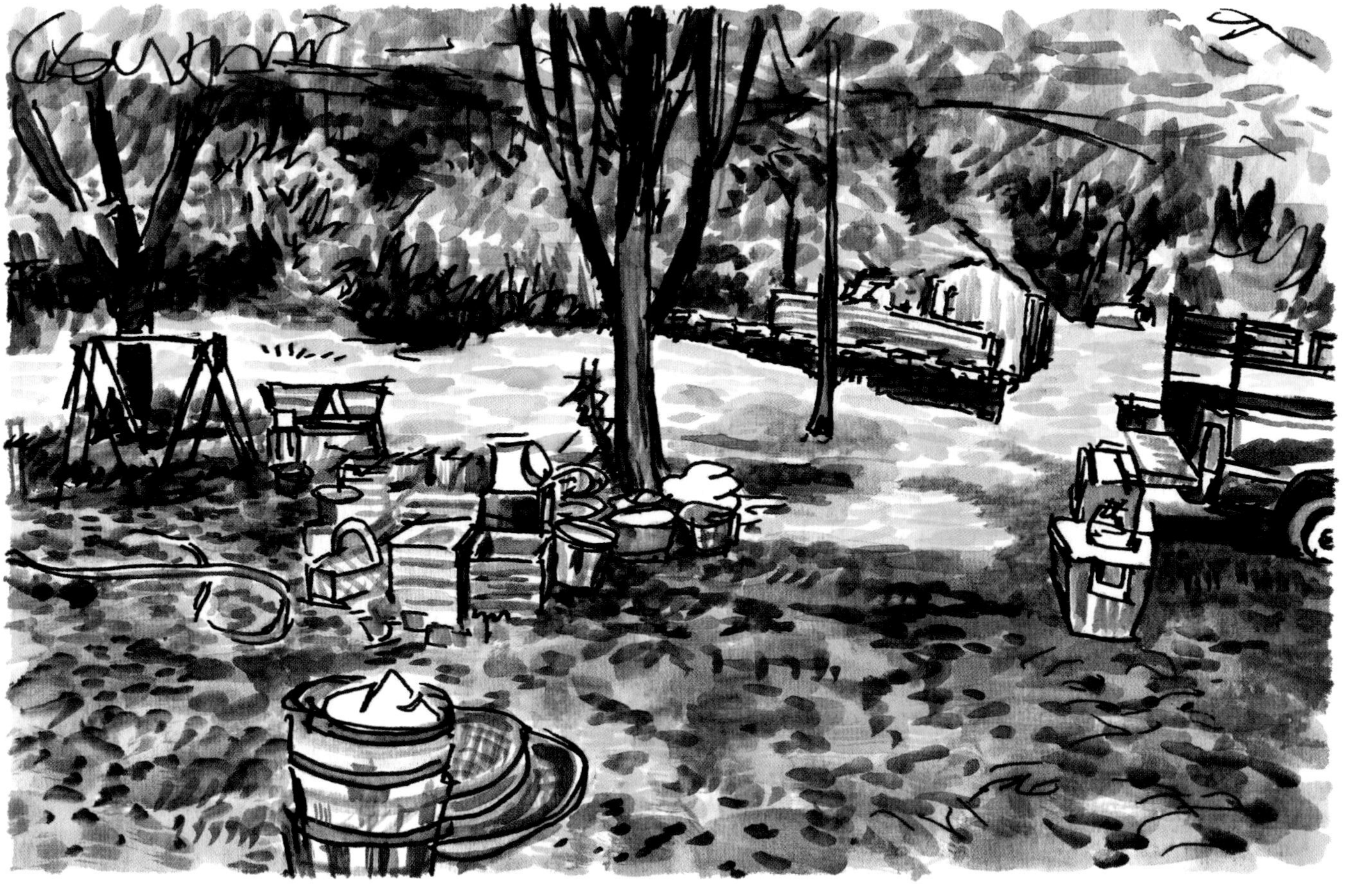

Saturday, July 27

People inevitably wind up talking about their gardens at arts gatherings in rural Kentucky. The same is often true in Lexington, the state's second-largest city. At a literary event there in May, I had conversations with three different people about what a good year it was for strawberries. Now, at the Morehead Old-Time Music Festival, people talk tomatoes and peaches.

Anna and Sarah are about to take the stage with the Briar Ticklers for the string band competition. Sarah is a singer and banjo player. She teaches high school Spanish here in Nicholas County and lives on a farm one county over. Anna now lives in Virginia, but she's originally from somewhere in the Northeast. She grew up playing classical violin and fell in love with Appalachian fiddling in college. She's done deep research into the work of great women fiddlers, who often only played in the privacy of their own homes. Earlier today, Anna won the fiddle contest here—the first woman ever to do so. She and Sarah wind up taking first place in the string band competition, too.

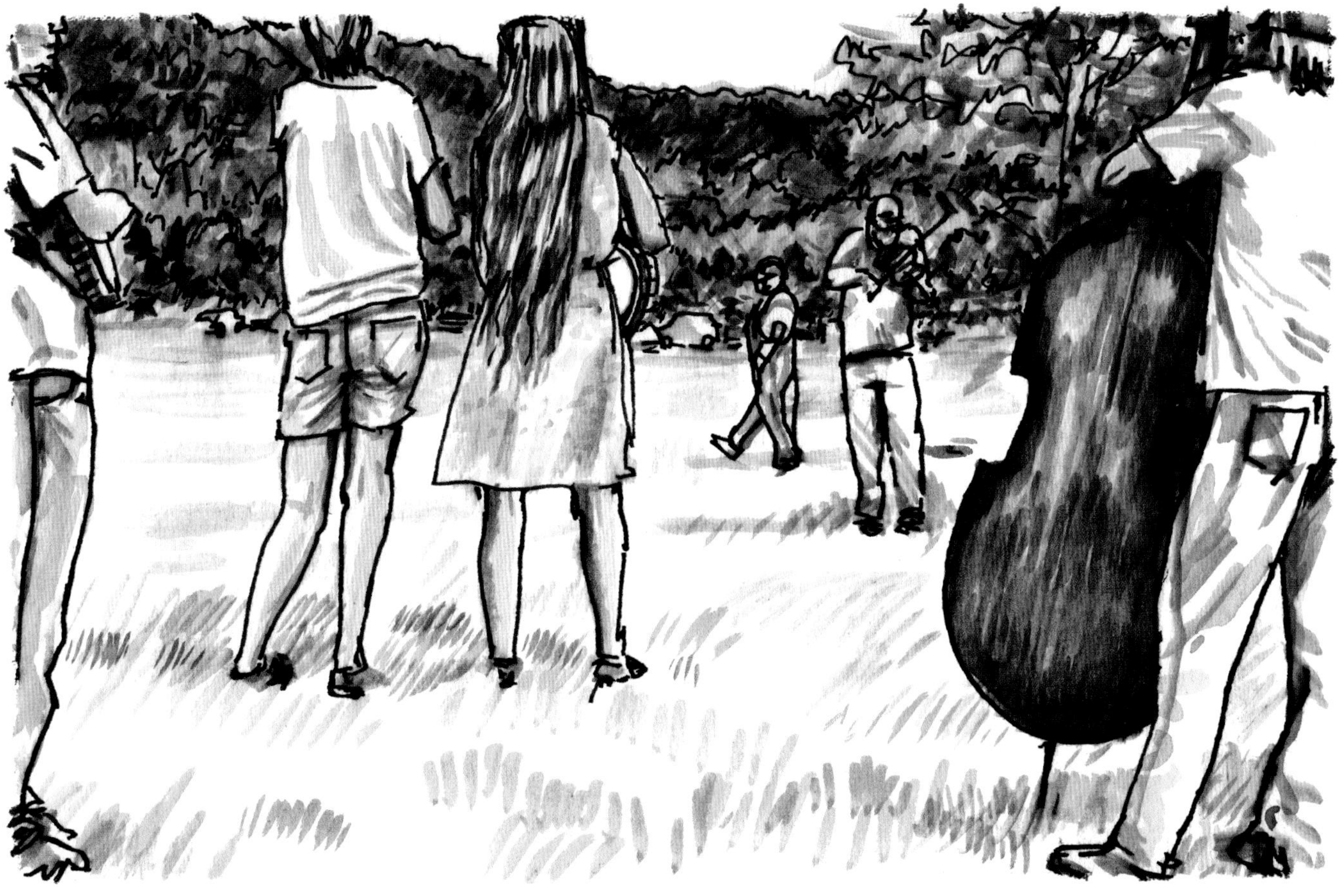

Sunday, July 28

When we finished harvesting strawberries in late June, I patted myself on the back for a job well done. The patch bore abundant fruit, and I felt safe to put it out of my mind for a time. We mowed and tilled between the rows, and now, a month later, the patch has become so choked with weeds that many of the strawberry crowns have rotted away. I weed to save what I can. I battle mostly with shaggy soldier, or *galinsoga quadriradiata*, which seemed innocent enough when it appeared in our fields years ago, with a tiny white flower and a pliant willingness to be pulled up. But piles of galinsoga I've pulled have happily re-rooted a week later. Shaggy soldier is a human commensal, following in our global footsteps. By tilling soil that was in grass for decades, we set a place for the soldier at our farm's table, and the troops followed.

It's almost impossible to draw a garden bed taken over by weeds. If you draw a hand around a weed, you've provided a focal point, but how then do you convey the sense of how small the hand is, compared to the power of weeds? A single weed has form and structure, but drawing it alone perpetuates an illusion of control, because it is a form that can be grasped. A single weed can be overcome, but ten thousand, a hundred thousand, against one pair of hands, two pairs…

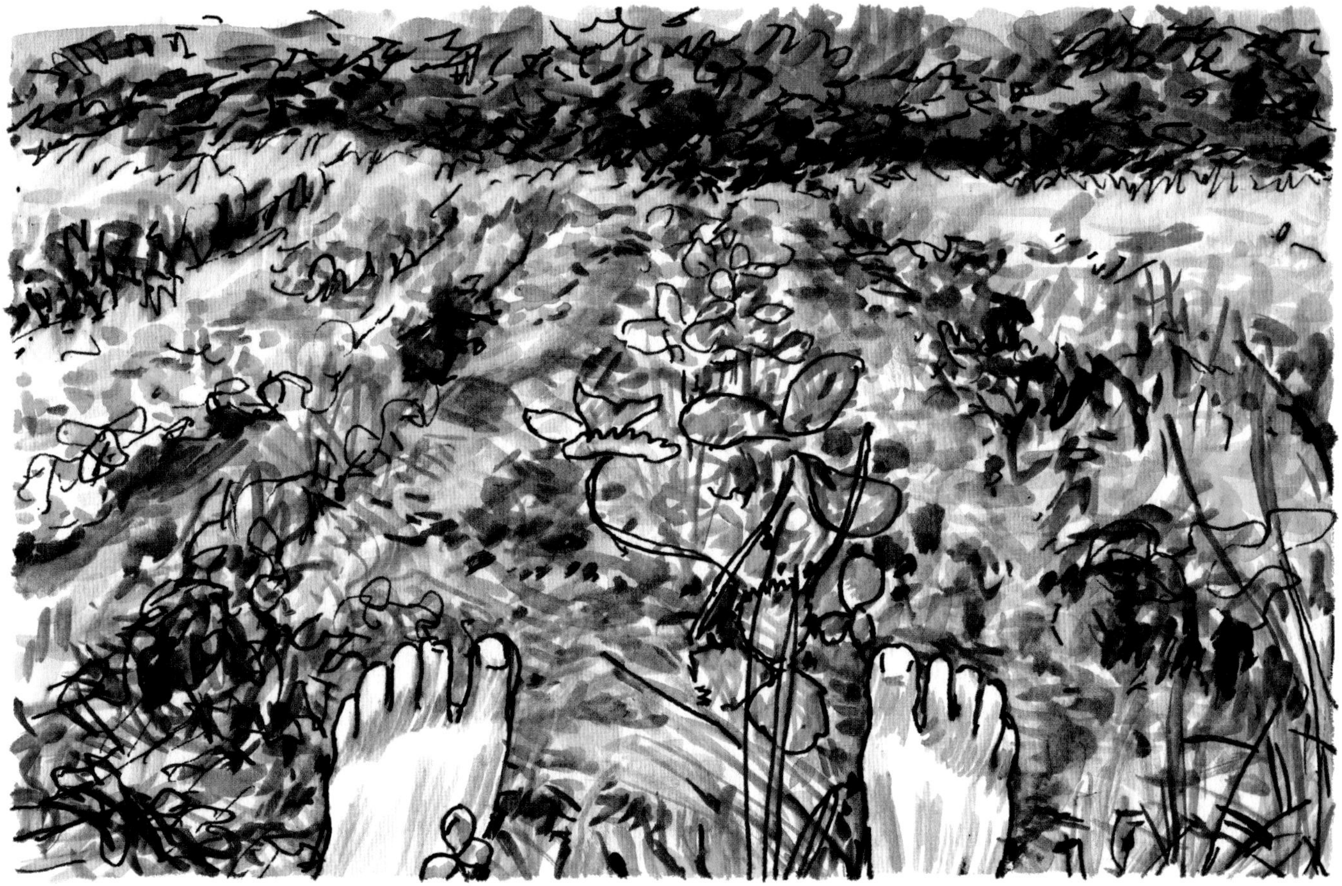

MONDAY, JULY 29

We still haven't finished trellising the tomatoes, yet the first ones are ripening. After breakfast, we harvest squash, cucumbers, and okra, and get to work. Tomatoes are such generous plants: you come away with more than just fruit when you rifle through the patch. They give you the iridescent yellow powder that dusts the stems, leaves, and fruit, loading it onto your skin and the hairs on your arms until each follicle stands yellow and straight. You will smell like a tomato all day long. They paint their dust on your clothes—no fabric that ventures into a tomato patch will ever be the same. But just what color is tomato powder? When you tie your first stems, your fingers turn yellow. Soon, they are greenish, then brown. After a few hours' work, you have a black crust over your fingers, as if you've dipped them in tar. When you wash your hands, the soapsuds will be bright yellow again. The powder is magic dust, a master of illusion.

I sit in the shade of a pear tree and eat, with tar-dipped fingers, bird-pecked Italian heirlooms for lunch.

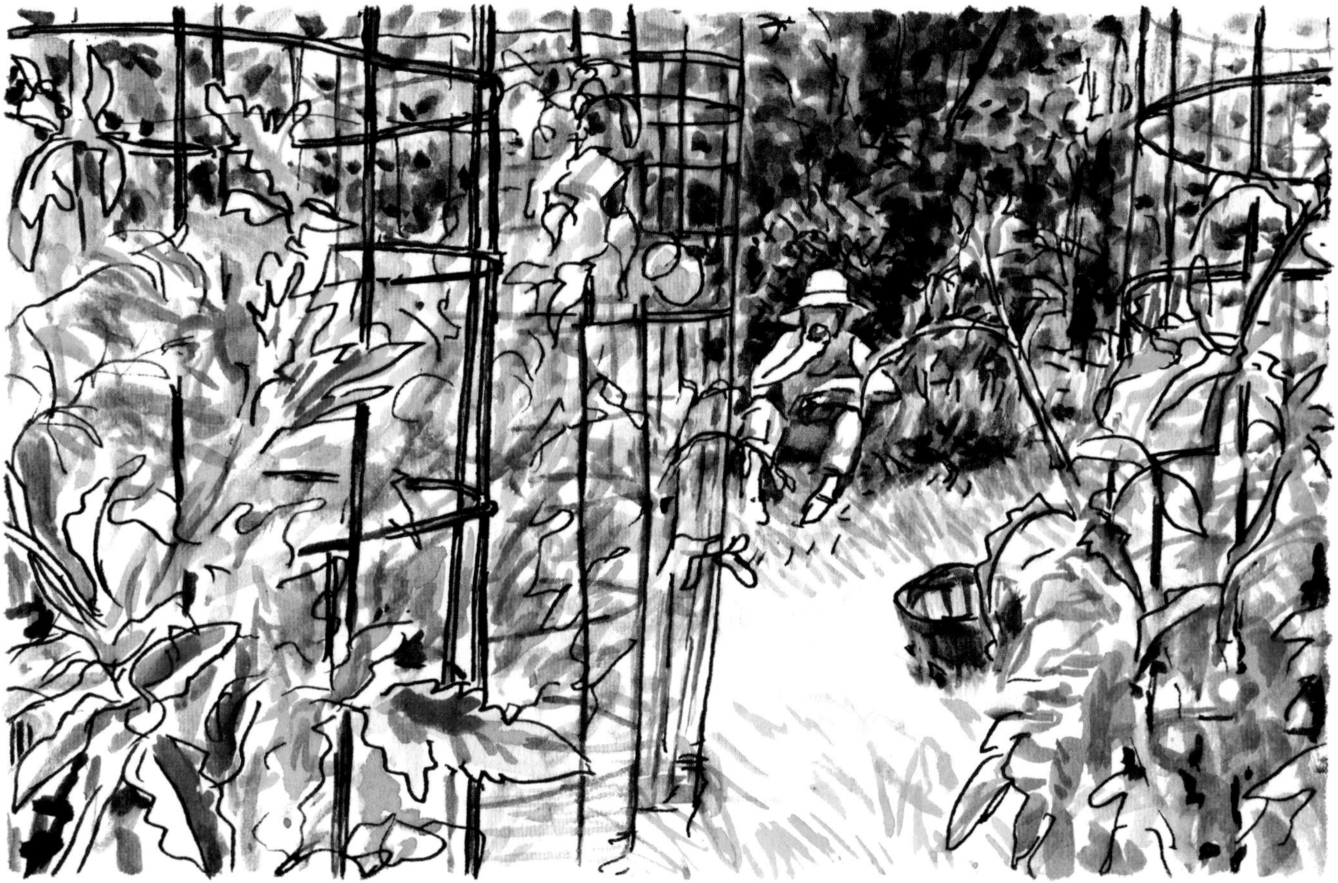

Tuesday, July 30

I've started posting drawings of our daily lives on the farm on my website. This is not possible to do over dial-up, an antiquated yet affordable system whereby we connect our phone line to our computer and listen for a warpy electronic sound that suggests an effort to make a connection. Then a digital clock appears onscreen and begins counting the seconds we're on the internet, prodding us to finish up and go do something else, preferably outdoors.

Mostly, I save up my internet-related work for days in town, but Ms. Helen and Mr. Charlie recently had a satellite dish installed, so sometimes I go to their house instead. If I cut across the fields and wade through the creek to get there, it's less than a half-mile away. I like the opportunity to visit with Ms. Helen, although I can't just waltz in and use her internet and then waltz out again without helping her make some progress on a jigsaw puzzle. It's good to visit, but I'd like to have better internet at home, so we decided to get a dish. Raul, the installer, says that the only place that will work is the middle of our front lawn. David makes a quick decision to cut down two trees so that we can put the dish behind the house. The walnut falls in the wrong direction and takes out our clothesline.

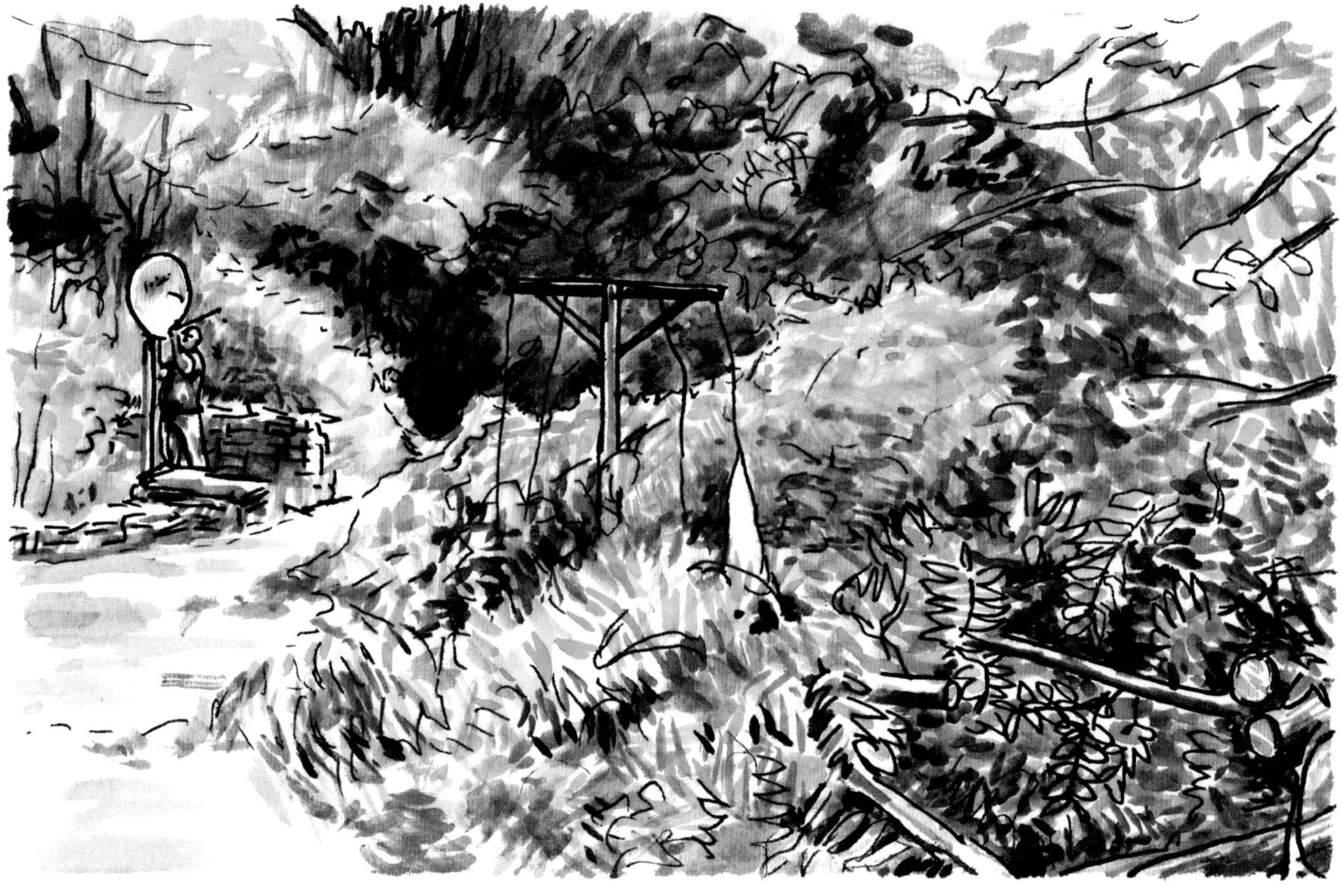

Sunday, August 4

David mows the towering horseweed, ironweed, and poison hemlock beside the lane, and mows around the new plantings of blackberries and the established blueberries and gooseberries. He uses the sickle bar attachment on our walk-behind tractor, which he likes because it allows him to work with his feet on the ground.

In our early years here, I did much of the mowing, with a small gas-powered machine that often choked and stalled, as if the poor thing were gagging on grass, but I forced it to keep eating. Also, it was too small for the vast expanse that regularly needs cutting. It was like scrubbing the floor with a toothbrush. David and I argued over it: he saw me struggle and thought I should leave the mowing to him. But I didn't want our work to be divided so neatly along traditional gender lines, so I kept mowing.

When the little machine broke down for good, David got a deck-mowing attachment for the tractor. It's far more efficient than the push mower was, but I've never learned to use it. I'm learning to yield to the gratitude of our arrangement. Right now, I am drawing and writing about David toiling, while David toils.

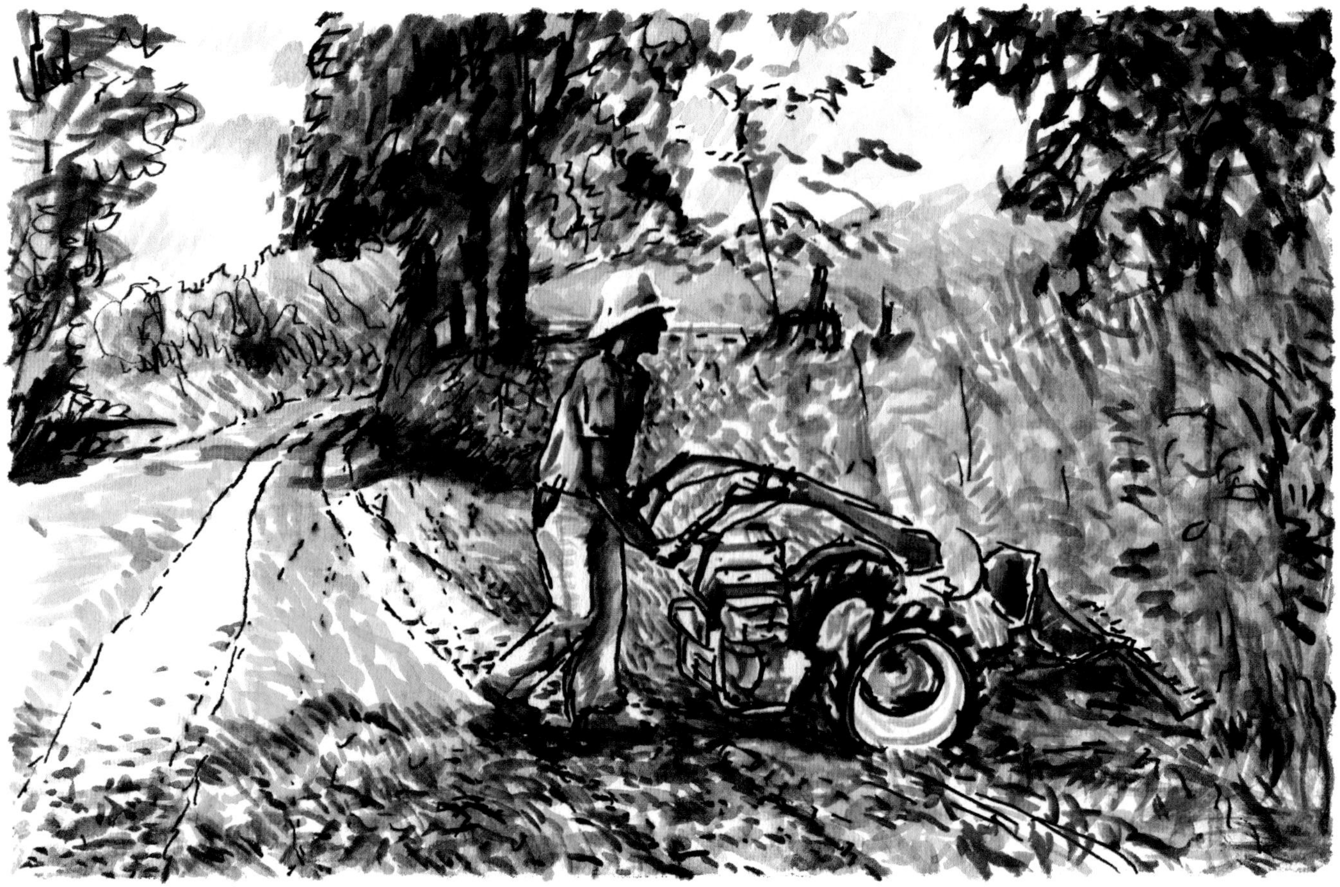

TUESDAY, AUGUST 6

Today is our first big tomato harvest of the year. Yellowing, blighted leaves suggest the tomato patch's decline, even while most fruits are still green. We have a row of fifteen pear trees in fruit, and raccoons have found all but one. The ground is littered with small, hard pears, a scratchy bite or two taken from each. What should we do, we wonder? Harvest the rest unripe, and hope for the best? Each night, we lose about another ten percent of the crop. We've planted dozens of apple, peach, cherry, and plum trees since moving here. None have produced, and we've given up on everything but these pears. A week ago, we went to a nearby orchard to pick peaches for our customers and ourselves. The orchard wasn't open to the public that day, but the owners are friends, and they let us come anyway. They showed us where to pick and warned us to steer clear of the raccoon traps, which, they told us, could break an arm. I guess they wouldn't want their customers to know that the lives of hungry raccoons are collateral damage for the fruit we love.

"We could trap the raccoons," I say to David, "drive them somewhere else, and let them go." He shakes his head. "We're surrounded by nothing but farms. I don't want to dump the problem in someone else's lap."

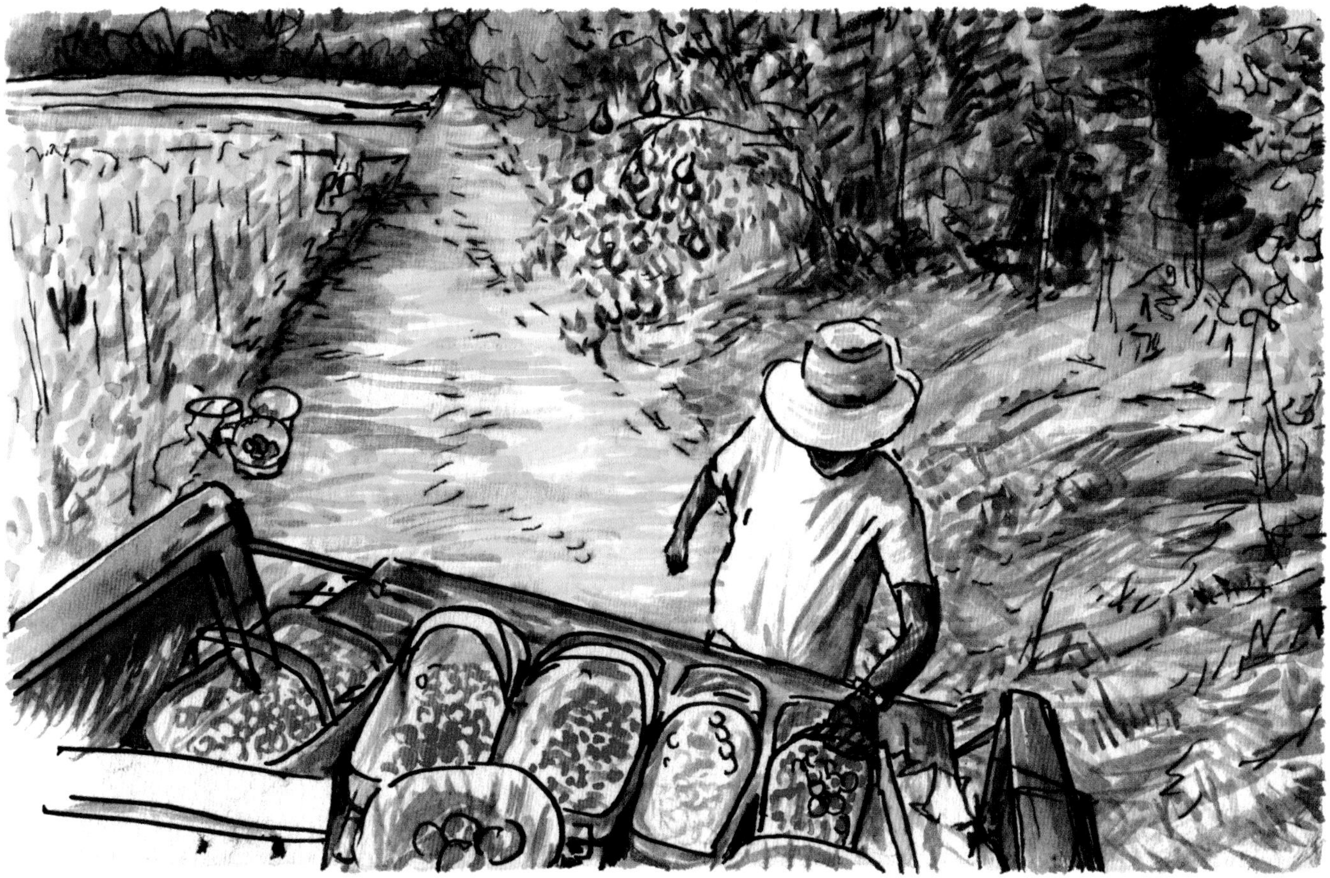

THURSDAY, AUGUST 8

Crates from yesterday's harvest are still out, and the delivery truck is not yet unloaded. August is a time of abundant, singing life, day and night, most of it bugsong, so I guess it figures that David looks to me like some sophisticated insect, sawing his elaborate tune. He puts down the fiddle, closes it in its case, and the air thickens with the rattle of cicadas, a sound skimmed over by the grasshoppers' high scraping pulse.

The katydids call to one another all night, then go quiet just about an hour before the birds sing up the sun. One recent early morning, I woke to dark silence, then a single katydid called once, slowly and tentatively—*Kate–ee–did?* Another answered—*Kate–ee–did. Kate–ee–did–it.* This triggered the first to let loose a feral tattoo of notes, as if it had been holding its breath, waiting for permission. Apparently, they had decided that the night was not quite finished, so I went back to sleep.

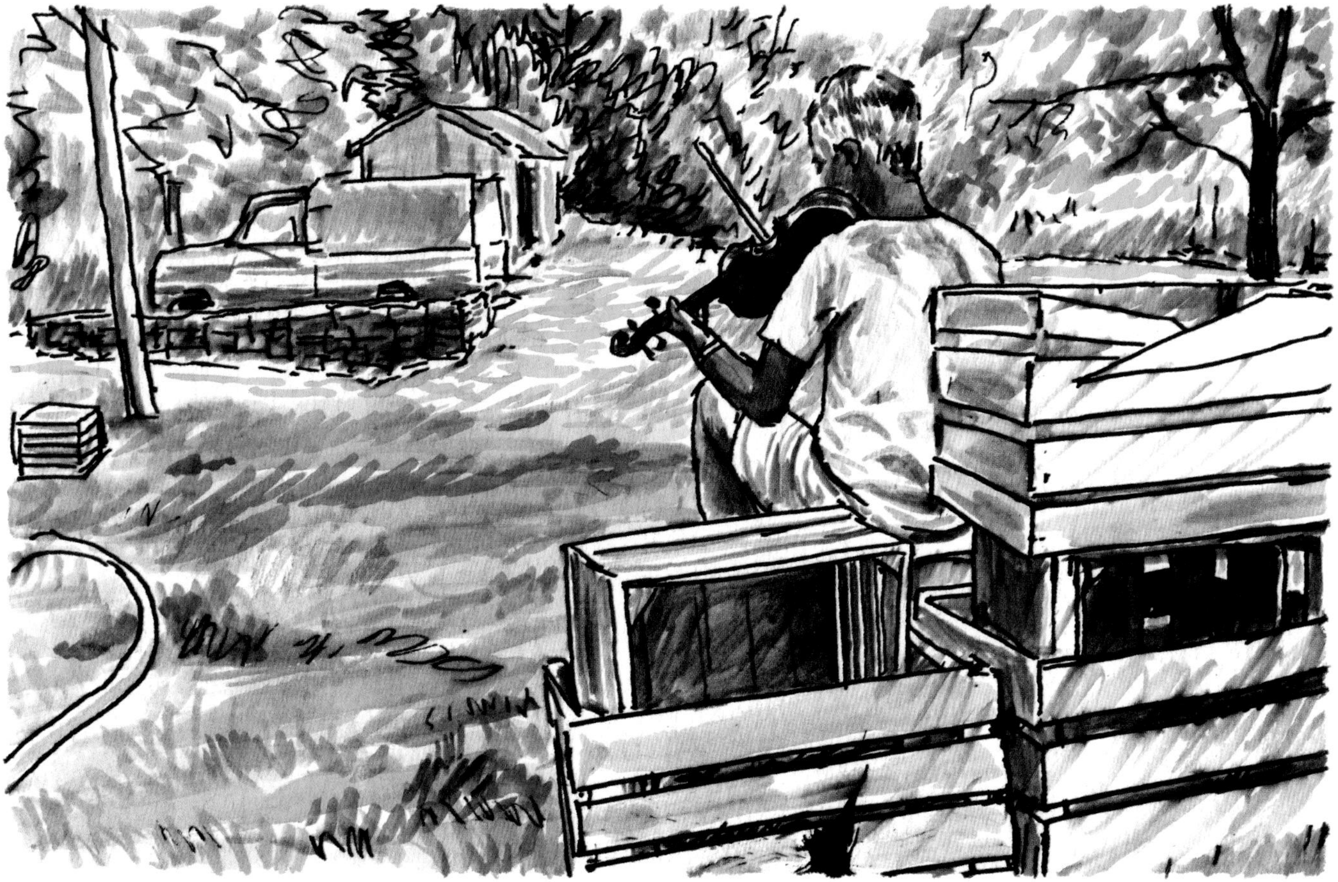

FRIDAY, AUGUST 9

Yesterday, there were twelve half-bushel baskets of produce on the floor of our shotgun kitchen. I've whittled it down to three. Edamame: blanched and frozen. Beets: some eaten, some refrigerated. Tomatoes, tomatillos, peppers, onions: I make a double-batch of salsa, twelve pints, and process the jars in the pressure canner. It's satisfying to extract the food we grow from the desolation of time by sealing it in a jar and setting it on the shelf: quarts of tomatoes, pints of tomato chutney, salsa, ketchup, pear-ginger chutney, spiced beets, pickled green dilly beans, roasted and pickled eggplants, sweet peppers, applesauce, peach and pear halves, gemlike jars of clear pale yellow white-currant jelly, rosy gooseberry preserves, bright red currant and deep red strawberry and raspberry, honey, apple and pear butter, maple syrup... I wander over to stare, sometimes, at the gradations of tone and hue, the flecks of texture I can see through the jars' quilted facets or grooves or plain smooth walls. Those jars cast a wicked spell on my weak mind. They whisper enticingly to my inner squirrel.

Today is Phoebe's first day of fifth grade. After removing the jars of salsa from the canner, I walk to meet the bus.

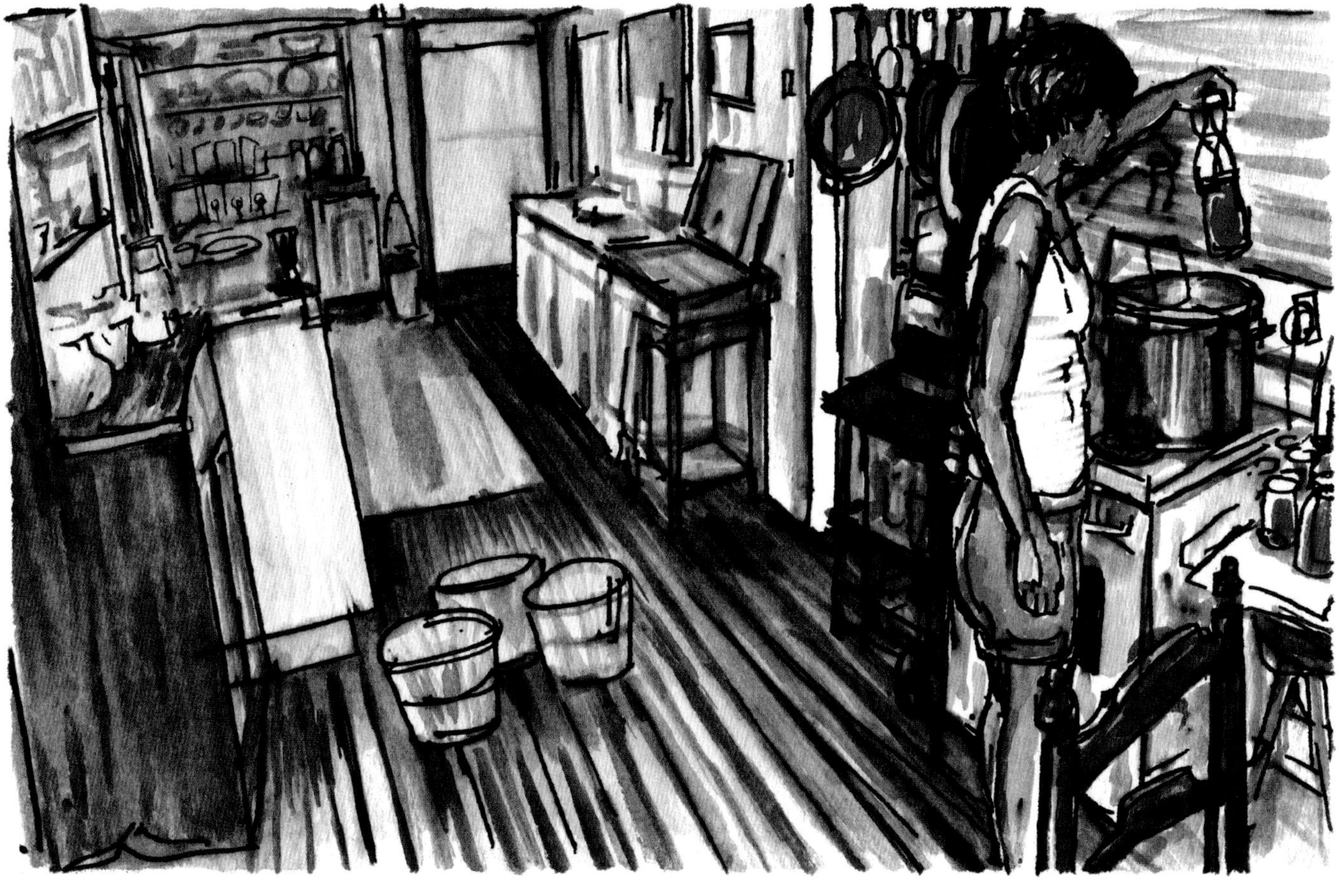

TUESDAY, AUGUST 13

At the end of the day, Phoebe catches the young hens and puts them back in for the night. Soon, they'll develop the habit of going into their roosts when darkness begins to fall.

Our girl's first days of school have been challenging. She had two new friends for a sleepover on Saturday night who have been in class with Phoebe since kindergarten, but neither had ever been to our house before. Phoebe told me they've asked a few times how much money she has. No student at her school is rich: Some don't even get enough to eat. Were these girls coming over to peg where our family fits into the hierarchy of wealth, and to use their findings as weapons against our daughter?

The girls checked out the house carefully. One of them called it "Amish-like." Later, Phoebe told me that the subject of Jesus' divinity came up during the visit. "I don't believe Jesus is God," Phoebe said. "I'm telling your mom you're on the devil's side," one of the new friends said. "She won't care, she's Jewish," Phoebe shrugged.

Yesterday at school, that new friend held up a Hello Kitty doll in front of a group of kids and pointed to its bottom. "This smells like Phoebe's house," she said, and then pointed to the bow on its head. "This smells like my house."

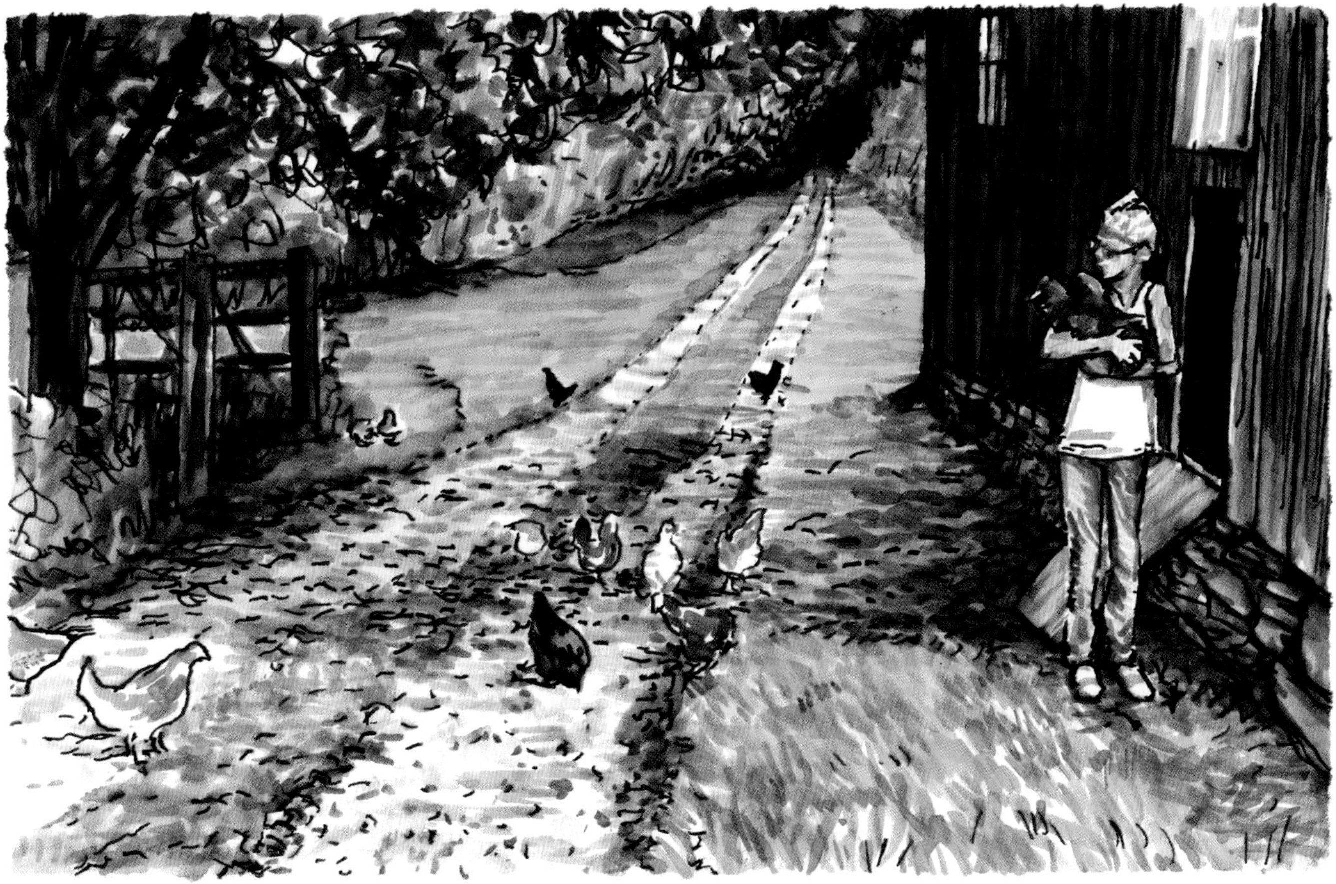

Saturday, August 17

We've kept a small herd of Nubian dairy goats for over ten years. After our goat-keeping neighbor died a couple of years ago, we lost easy access to bucks for breeding, so our does have had a break from bearing kids, and from milking. Lily, our Jersey cow, is due to calve next month. For now, we make do with store-bought milk.

A few years ago, we included chevre in our CSA baskets. It was a folly: in addition to the time spent hand-milking four or five goats, we spent two hours each day culturing milk, washing equipment, spooning out curds, salting and curing the cheese, and wrapping each finished disc in cellophane to refrigerate until delivery. We didn't charge extra for the cheese. It was a worthy thing to do, something that set us apart. It was also not legal. Meeting USDA standards would be prohibitively expensive. In the midst of our experiment, we met a professional cheesemaker who told us we were nuts. "If any of your customers get sick," she said, "they could sue you, and you could lose your farm." We don't bring chevre to our customers anymore, and I'm not sure any of them have forgiven us for it.

After feeding the goats, I squat to visit with Myrtle, and she takes a bite out of my straw hat.

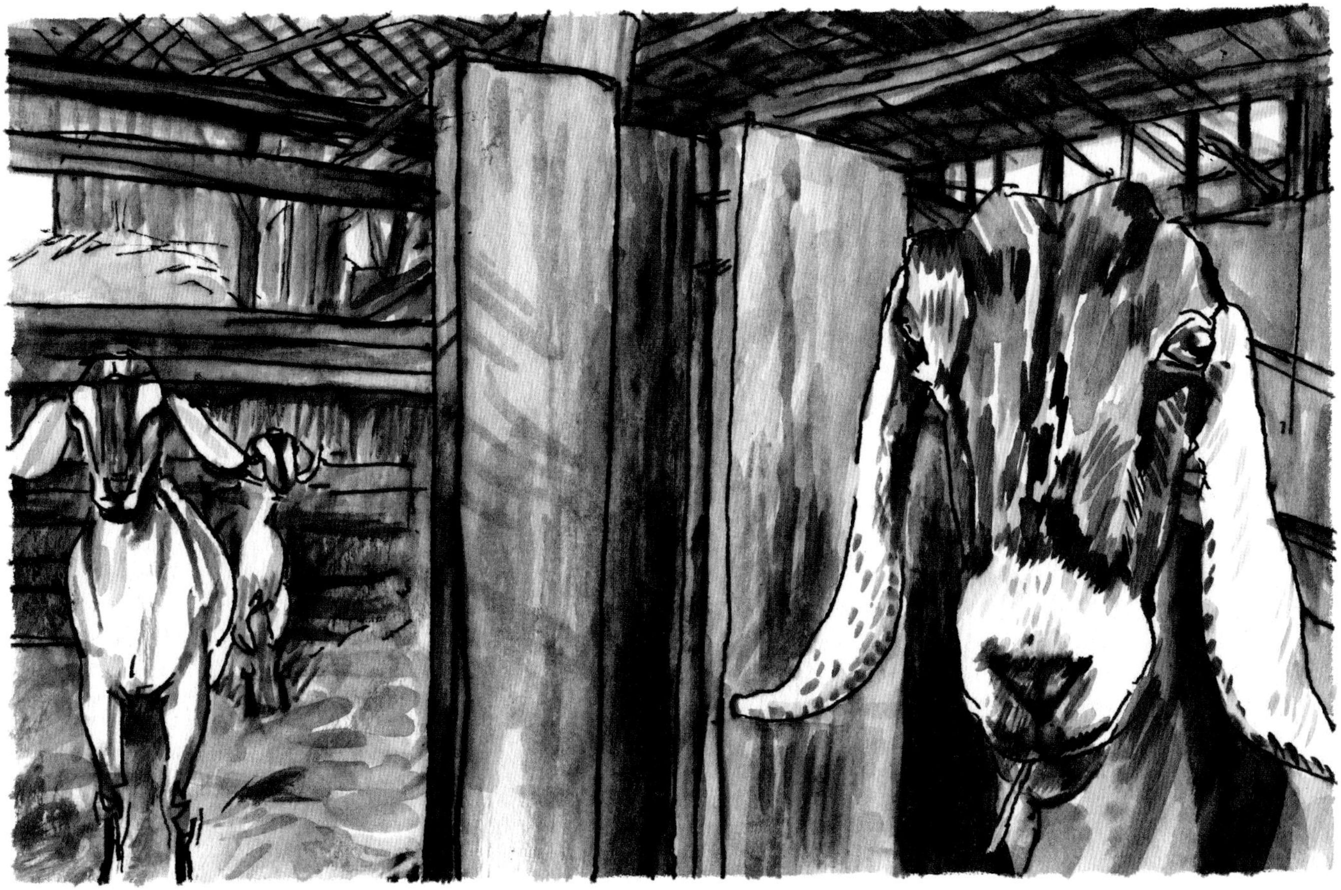

SATURDAY, AUGUST 24

Even after distributing several pounds to each of our customers, the kitchen floor is packed with baskets of tomatoes: green zebras, red zebras, Italian heirlooms, pink beauties, giant yellow Dr. Wyche's, estivas, Martino's romas, black plums, desters, dafels, pink-yellow hillbillies, and a few types of cherries. The smallest are the size of blueberries; the largest have the heft of grapefruits. I spend much of the day canning: fourteen quarts for the pantry shelves. The chickens get their fill of bruised tomatoes. I've given two baskets to a friend and still have five baskets left.

We picked peaches on Tuesday. CSA baskets were heavy on tomatoes and peaches this week. We scraped the bottom of the barrel, trying to include more variety: small and rangy lettuces, some green beans, a little summer squash, a few eggplants. In late August of last year, the baskets were packed with tomatoes, green and red peppers, a choice of cabbage or chard, a variety of eggplants, squash, fresh herbs, and lettuce. Some of the difference between last year and this one has been chance and weather, but some is due to having had so many hands at work then—five full-time interns— and so few now. Still, David, who oversaw their work, is happy to be free of that duty.

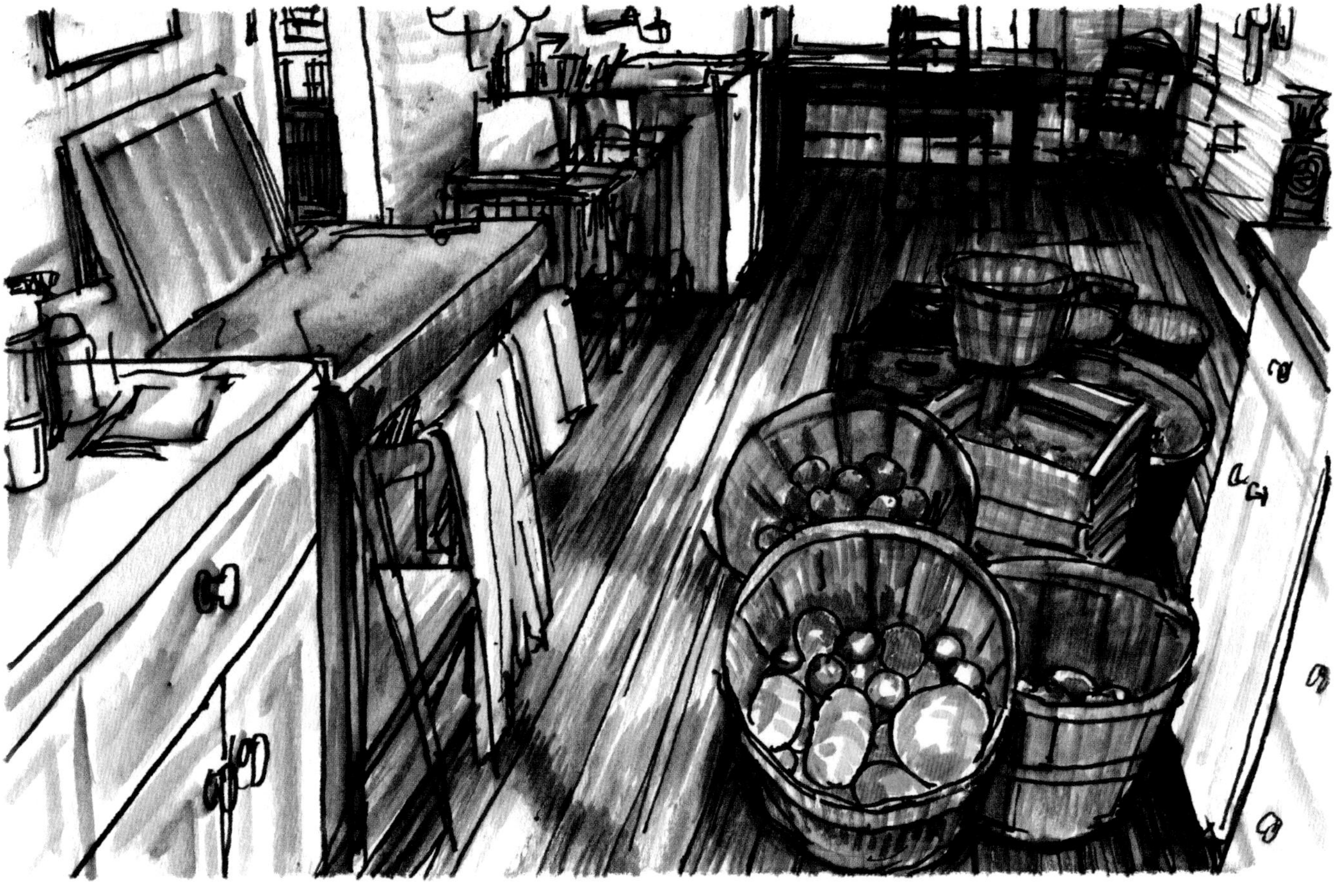

TUESDAY, AUGUST 27

Before dinner, the three of us drive to the field with a load of baskets for cherry tomatoes. Phoebe is immersed in her book, and we allow her that grace. David brings her a sungold—a sweet bonbon of a cherry tomato—to let her know he's glad she came along. Will it inspire her to put down her book and join us? We don't want our daughter to hate farming, so we don't push her much. We've heard many stories of kids who grew up toiling on farms and were eager to leave. David's father, Ron, was one of those kids. He grew up on a farm in Bourbon County, about 30 miles from here, and later became the first person in his family to earn a college degree.

We pick sixty quarts of cherry tomatoes: possibly our biggest single harvest ever. Phoebe reads the whole time. Maybe we should push her more. Back at the house, I make four salads: one of red, green, and gold tomatoes with feta and basil; one of steamed beets, radicchio, thin slices of fennel, and spring onions; one of baby summer squash and eggplant, broiled and marinated in lemon juice, garlic, and olive oil, with plenty of parsley; one of cubed cucumber with rice vinegar, toasted sesame seeds, and red chile flakes. I haven't worked the pile of okra left over from last week's harvest into our meal, so we're still not eating enough vegetables.

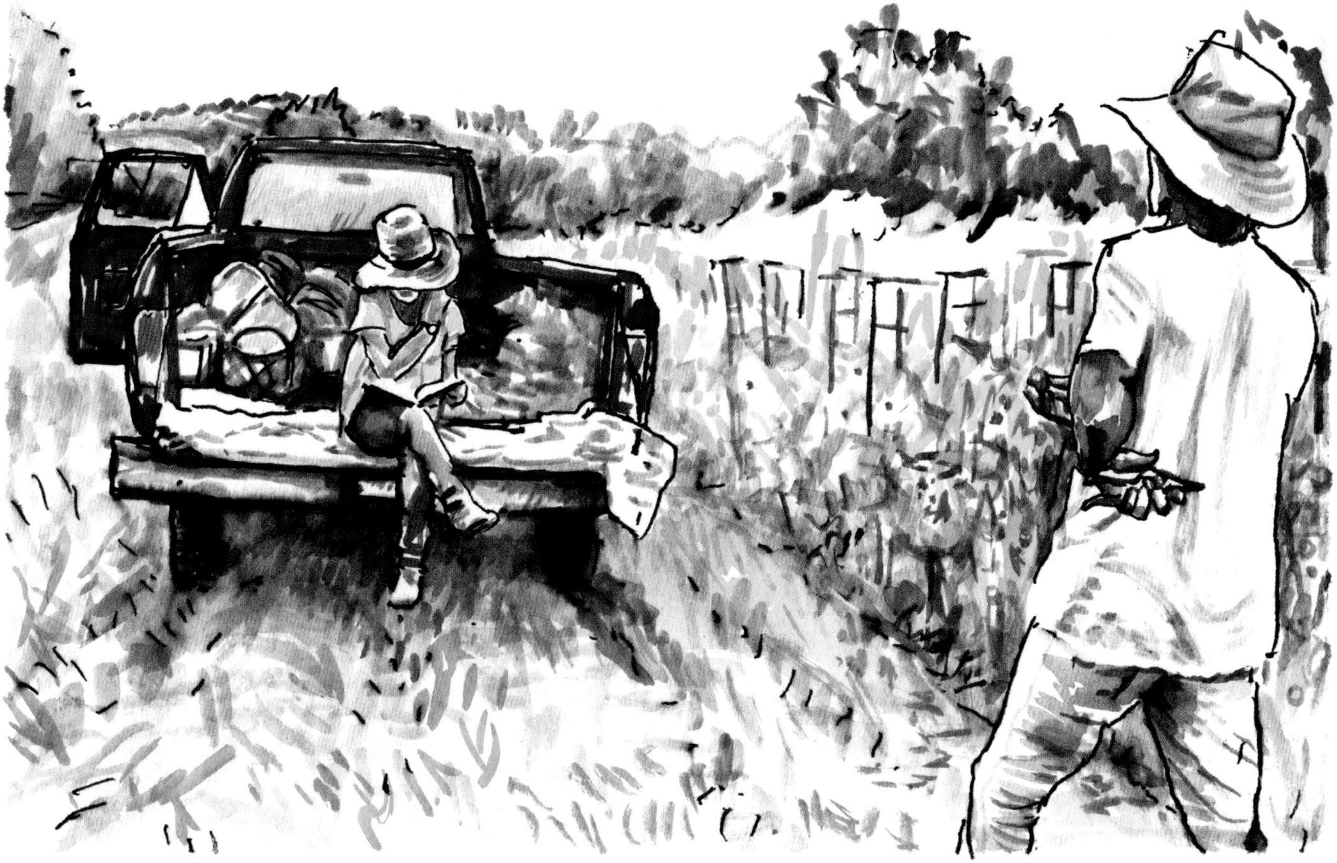

FRIDAY, AUGUST 30

Phoebe is sleeping tonight at the house that smells like Hello Kitty's bow. We drive eighteen miles from the northwest side of the county, where we live, to the southeast side. As we leave the hills and woods of the Crooked Creek valley, we see large fields of mature tobacco, and some that have already been harvested. Stray tobacco leaves litter the roads, fallen during transport from field to barn. Many barns, like those beside the gravel lane leading to the new friend's farmhouse, are full of drying burley.

When we moved to Kentucky in 1997, many of our neighbors grew modest patches of tobacco on their small farms. Federal price supports for tobacco growers were in place until 2004, after which farmers needed to get big or get out. There are no tobacco patches along Crooked Creek anymore. Somewhere under the economic umbrella of Big Tobacco, alongside the destructive forces of a global industry that thrives on making people sick, there were small family farms that resisted industrialism, where neighbors worked together to bring in the crop, and where families gathered in warm stripping rooms on cold winter days to work and tell stories.

It is informative to see the outside of the new friend's house, which is just as humble as our own.

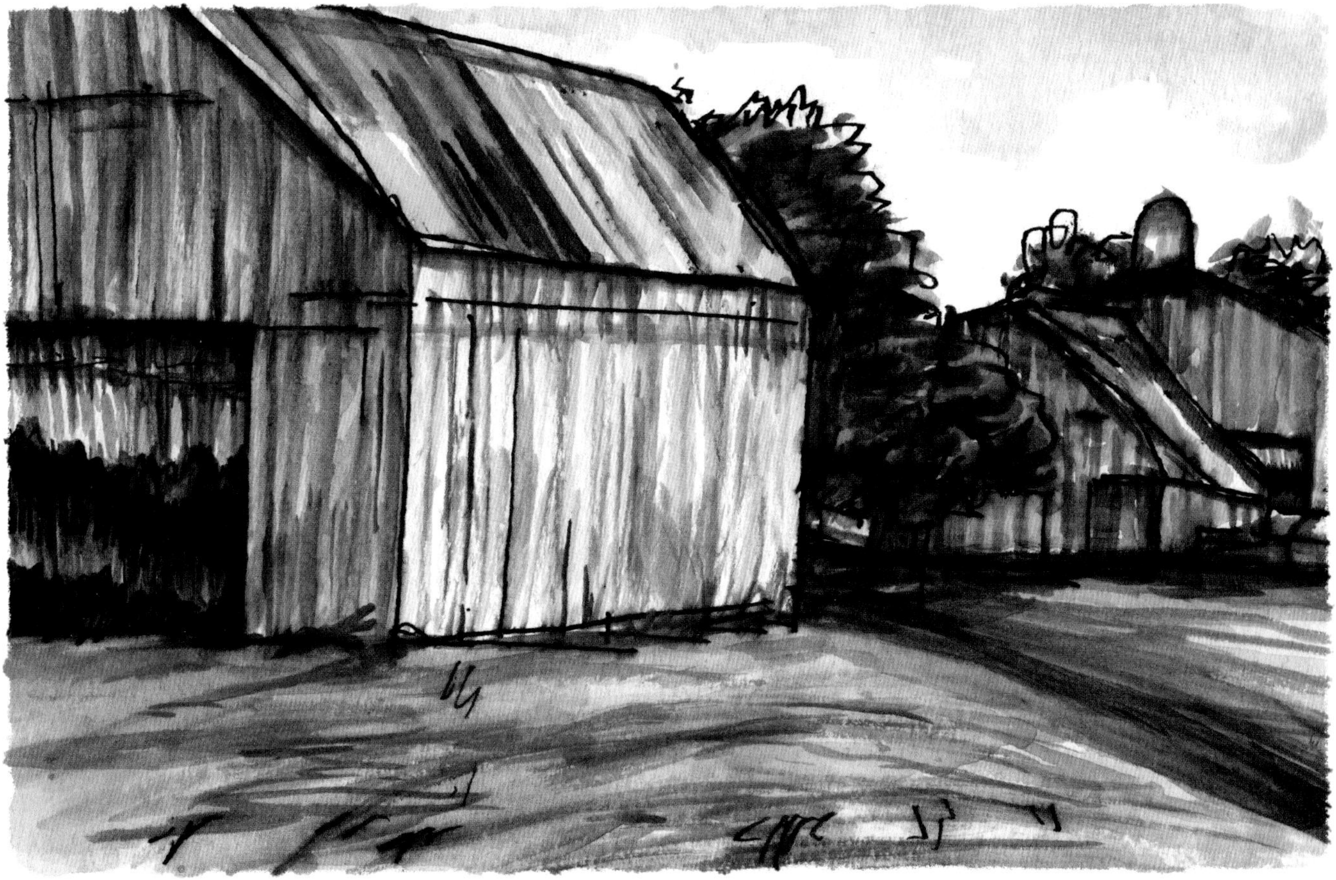

Saturday, August 31

Lily gives birth to a tiny bull calf. She was bred by a miniature Hereford bull: a little guy compared to our Lily, but he got the job done. The calf has come earlier than expected, probably because of his small size. One day last November, when Lily was in heat, the bull made his way from a neighbor's farm to ours through a hole in the fence. Our neighbor allowed him to stay with our cows for a week or two before returning to his own herd: a working vacation of sorts. Cassie, our other cow, is due any day now.

When cows are ready to calve, they prefer a secluded spot, and Lily made her way to a wooded patch at the top of the farm's northeasternmost hill. She has been working so hard licking her little one clean that her neck must be sore. When Phoebe and I arrive to check in on her, she rests for a moment, swinging her head up for a good stretch.

The ironweed and goldenrod, harbingers of fall, are in full bloom on the pasture hill. Phoebe says she had fun at her sleepover last night. She heads down the hill before me, surrounded by royal purple and gold.

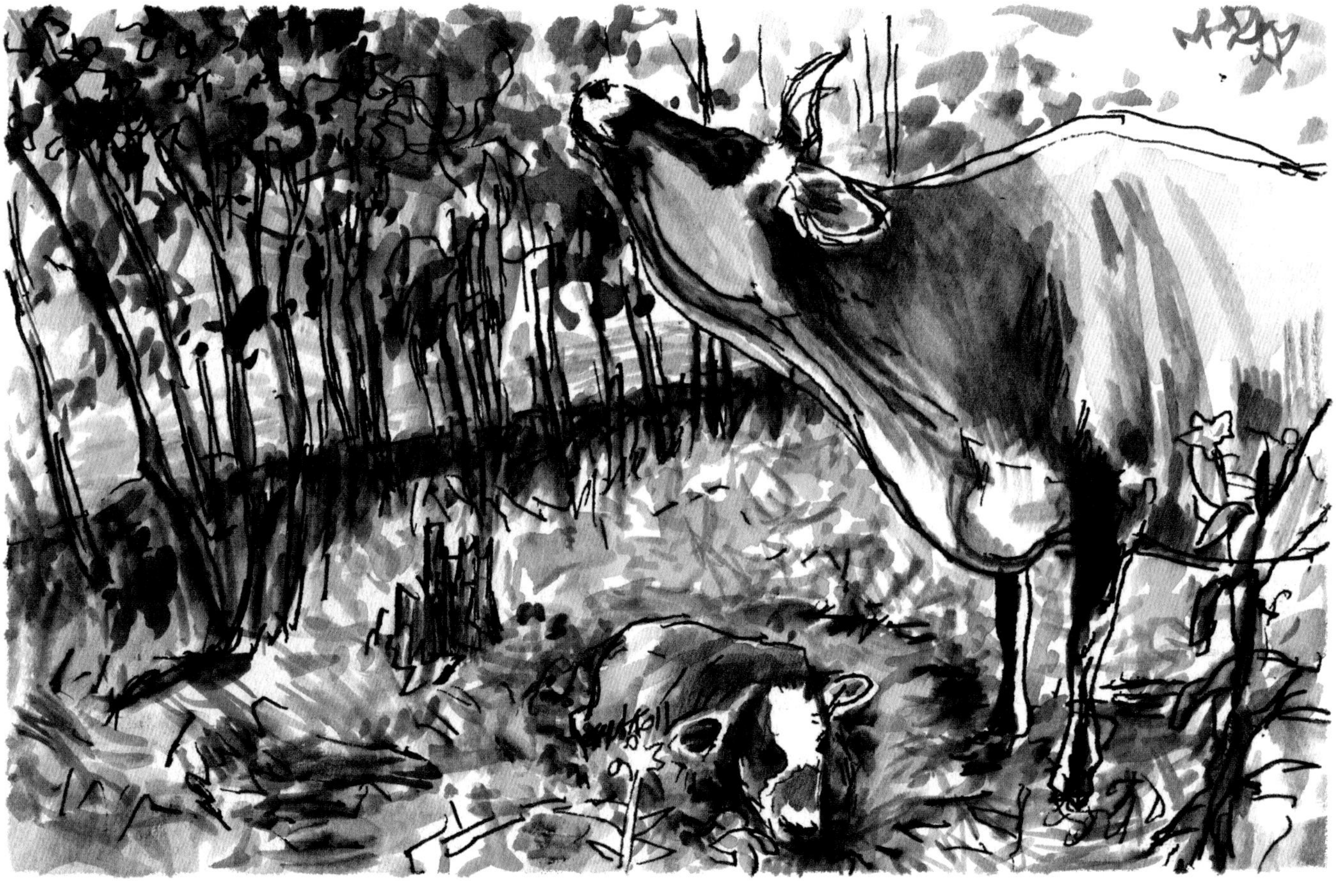

THURSDAY, SEPTEMBER 5

David's dad Ron comes over for a visit. We drive down Crooked Creek Road and up the Polk-Waggoner Hill to look at the old Waggoner homeplaces and burial grounds. The cemetery at the Mount Pleasant Methodist Church is full of ancestors' bones, including those of Godfrey and Elizabeth Waggoner, whose pocked and worn headstones bear the dates of their births and deaths: 1818, 1818; 1891, 1890. Godfrey's father came here from Pennsylvania in the early 1800s. His father had been killed in action during the Revolutionary War. Godfrey and Elizabeth's son, John Samuel, was David's great-great-grandfather. He dropped the second "G" in the family's surname. He owned a gristmill on Crooked Creek, near the community of Barefoot, which once had its own one-room school and post office. John Samuel and his wife Nancy Ellen had seven sons, whose descendants gather yearly in color-coded shirts—seven colors, one for each son—at a park in Bourbon County.

A man named Jimmy now lives where John Samuel and Nancy Ellen's gristmill once stood. Jimmy is what David calls an "accumulator": his trailer sits on a rise overlooking the road and is surrounded by rusted cars, stacks of lumber and firewood, oil drums, paint buckets, lawnmowers, heaps of scrap metal, and other items too sundry to name. In front of the trailer, a horse grazes the one patch of grass left clear.

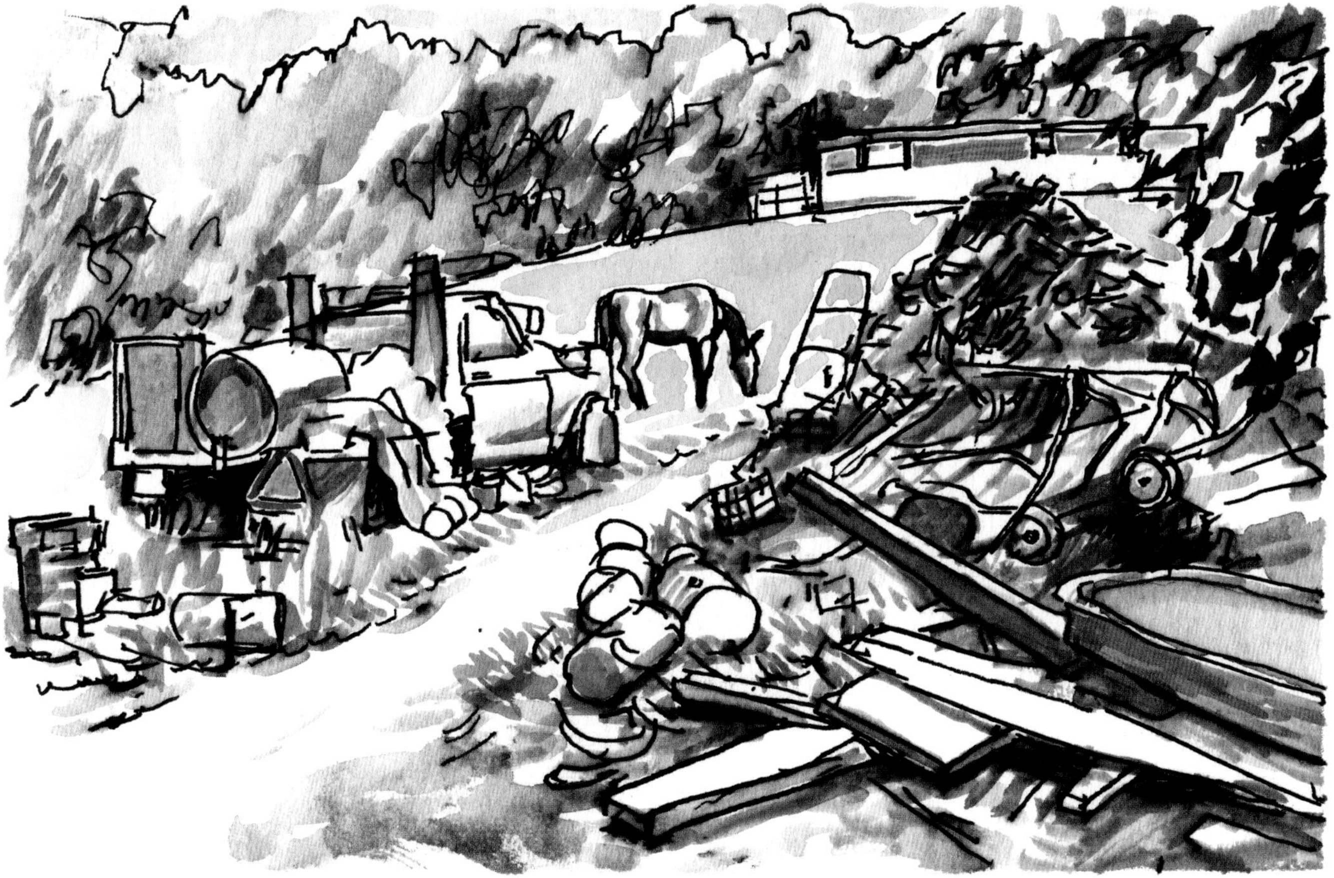

TUESDAY, SEPTEMBER 10

Lily's milk still has too much colostrum: David milks to relieve pressure, since her calf doesn't need nearly as much as she produces. Cassie gave birth to a heifer calf on Thursday night. We loosely tie Lily's head to a post so she won't move too much during milking. Afterwards, David castrates Lily's calf by binding the neck of his scrotum with a heavy elastic band, which cuts off blood flow to the testes. Soon, they will slough off. The calf lies still, before the job and after.

Out in the field by the pear trees, we've caught a raccoon in a Havahart trap, but we don't have a heart. David will shoot it in the head. To make this an ethical act, we should eat this creature, but we're not that hungry.

Today has been an ordinary day on the farm. We tied our cow's head to a post. We put a tight rubber band around her baby calf's nuts so they will shrivel and fall off. We shot a raccoon in the head. We do all of this with the aim of producing our own food, taking responsibility for our actions, not leaving the difficult decisions and dirty work to someone else. That explanation does not exculpate my sense of failure at being good. Often it seems that goodness is perched on a razor's edge.

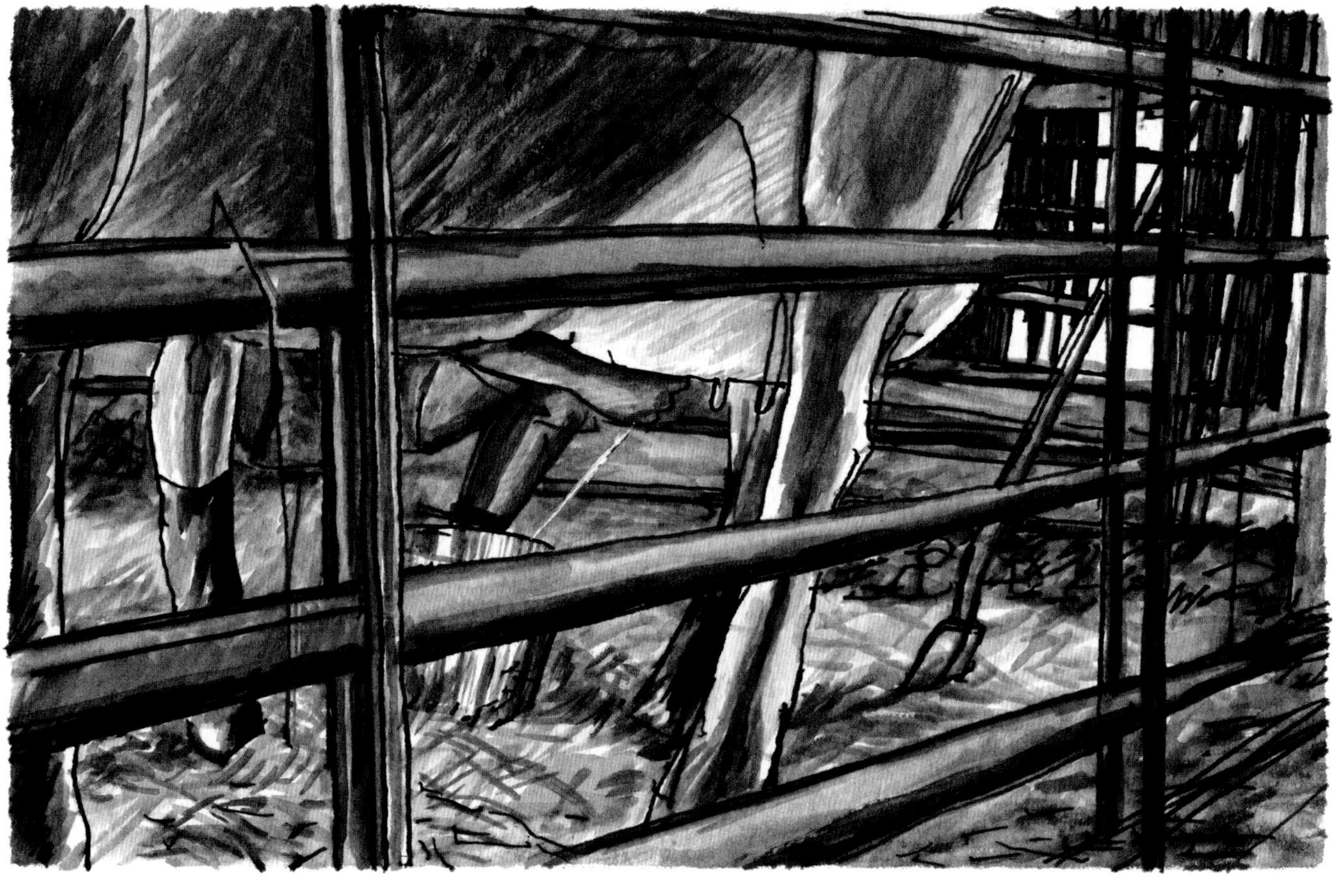

WEDNESDAY, SEPTEMBER 11

When our deer problem was at its worst, David slept in the fields with the dogs to protect the crops. Eventually, deer learned to graze just beyond the reach of the dog's tether. Then, the year Phoebe was born, we built a fence around the fields. It's eight feet high, surrounds two acres of bottomland, and took the whole year to get done. David closes the wire gate after we harvest. Sweet peppers and okra are coming on strong, and as the nights grow cooler, a fresh flush of greens has found its footing.

Back at the house, the phone rings. It's the mother of one of Phoebe's school friends. She's been reading my book about Holocaust survivors who settled in Kentucky. Her church has a new pastor, she says. The last one was good, but he's gone: "He was too smart to stay here. Anyone who has a better choice will leave." The new pastor has been saying things about the Holocaust being punishment for the Jews' sin of unbelieving. She wants me to talk to the congregation about Kentucky's Holocaust survivors. "I don't think I can do that," I say. "The pastor would have to want me to be there." She understands. We change the subject.

After hanging up, it's the words "anyone who has a better choice will leave" that won't give me peace. Let us give this good land due respect, I want to tell her. Let us honor those who choose to stay.

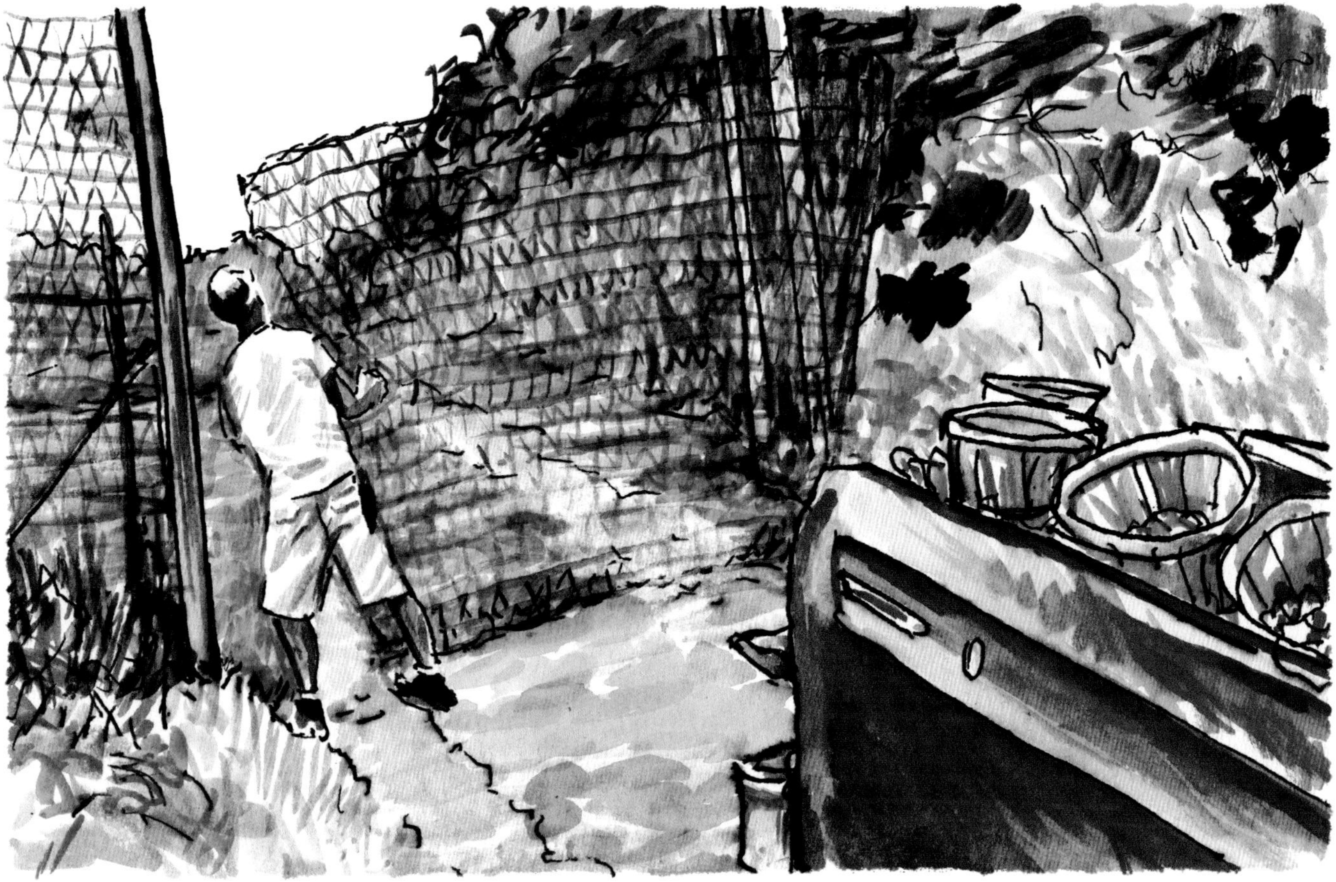

FRIDAY, SEPTEMBER 13

Most of the farm's animals—four goats, four cows, two humans, and a dog—lounge in the shade of a shagbark hickory on the hill above the barn at midday. Lily's calf rests with the goats. Cassie's frolics, challenging her mother to keep track. Cassie spends most of her non-grazing daylight hours battling flies. They settle on her back, she flings her head and tail at them, they fly up in a cloud and settle again.

The dog is in our laps, belly up, tongue lolling. In a few hours, one of us will walk out to meet Phoebe's school bus, and Bando will trot along beside us. Does he anticipate the winter, as the nights lengthen and grow colder? We share our lives with this devoted and mysterious creature. "Our lives are woven together with all the farm animals that way," David says. In some ways, we're more intimate with them than we are with people in our lives, however beloved, who don't live here.

"But sometimes we kill them," I say.

David is quiet for a while. "I know this isn't likely to happen," he says, "but I like the image of my body being left up on that ridge after I die, and the buzzards come and disperse it in all directions."

"I don't like that image at all," I say.

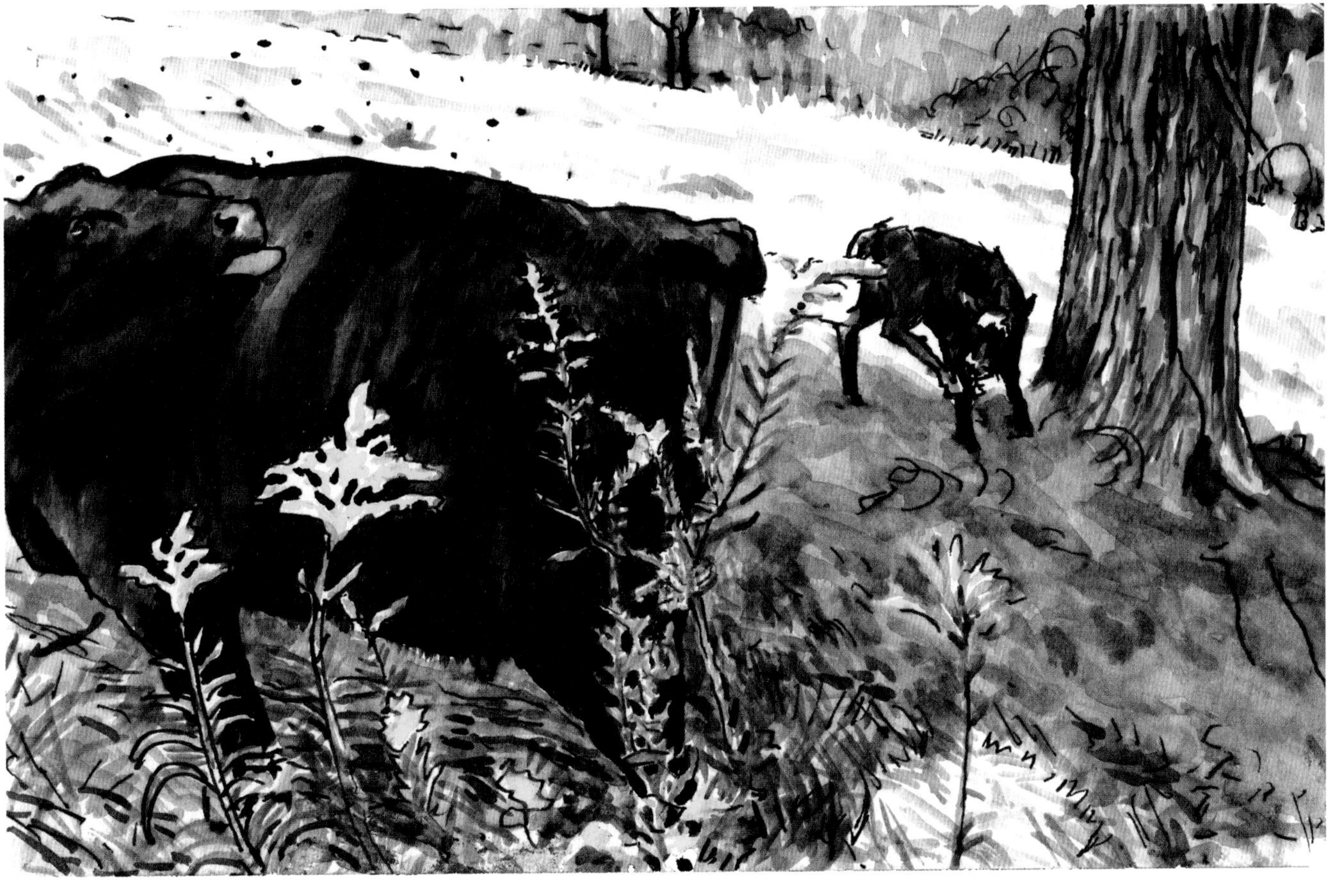

Friday, September 13

Before dusk, I head to the woods in search of pawpaws. Here are about a half-acre of spindly trees whose velvety leaves fan like broad green hands, aglow in the filtered light left by taller oaks, sugar maples, and beeches. Squirrels and raccoons usually beat us to the picking, so there is not much to find. The mango-like fruit hangs in the hardest-to-reach branches. I work with a long stick in one hand to bend branches down, and grab the fruit with the other hand. It's almost as fun as swinging from the wild grapevines that populate these woods, and marginally more productive. I wander for a good hour, and return to the house with a hatful of hard green rocks.

Pawpaws are our largest indigenous fruit, fleshy and sweet, dangling from graceful trees we've done nothing to propagate, with custardy pale yellow flesh in which plenty of glossy brown seeds the size of a thumbnail are embedded. I want to love them, but only once did I find the fruit delicious. It was our first find, and a lucky one: a few had ripened on the tree. The flesh was delicately fragrant, yolk-yellow, the texture of creme brulee. Maybe I was seduced by the surprise, and didn't notice the cloying sweetness or the musky-bitter aftertaste that jades me now. Or maybe their flavor changes when they ripen off the tree. Still, we'll eat them all, somehow.

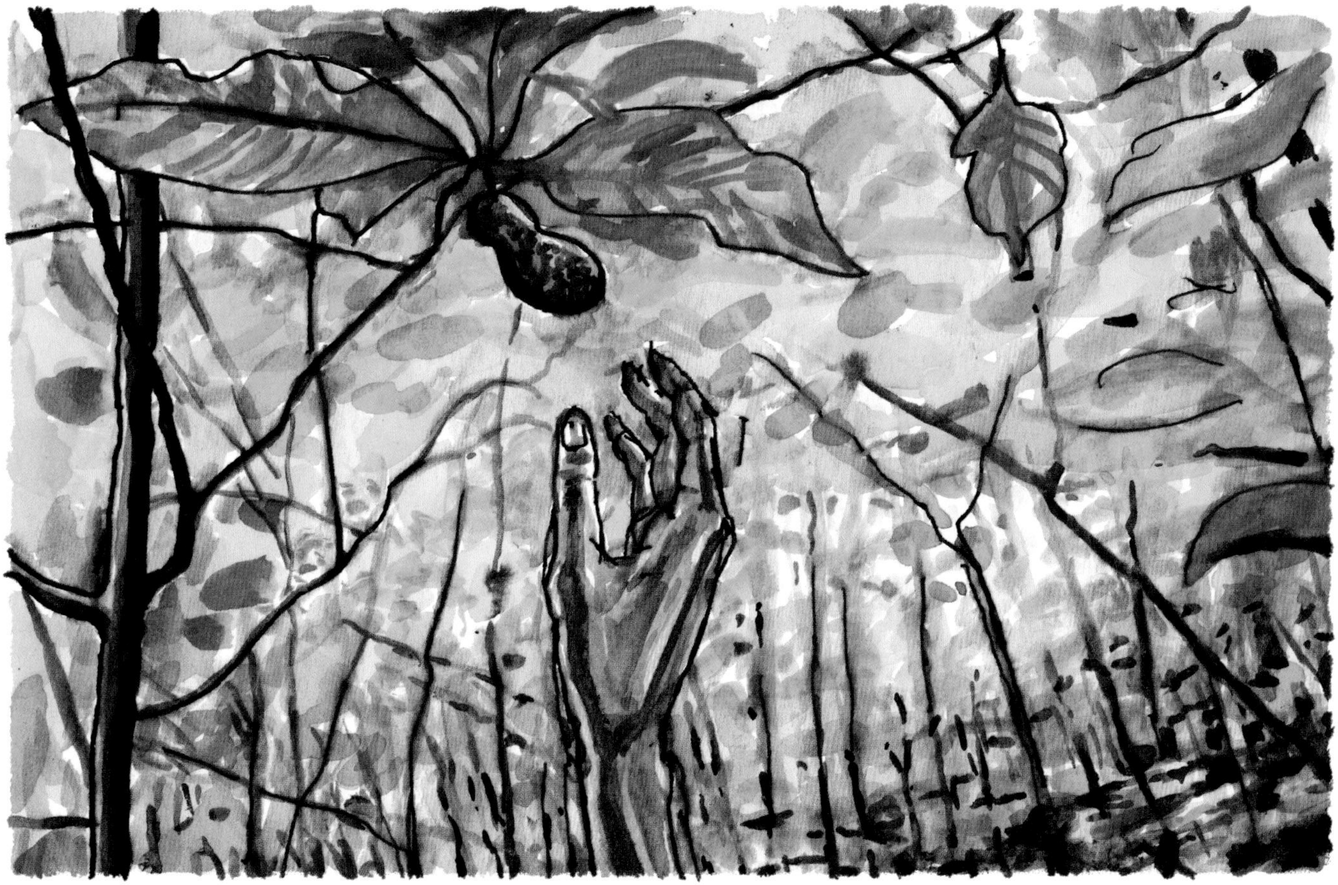

THURSDAY, SEPTEMBER 19

Two gallons of milk in the fridge, and more to come tomorrow. Lily, that monolithic cow, is both gentle and terrifying. When you stand beside her and she flings back her horned anvil of a head to knock out a fly, you must step back quick. She barrels toward her grain, head down, horns leveled at your ribcage, before you're quite ready to give it to her. She gored one of our goats once: poor Andromeda didn't survive it. But Lily shows affection and trust when you brush her, lean against her, scratch around her horns. I like to put my ear against her side and watch the milk strike the pail. I like her warmth and the sweet cream she gives us, although she habitually holds the richest hindmilk back for her calf.

After I meet her bus at the end of the lane, Phoebe and I say hello to the cows, then I go back to the house and make a batch of paneer. I'll pull some of our spring green peas from the freezer and get Phoebe to help make mattar paneer with basmati rice. It will probably be the first time this dish has ever been prepared in the Crooked Creek valley. This is just one of the small and forgettable ways we make history.

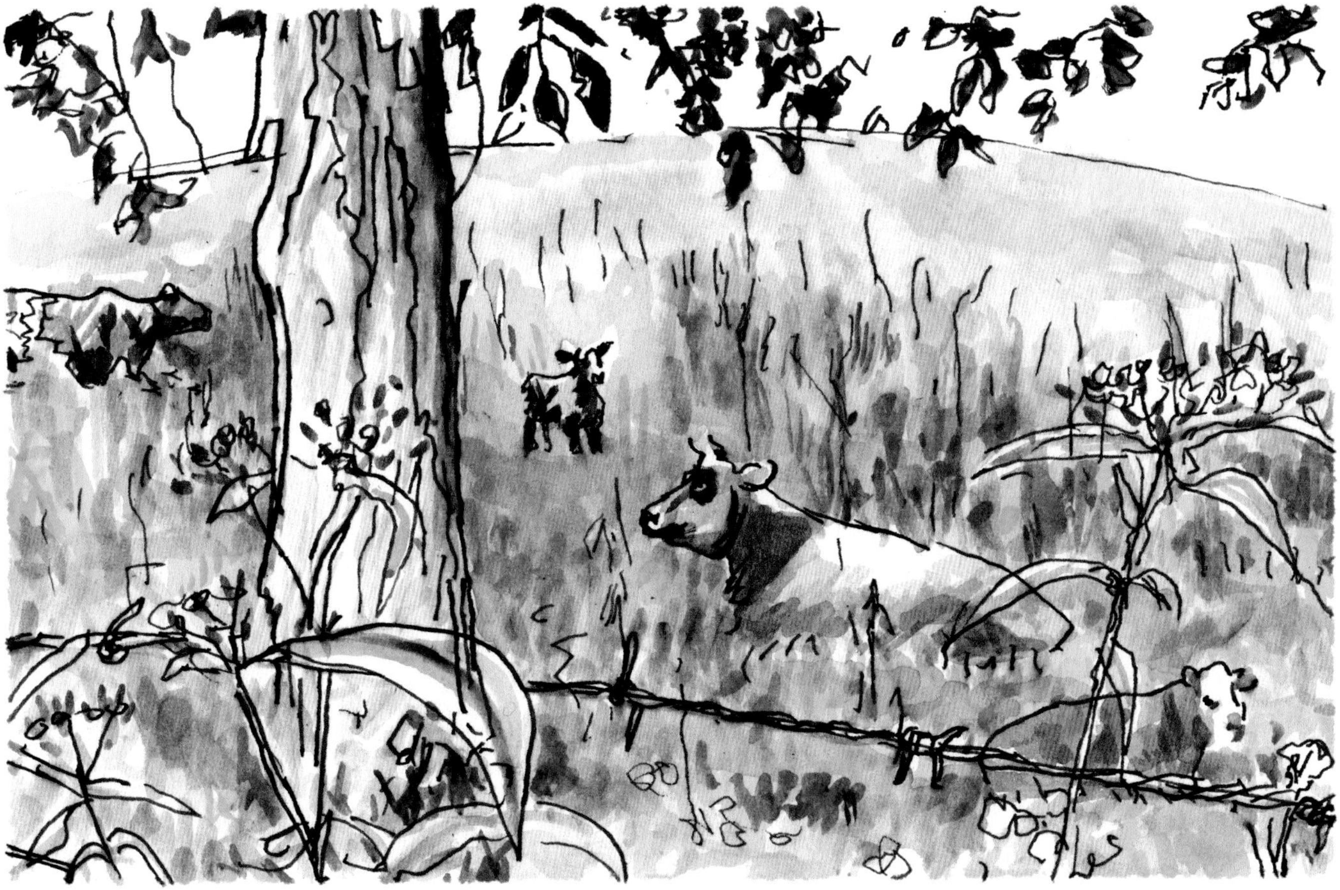

Monday, September 23

As I walk to meet the bus, David drives out with a load of trash that fills the truck bed and trailer. We make contributions to the Nicholas County landfill a few times a year. Trash service and dump deliveries cost money, and many of our fellow accumulators on Crooked Creek burn their garbage, no matter what it's made of.

The bus arrives and Phoebe marches off it, scowling after a hard day at school. We walk back up the lane, leave school stuff on the porch, and head straight to the raspberry patch. This variety bears in early summer and again in early fall. As we pick, Phoebe tells me she loves being home. I am happy. "Let's homeschool next year," I say. She's reluctant, afraid of change, but I work at talking her into it. There's a troubling undertow to my happiness, though. It's that "anyone who has a better choice will leave" problem. For the moment, yes, homeschooling would mean keeping my child close, but aren't I really aiming to give her a clear path out of here, knowing that the best opportunities for her lie elsewhere?

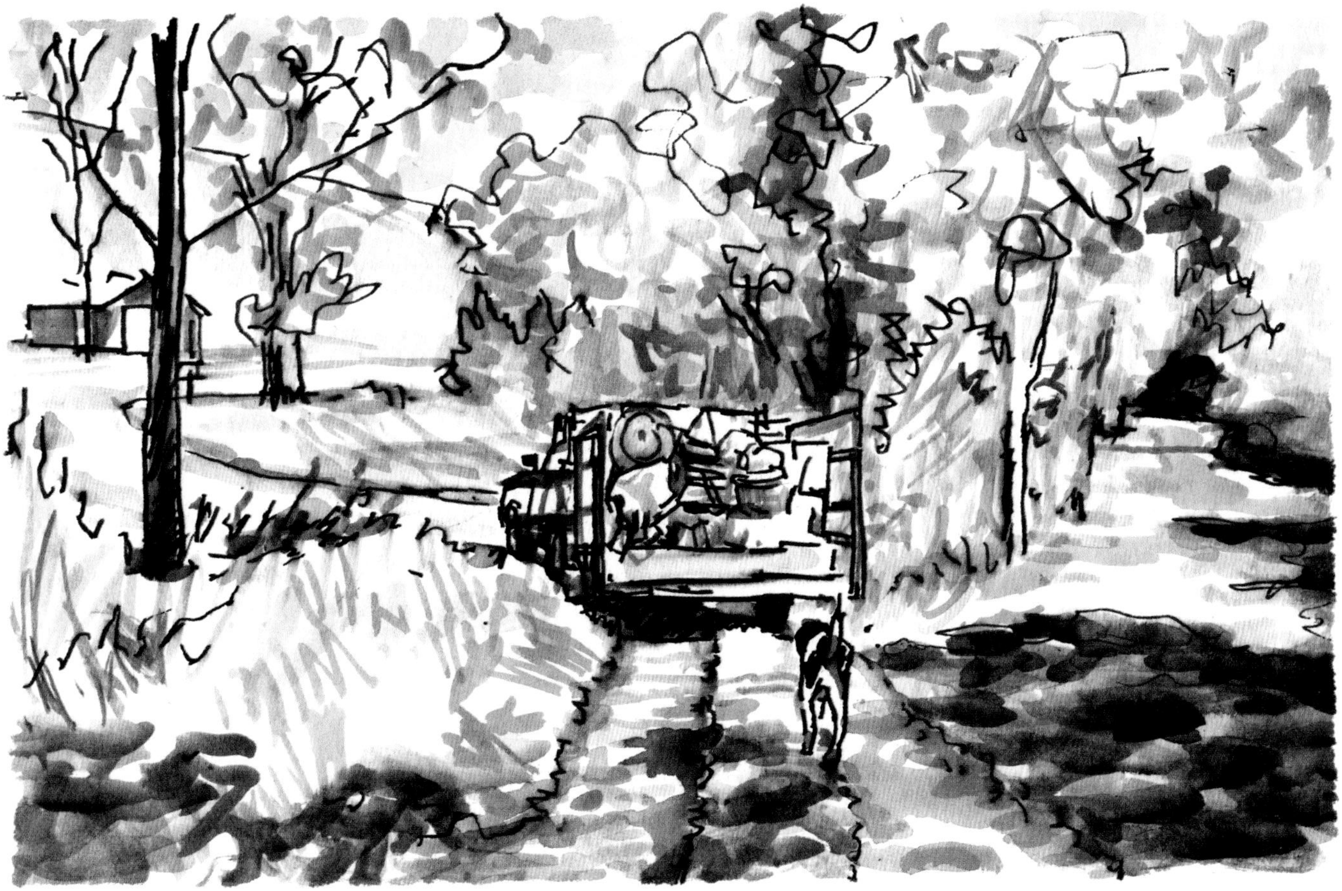

MONDAY, SEPTEMBER 23

The season of wood is upon us again. Last year's hickory logs—too tough and green to split, too large to fit in our stove—sat on the stone landing off the front porch all these months. David took the monster maul to them, and now they're ready to burn. The logs made a mockery of my efforts with the lighter maul, which bounced off the wood.

Cleaning up the logs inspired David to build steps off the side porch. The season of wood is a season of burning and of building, as the field requires less of us. We have fire in the hearth again. It's magnetic: I find myself sitting and reading, or watching the fire. Sometimes in the colder months, I feel we exist to feed logs to the hungry stove, a squat iron god granting us heat in exchange for our offerings. Of course, in order to feed it, we must feed ourselves.

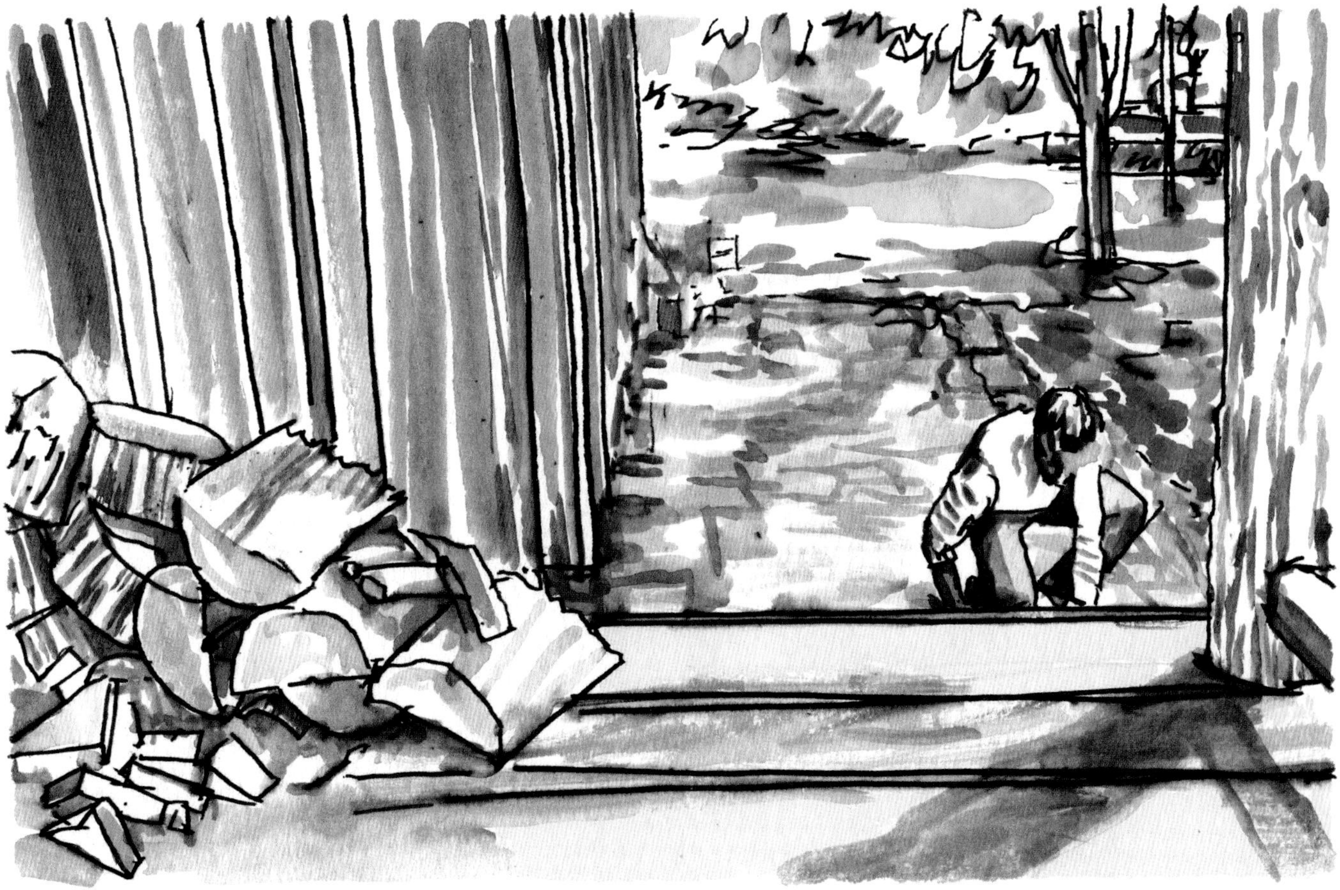

Tuesday, September 24

A moment of rest before we get to work: harvest today includes winter squash, various peppers, the remains of the tomatoes, green beans, and okra. Tomorrow we'll harvest greens—arugula, lettuce, mizuna, tatsoi—suddenly abundant again, though it hasn't rained. There is always a second spring in the fall. When the nights grow long and cool, the greens go suddenly lush. They shake off the bugs' oppression, and the rank smell that hovers around the kale and cabbage during the heat of summer edges into sweetness. This lasts for several weeks, a green oasis, until night temperatures dip into the twenties.

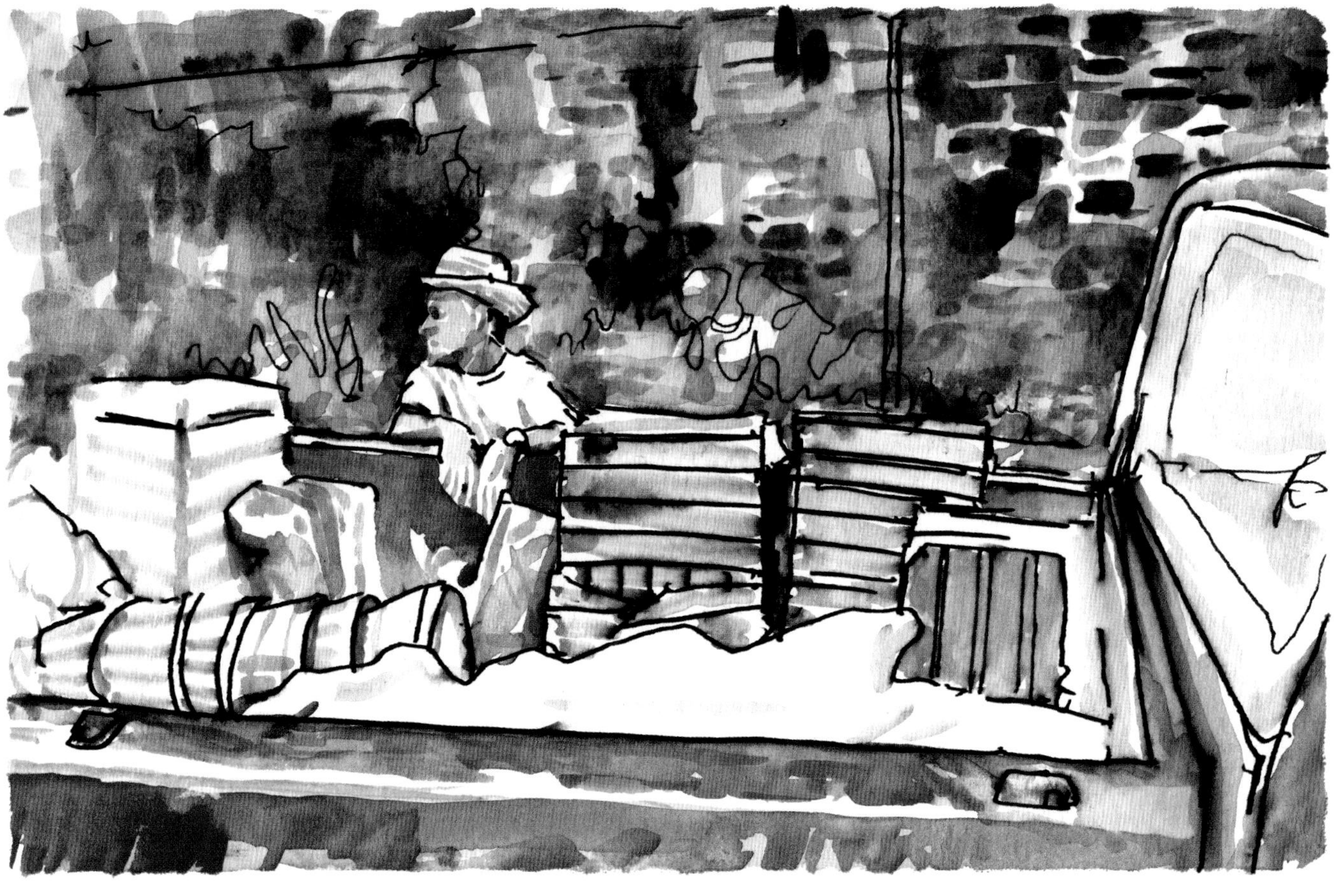

SATURDAY, SEPTEMBER 28

Sometimes we need to get into the city. Our wedding anniversary is a good excuse, and we've come to Louisville. We sit and drink a beer at a pub on Bardstown Road, talking about what we're doing with our lives. Cities are great burners of money, and we feed the fire. Living where we live, we get by on very little. Here, there are so many people, so many shops, at work to sell us a measure of pleasure. We have no retirement savings, no health insurance, no sight on the horizon of an easier life in our old age. Still, isn't it something that we can live like this, here and now, surrounded by such riches?

We've been farming in more or less the same way, with the same business model, for the last fourteen years. Where do we go from here? Do we come up with something new, or just shift things around and see what takes shape? How long can we go on like this? The more questions we ask, the more we have.

We are sitting at a sidewalk table beside the pub's plate-glass window. David spots a honeybee stuck inside, wandering the glass. He ducks in and returns with the bee in his hand and feeds her sugar until she has the strength to fly.

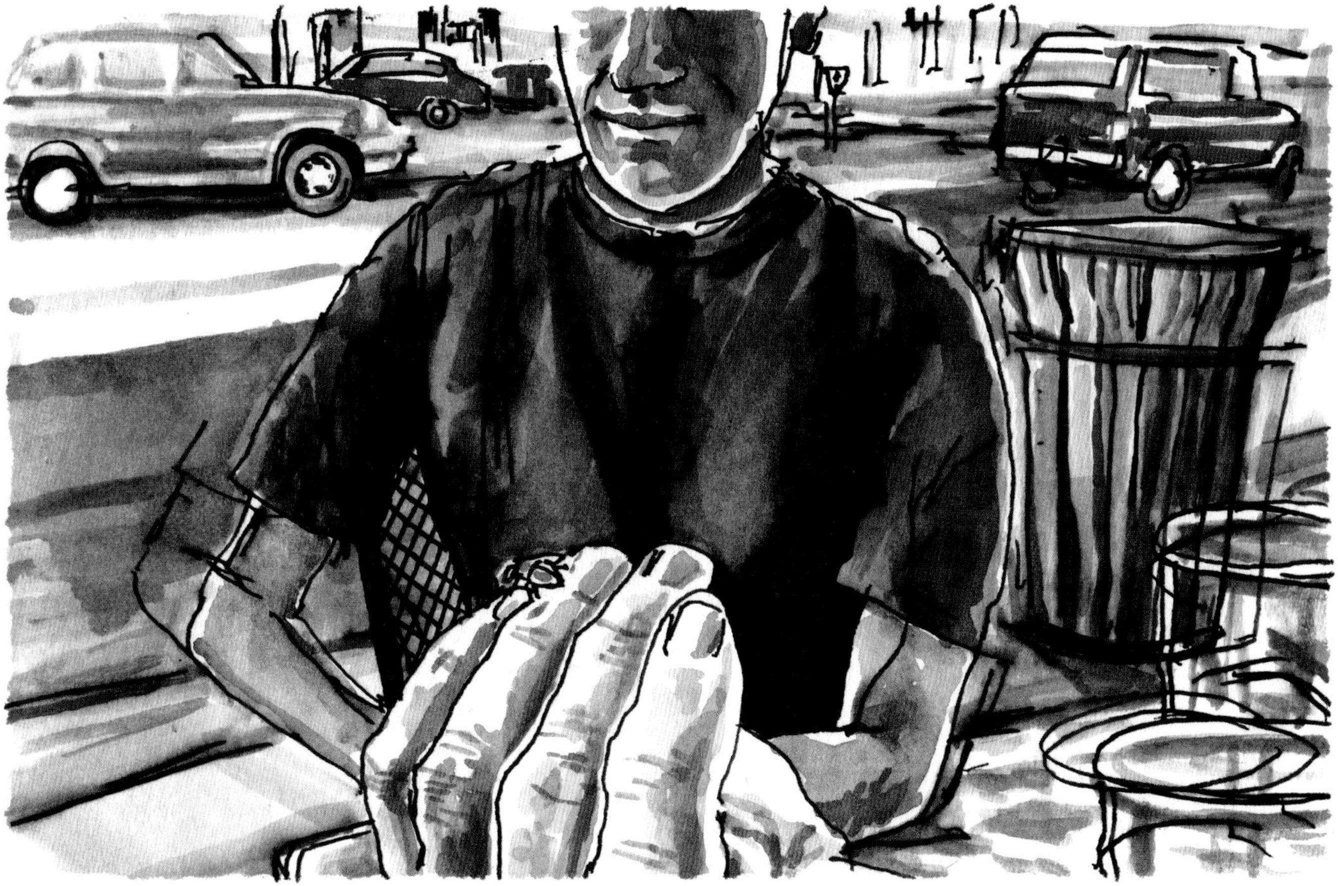

MONDAY, SEPTEMBER 30

Ms. Helen used to walk along the road every day, but she has been in pain lately, and a doctor told her she needs a knee replacement. The last time I visited, I told her I'd do what I could to help. I want to check in to see if she's made an appointment for the surgery, so after Phoebe gets off the bus, she and I walk over. When we step in the door, though, Ms. Helen is in tears. One of her grandsons had an accident on his four-wheeler on Friday night. His neck is broken, and he's paralyzed from the waist down.

We leave, and I feel sad and unmoored, not wanting to go back home, so we walk past our own lane and up to Lucy's place. Phoebe feeds blades of grass to the ducks while Lucy and I talk. She's starting a seasonal job at the Amazon warehouse in Lexington tonight. She doesn't ride her own four-wheeler much anymore, Lucy says, ever since two boys were almost killed in an accident a couple of months ago up on Johnson Road. We shake our heads over how the manufacturers of these dangerous machines don't do a thing to make them safer.

Lucy gives us a dozen duck eggs and won't let us pay. On our way back to the house, Phoebe gathers a shirtful of eggs from our own hens.

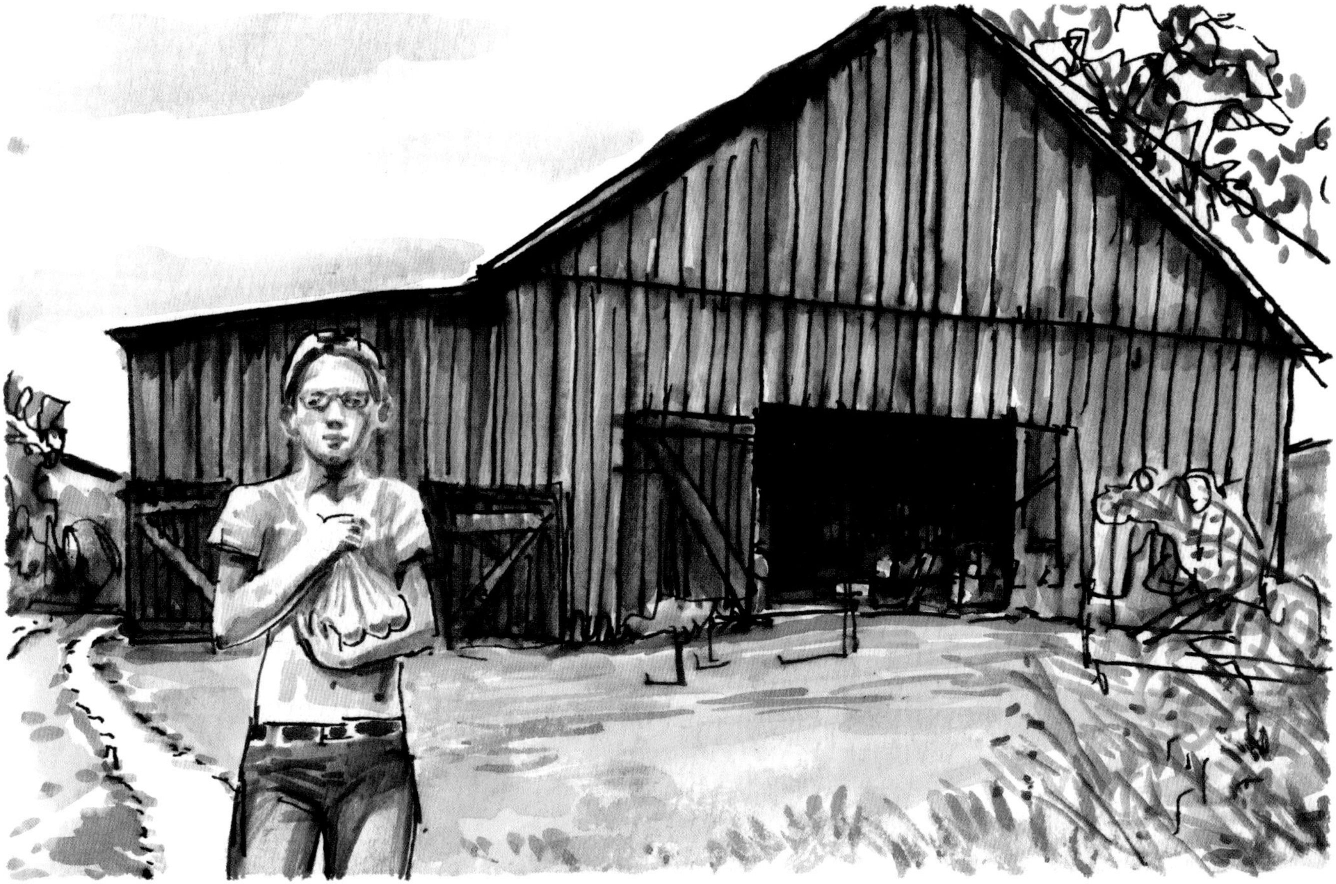

FRIDAY, OCTOBER 4

Our last CSA delivery of the year was on Wednesday. David stands among the rinsed and drying coolers, crates, and baskets. On the porch bench and kitchen floor: baskets of pears, peppers, winter squash, potatoes, sweet potatoes. Our fifteenth year of growing produce for market was, in some ways, like our very first: we two (occasionally three) do the work of the farm alone together. That's given us the chance to visit every harvest day while we work, to reflect on the pattern of our lives.

That pattern is defined by the swinging wheel of seasons. Our own wills are swept off by the wind of the wheel's turning. Winter's dormancy nurtures hope and hunger. Optimism takes root in spring, flushing fresh and green. Summer's setting of seed and fruit lays bare our inadequacies: we are in the weeds. Much of what we wanted to thrive has withered; much of what foils us has thrived. Now, in autumn, we reckon with reality. How can we do better next year? We plan and scheme but know by now that failure is part of the pattern. We might as well greet it as we would a faithful friend.

I begin to avoid weeding, to protect crops from exposure to deer and insects. A freeze will soon kill everything anyway. What's the best possible method of failure, here? The one that requires least work.

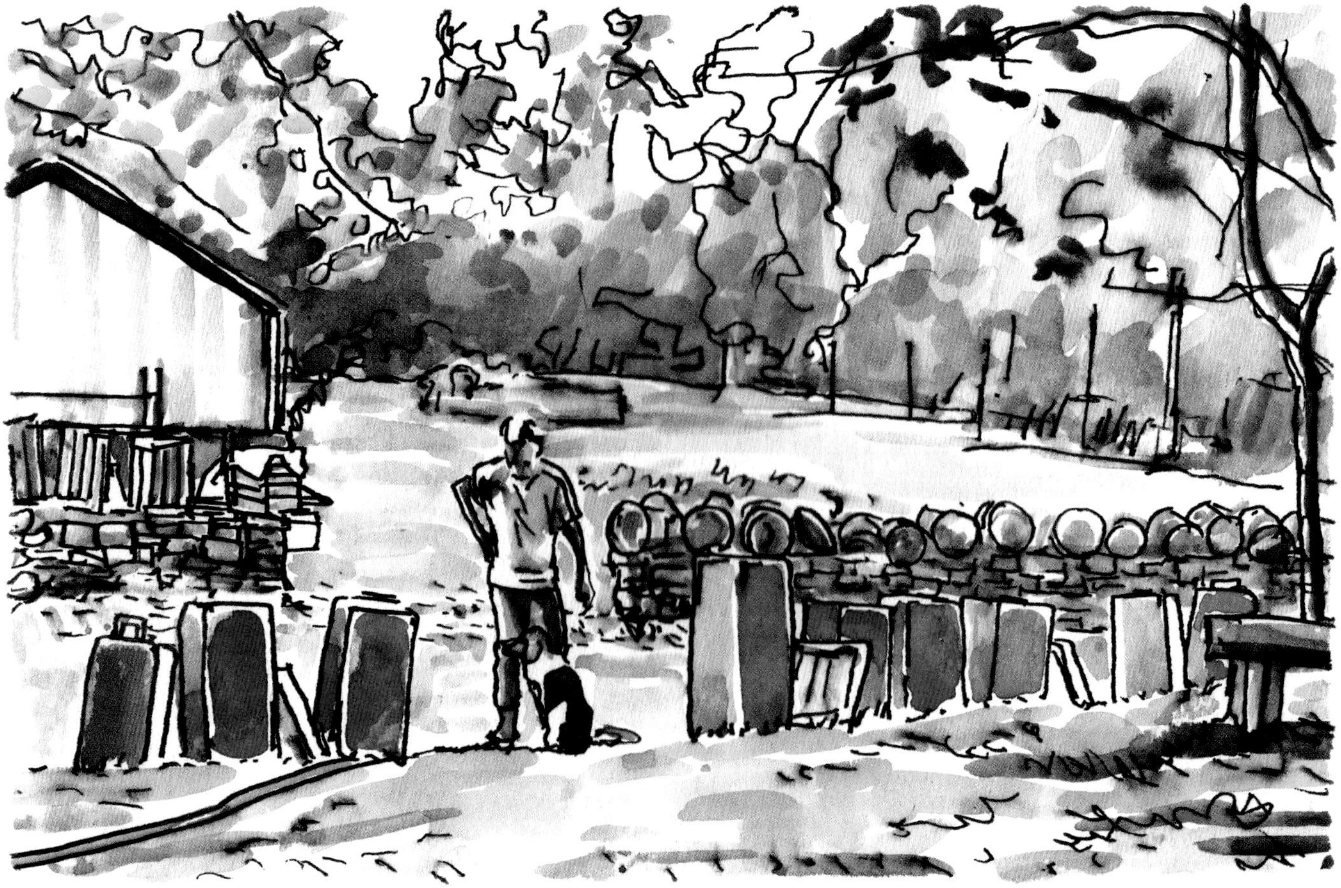

Sunday, October 13

A fallen-down tobacco barn, surrounded by young trees, is a key feature of our woods. Living among abandoned and decrepit barns, I've learned that they tend not to fall all at once, but to slump slowly to the earth over a matter of years. One after the other, like houses of cards collapsing in slow motion, we watch them go.

A century ago, these woodlands were inhabited by David's ancestors, among others. It was marginal land for farming, but the rocky slopes were tilled by horse-drawn plow and planted in corn, tobacco, or wheat. Eventually, the soil eroded, and those who lived here moved on. Chunks of limestone drawn up by the plow were gathered and placed in huge piles. Barns and piles of stone: monuments to a story of abandonment, artifacts of toil. As the soil washed from gully to creek, creek to river, river to sea, a tide of humans left this land for towns and cities. We've worked our way here, as if swimming upstream, yet we still feel the pull of that tide.

David has been cutting a lane through the woods for access to the piles of stones for building, and to trees for selective logging.

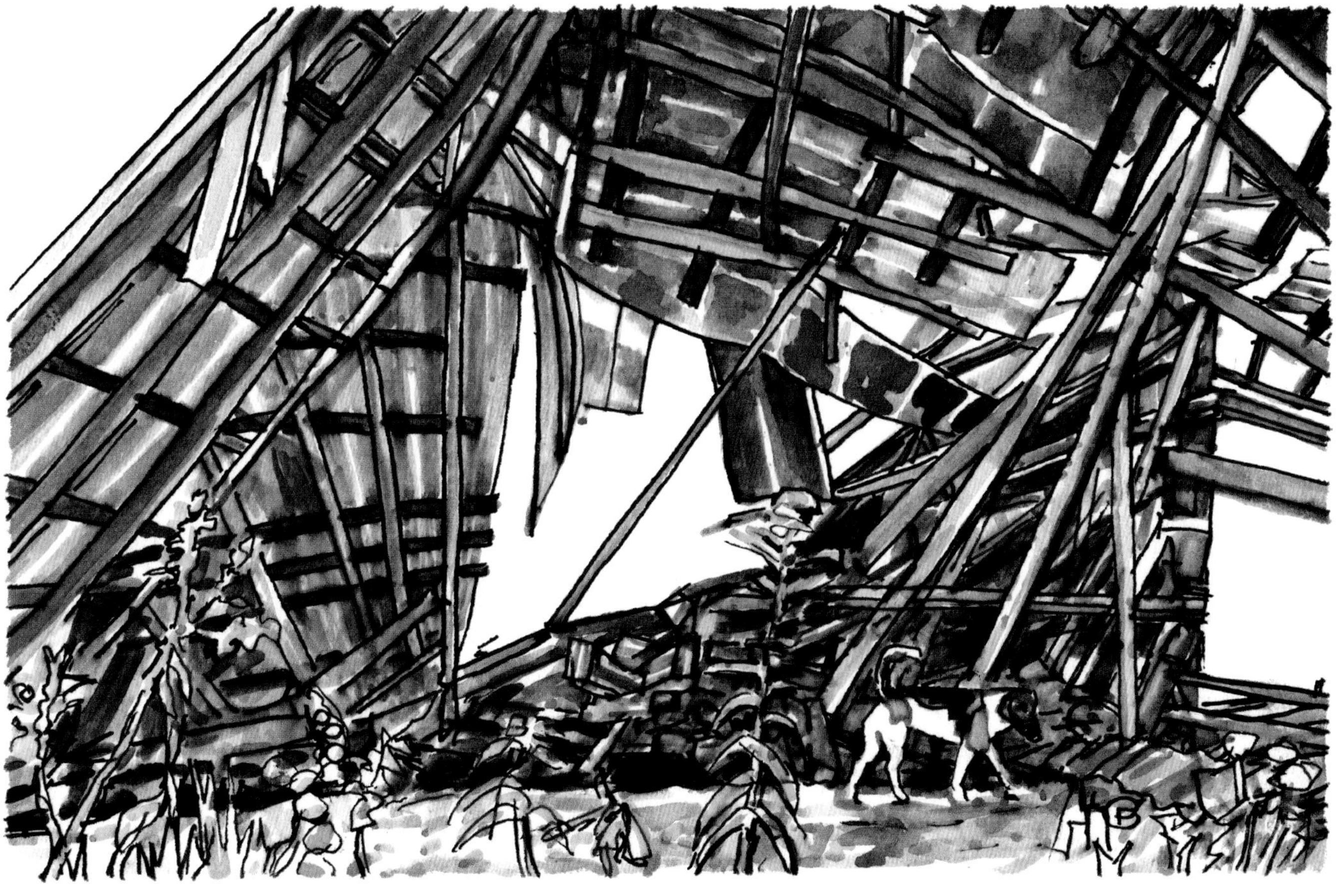

SATURDAY, OCTOBER 19

It's going to be cold tonight, possibly a killing frost, so we're out in the fields until after dark, harvesting tomatoes, peppers, lettuce, kale, arugula, and herbs.

Some frosts burn a few tender leaves, but they aren't game-changers, as killing frosts are. Early one morning each year, a great cold hand presses down and snuffs every tender thing. It kills what you've toiled over, and what you've not gotten to. What you've aimed to master, and what has mastered you. Peppers, basil, horseweed, stinkweed, prickly amaranth, shaggy soldier, knotweed, tomatoes reaching from the tops of their tall cages, the spindly eggplant, summer squash, okra, beans, corn, zinnias… all might be lifeless by morning. The sun will warm what remains: a row or two of lettuces, keeping the garden buttoned. Sprays of kale, a stubby carpet of grass. The lettuces and kale will be damaged by this frost, but some might live through the winter under two layers of row cover.

The frost has a palate-cleansing effect, clearing the congestion and clutter of summer. I'd be sorry to live without it.

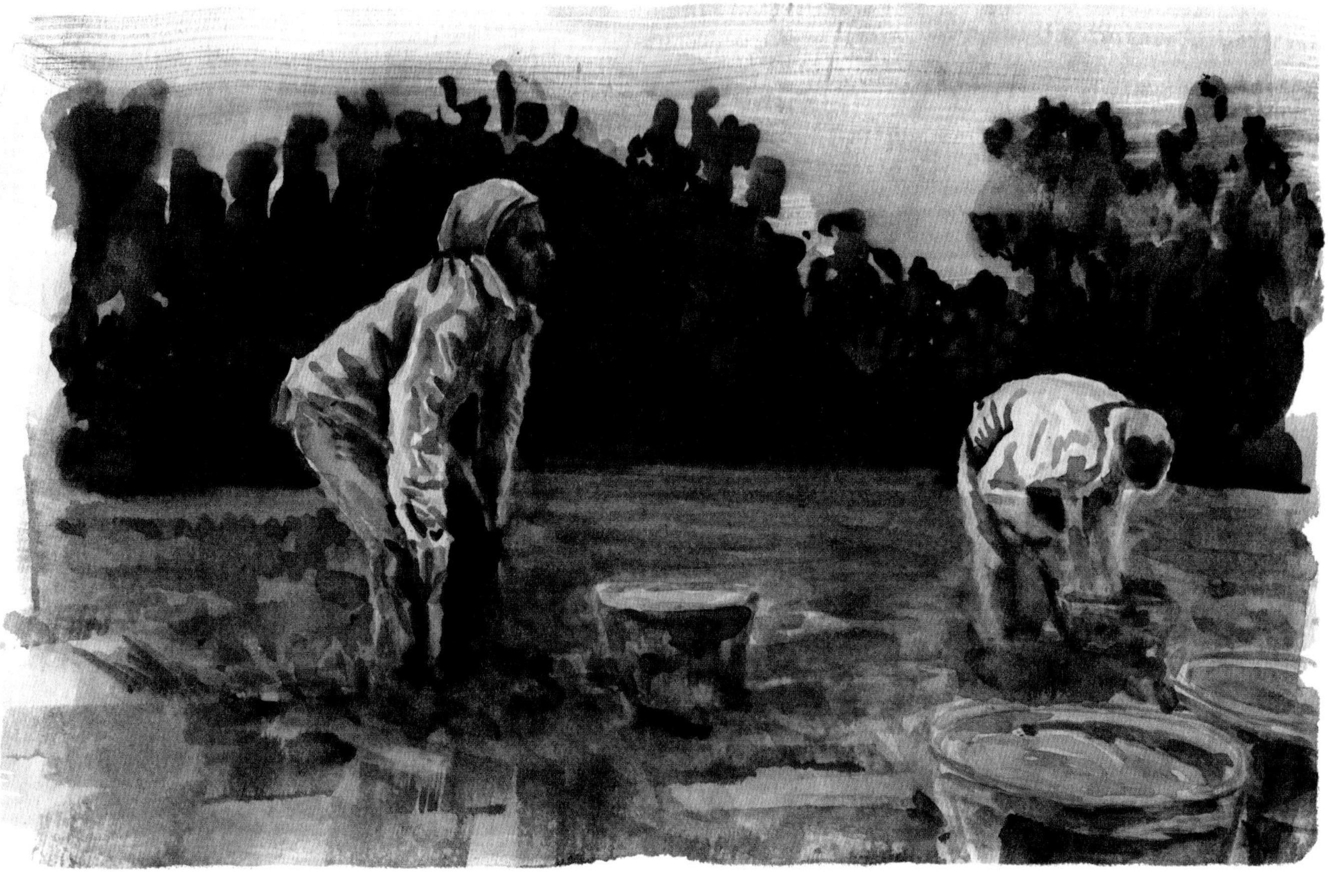

SUNDAY, OCTOBER 20

We host an end-of-season Farm Day for customers and friends. Our last one was three years ago: We used to feel obliged to do this every year, but it dawned on us that it's our call. This year, we're ready again to share this place. We tour the barnyard, fields, and woods, where we visit the rough little cabin David built. He put up a handrail and finished the steps for the occasion. Some guests skip the woodland walk and play music on the porch. The killing frost didn't come: Our flower garden weathered the thirty degrees we had this morning before dawn.

Leaves have begun to change color in the last few days. The house looks pretty. Clusters of mostly unripe cherry tomatoes—white, green, yellow, orange, red—hang from the old tin chandelier. On the table, a bowl of golden russet apples. Here and there, gourds and pumpkins and ears of popcorn. In vases, hyacinth bean vines, with deep pink flowers and purple pods, and plumes of rosy wheat celosia. A fire in the hearth, clean windows, and the golds, yellows, greens, and reds of the leaves outside, framed by the windows.

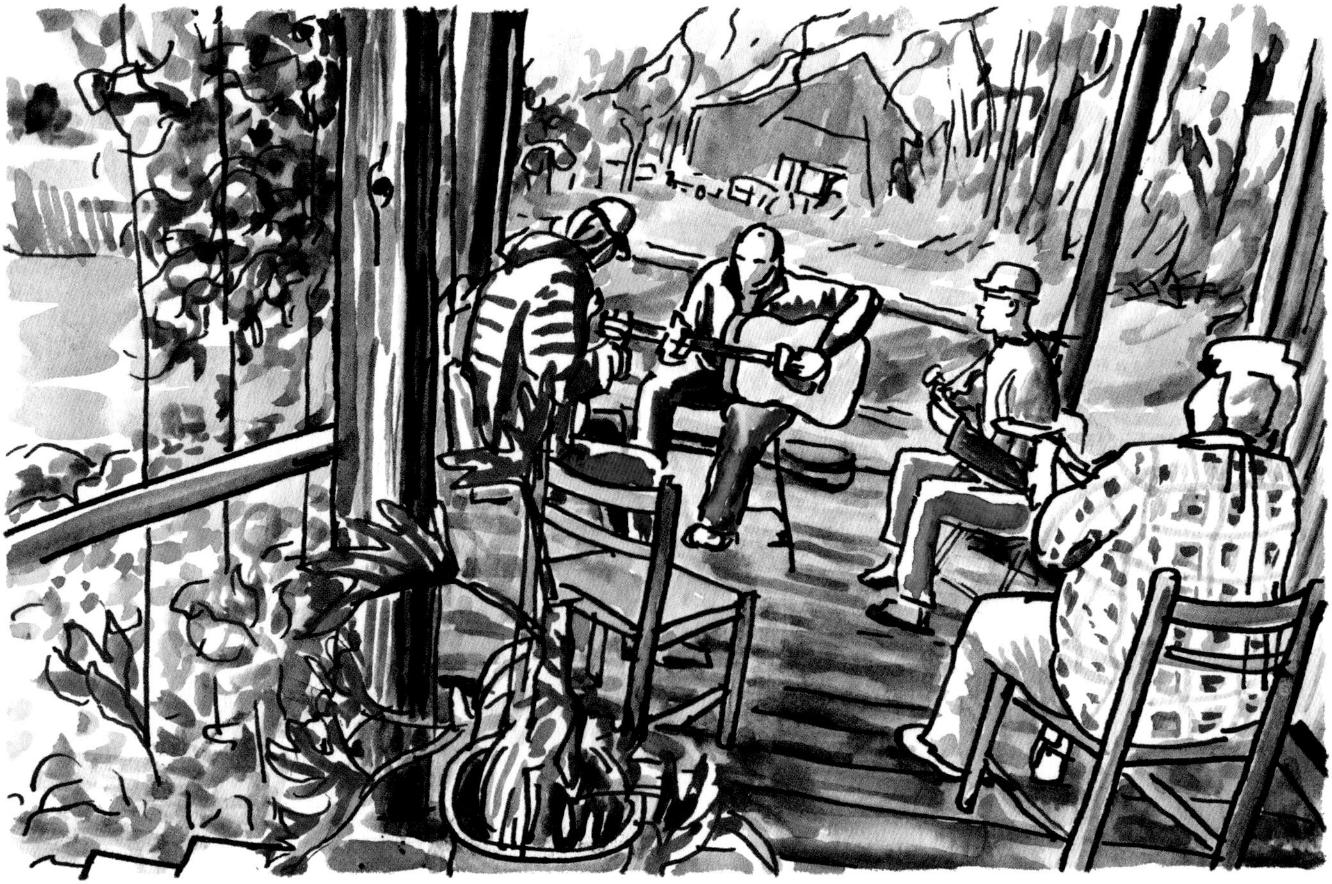

MONDAY, OCTOBER 21

My father is visiting from Santa Fe. He, David, and I walk in the woods together. A walk toward the source of Straight Run, is—in human terms, at least—a walk back in time. If we were to keep walking upstream, we would come upon a brambly meadow where a solid limestone chimney stands. This is where, we have been told, my daughter's great-great-great-great-grandmother once lived. There, she presumably gave birth to her children; drew water from a deep well, now covered with a large stone to keep the unwary from tumbling in; and planted irises that, generations later, form a mat as thick as grass, too crowded to bloom. I think of that place while walking behind David, who gathers leaves from unfamiliar trees as we go. Giving birth to my daughter here, in our home downstream, has stitched my body indelibly to this land, and to the woman who, on her Spring Equinox wedding day in 1839, signed her name with an X at the Nicholas County Courthouse, about twelve miles away. What did she see as a horse drew the newlyweds' carriage up Straight Run, towards her new home?

Once we return to the house, we identify the leaves David has gathered: we've found a few hazelnut trees we didn't know were here.

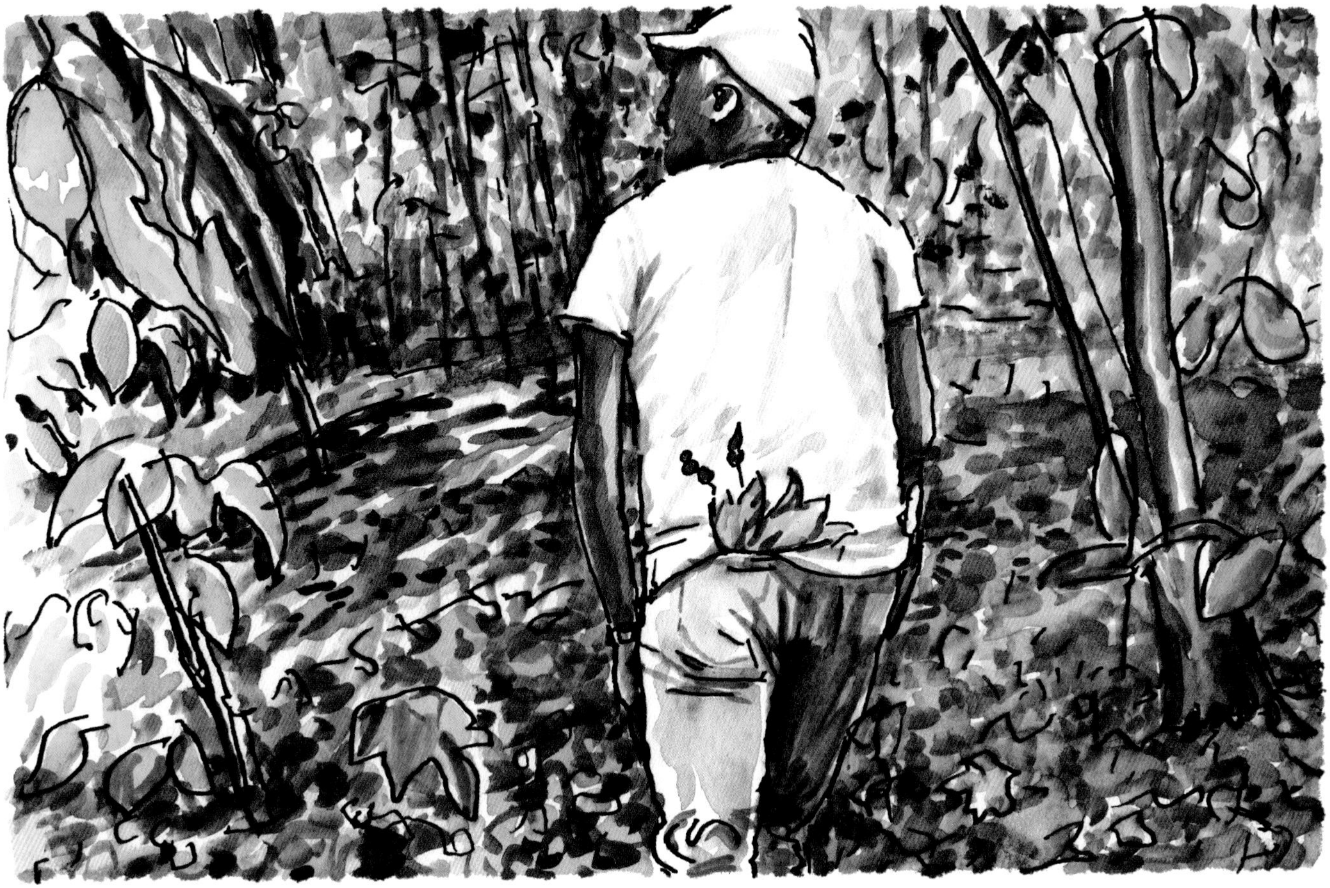

THURSDAY, OCTOBER 24

We load firewood into the barn shed's wooden mangers, originally built to feed hay to a herd of cattle. A windfall oak from the top of the hill, 113 years old, according to a count of rings. Gathering firewood is a job that should be done in spring, when green logs can be split, stacked, and left to season until winter. Who has time to gather firewood in spring? We must often burn some green wood before warm days return.

On the pantry shelves, time stands still in jars. In the hearth, 113 years burn in a single hour.

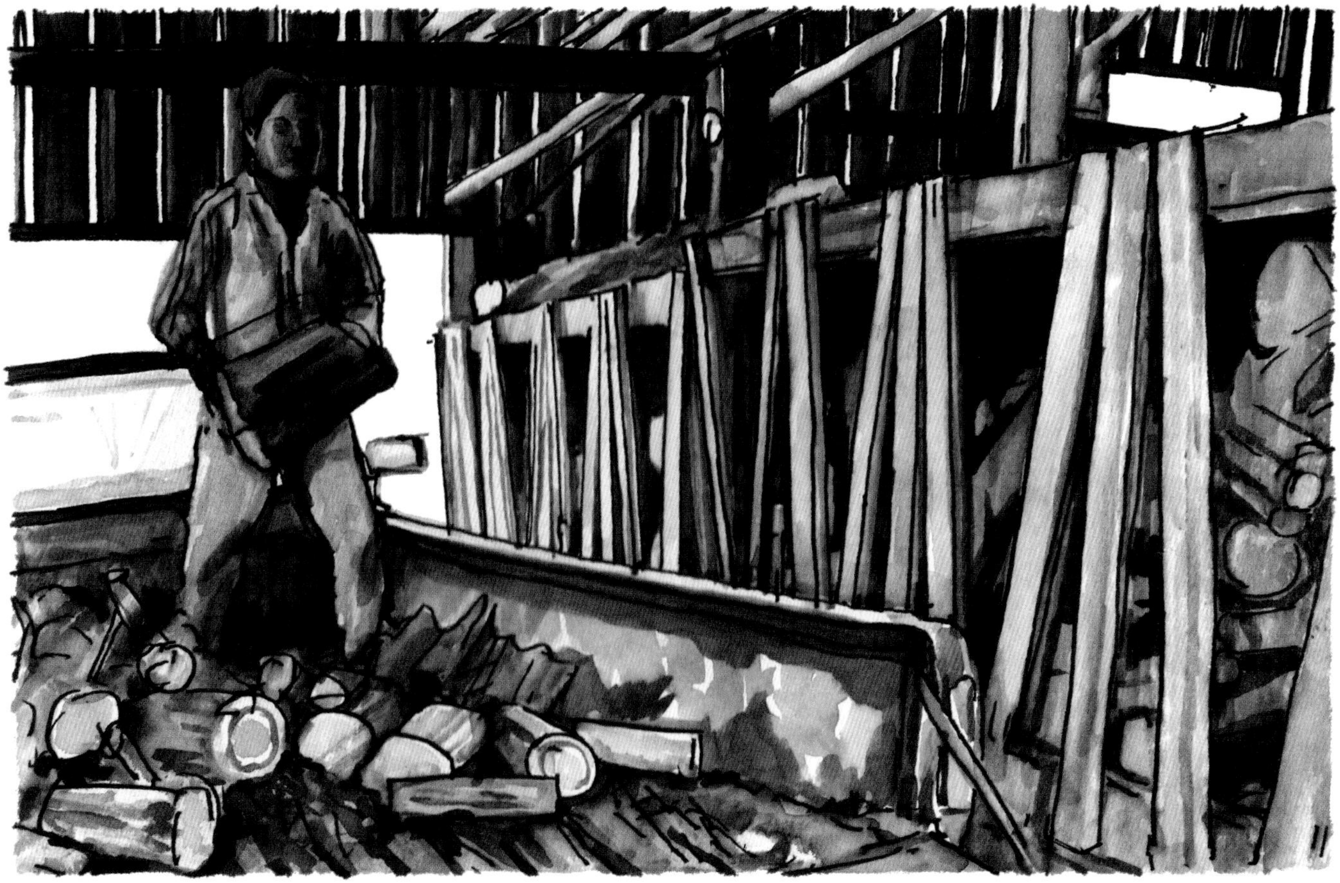

MONDAY, OCTOBER 28

Our goats are off to a farm in Clark County to be bred. David stops at school on the way to take Phoebe along for the ride. It's daunting to think that we'll have four does kidding at the same time next spring: a couple of gallons of milk per day. But because their milk is naturally homogenous, unlike cow's milk, it's easy to make into fresh chevre, which we miss.

We've quit milking Lily: her milk tasted off, and then her production dropped dramatically. Fresh milk from ruminants with unlimited access to pasture should taste better than any milk we could get from the store, right? But milk, at its best, is bland, and any unpleasant flavor stands out. This blank canvas onto which we project so many of our desires turns out to be an extraordinarily delicate instrument. A cow who breathes stinky air will produce stinky milk. Does your barn, perchance, smell like the animals that spend their days shitting in it? Oh lord, I give up.

But David doesn't. Getting all these dairy animals was his idea in the first place, and what's the point of haying and buying feed and mucking stalls and carrying water if we don't get milk in return?

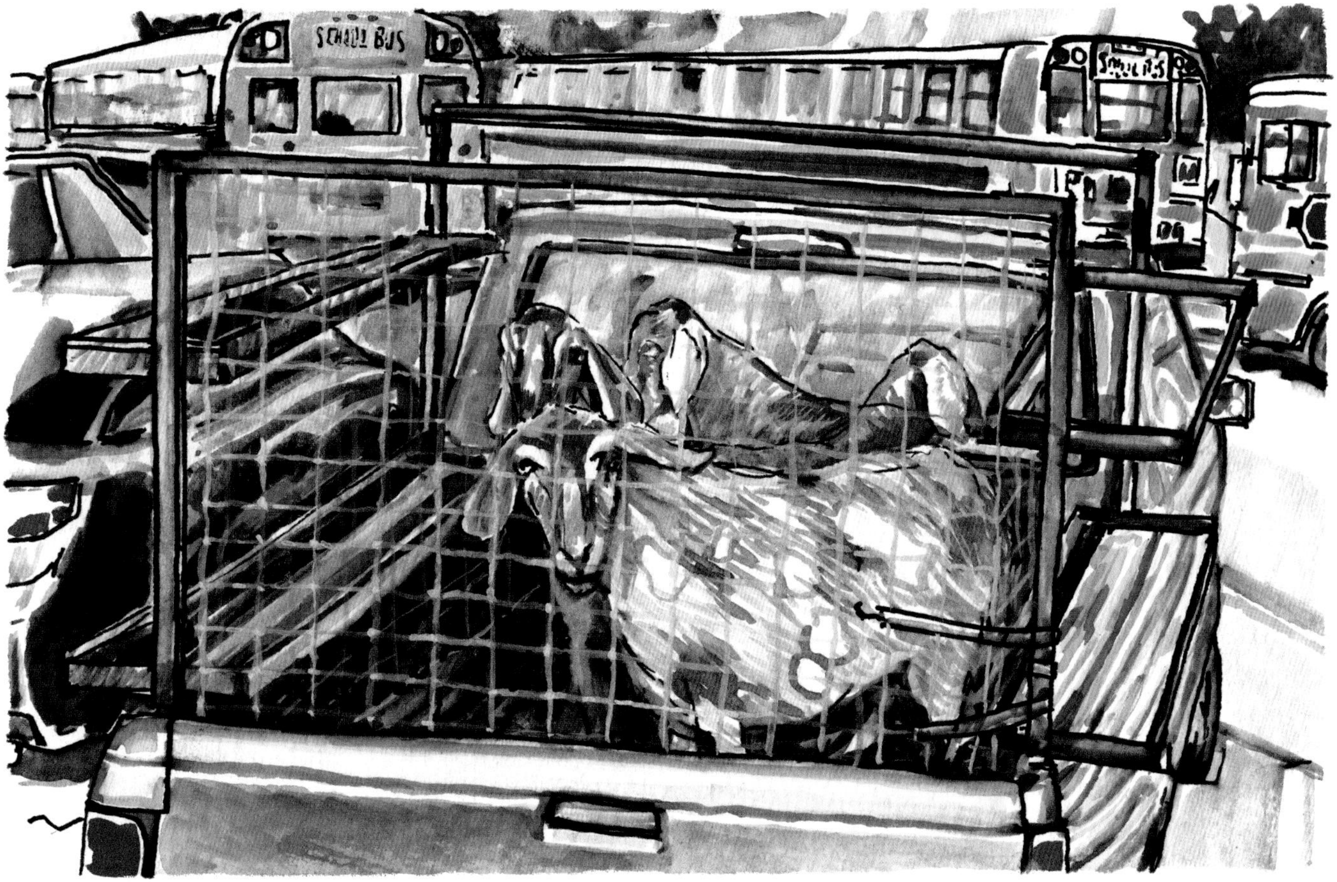
SCHOOL BUS

Monday, November 4

David always has a pair of red–handled pruners in a holster on his hip, like some agrarian cowboy on a mission to tame renegade woody growth. Waiting by the bridge for the schoolbus in the afternoon, he clears grapevines and wild blackberry brambles from around a little box elder. After years of these bus–waiting intervals, the landscape changes, each tree considered and tended.

I feel a surge of gratitude towards this private man who has allowed me to take photographs of him doing what he does for the last year. Only once did he drop his pants when the camera appeared and present his bare ass for its gaze.

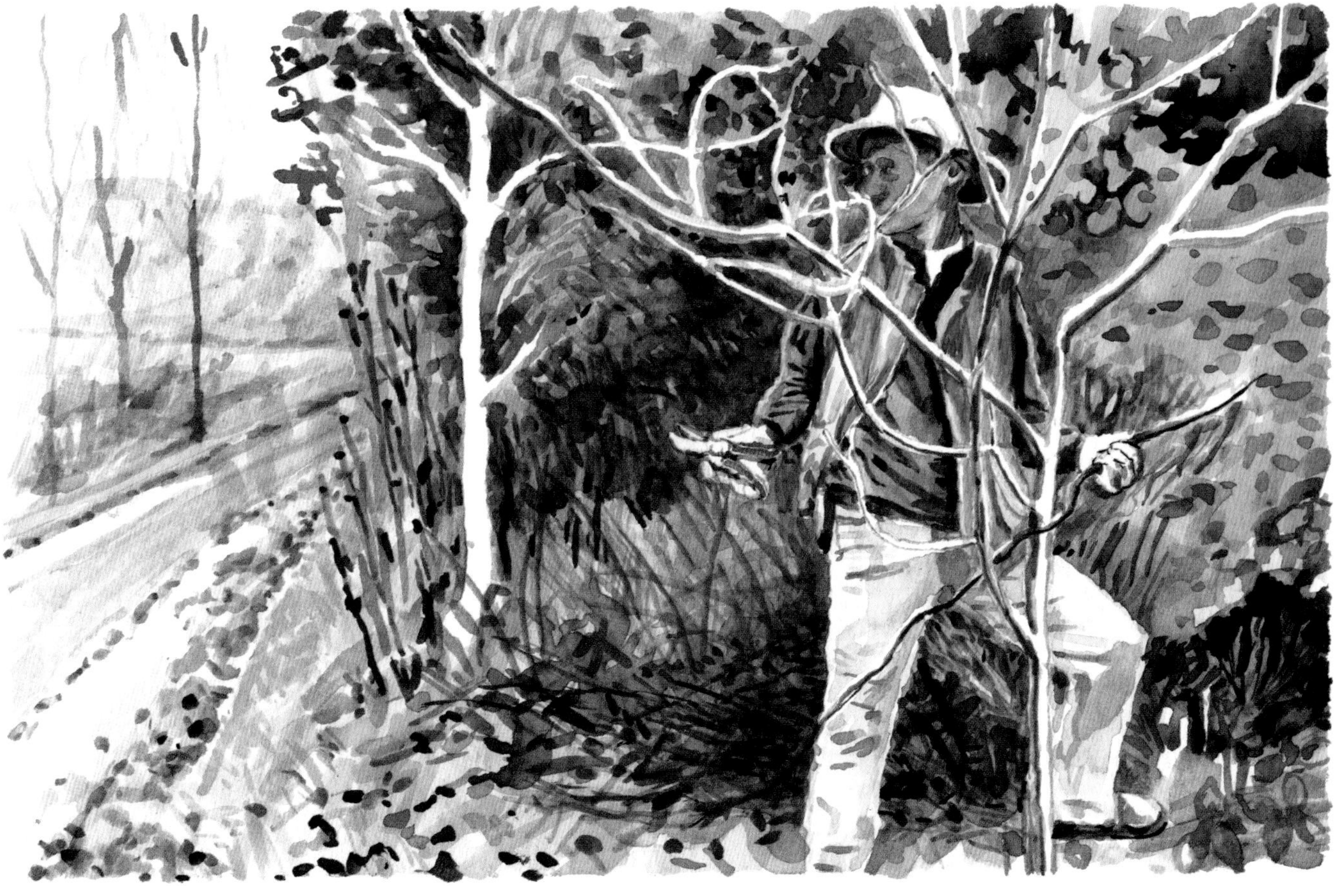

TUESDAY, NOVEMBER 5

After a four-month break, we're back to building the hoop house. It's been a little while since I've even seen the Green Bean. Yes, there is a young tree growing right through the floor of the side porch. Charlie teases us about it: "Don't have to go far for shade, now, do you?"

The program that's helping pay for the hoop house was established under the leadership of USDA chief Tom Vilsack. Some months ago, I read an Associated Press story that quoted Vilsack as saying rural America is "becoming less and less relevant."

What? Did our highest agricultural official really say that the countryside on which our cities are absolutely dependent are *less and less relevant?* Well, not exactly. He actually said that "rural America with a shrinking population is becoming less and less relevant to the politics of this country." There's a world of difference between what is actually relevant and what is relevant to politics.

Vilsack told an audience of industrial farmers that they must have a "growth mindset" and "embrace diversity." There is nothing rural America needs more than to embrace diversity, in its approach to culture and agriculture. But while capitalism requires limitless growth in a world of limited resources, embracing diversity demands making room for slowing down, reckoning with the historical reality of violent exploitation of land and people, and doing the hard work of repair.

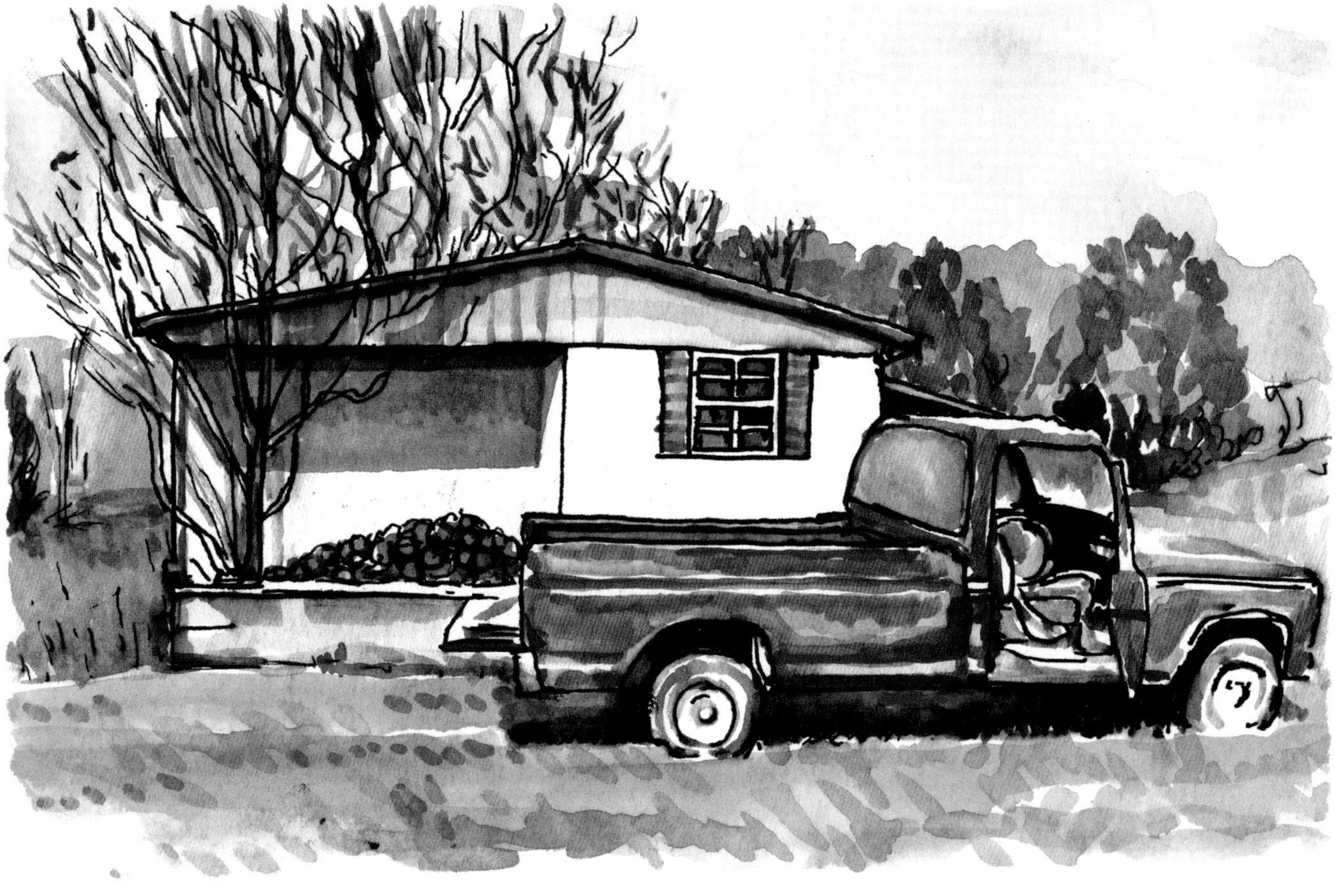

THURSDAY, NOVEMBER 7

Charlie wanders over from next door. He helps us unfold plastic film and pull it over the hoop house frame. Charlie is Mr. Charlie and Ms. Helen's eldest son. Long ago, a car accident damaged his memory and made it impossible for him to hold down a steady job. He used to work for us on harvest days, more than ten years ago. After David left with the delivery, Charlie would stay and clean up. I'd fix him a cup of coffee, and he'd offer me a cigarette.

One day, I asked about his son, who was around seventeen at the time. Charlie was wearing the brown shirt that matched his brown skin, brown hair, brown eyes, and big brown mustache. He seemed most himself when he wore that shirt, as if each of his features were disappearing into the other, and the whole disappeared into itself, the way Charlie does. The boy was not too good, Charlie told me. He stole a truck with some other boys. "Something's going to happen to him, I don't know what," he said.

Over the next few years, the boy fathered two children. He abandoned them to the care of his grandparents, who had also raised him. We rarely see him anymore: He seems to live his life on the run. Something's going to happen to him, I don't know what.

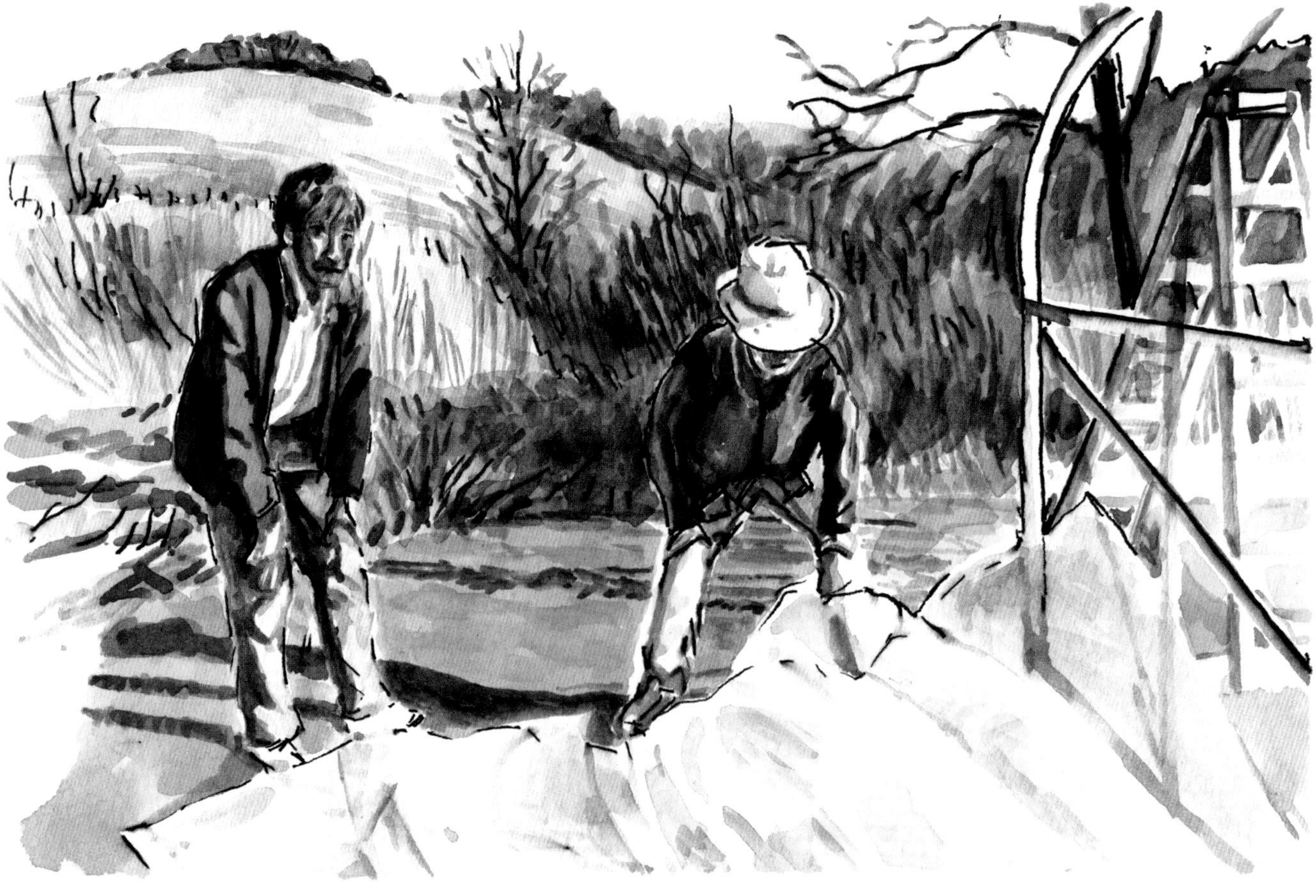

MONDAY, NOVEMBER 11

Phoebe was asked to play a patriotic song on her violin for her school's Veterans Day program. She's taught herself "America the Beautiful," which she performs for an audience of parents, students, and local veterans. There's a slideshow of veterans who are related to the students: I'm moved by how many there are.

Then it's back home and to the barn to fetch the braided row covers, which hang like the entrails of some enormous animal. We'll cover the rows just sowed in the newly completed hoop house to protect them on cold winter nights. When the wind blows, it will be nice not to go outside and find frozen lettuces and shredded row covers caught in treetops, not to have to reset the stones that weigh down corners and edges again and again through the winter.

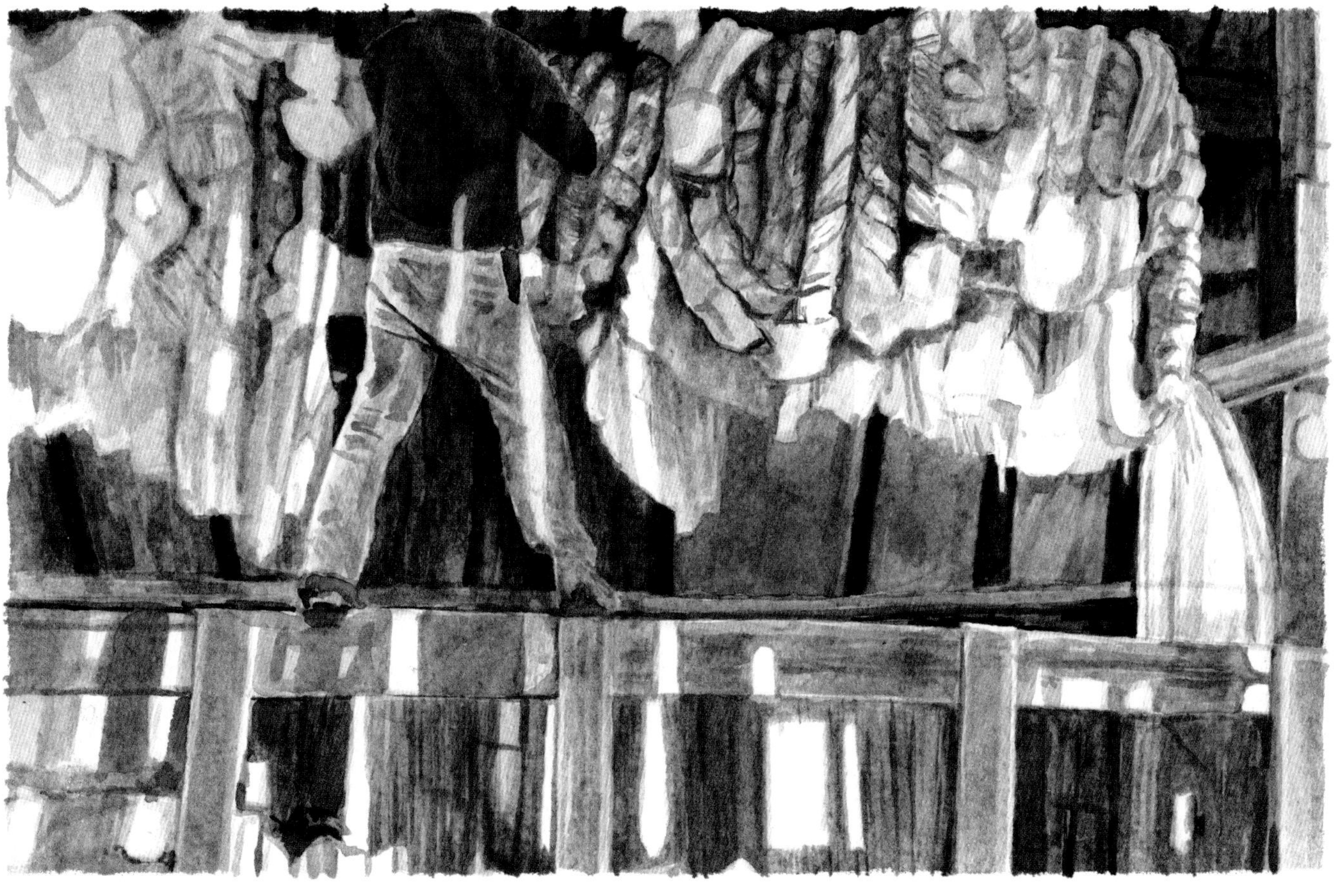

TUESDAY, NOVEMBER 12

David uses the low-wheel cultivator to make furrows just before sowing hardy greens in the hoop house. Outside, there's a mackerel sky over our new plastic bubble and bittersweet in berry on the fencerows. Walking home, we scare up a great blue heron fishing just above our bridge. David heads out to the fields, where he harvests squat, fat carrots, winter radishes, Jerusalem artichokes, beets, and turnips.

I am compelled to catalogue things that remain undone: the dead stalks of the flower garden; the bird netting on the chicken run, freighted with fallen leaves, that needs to be removed, as does the netting on the blueberry bushes; towering horseweed and stinkweed in the currant and gooseberry patch. There's the car-struck deer carcass in Crooked Creek: shouldn't we haul it somewhere? And of course, there's the deep cleaning the house calls for before Thanksgiving guests arrive. Cataloguing these things entrenches their state of not being done, and fortifies their entrenchment, because not only do I neglect them in favor of something else, I also commemorate the mess.

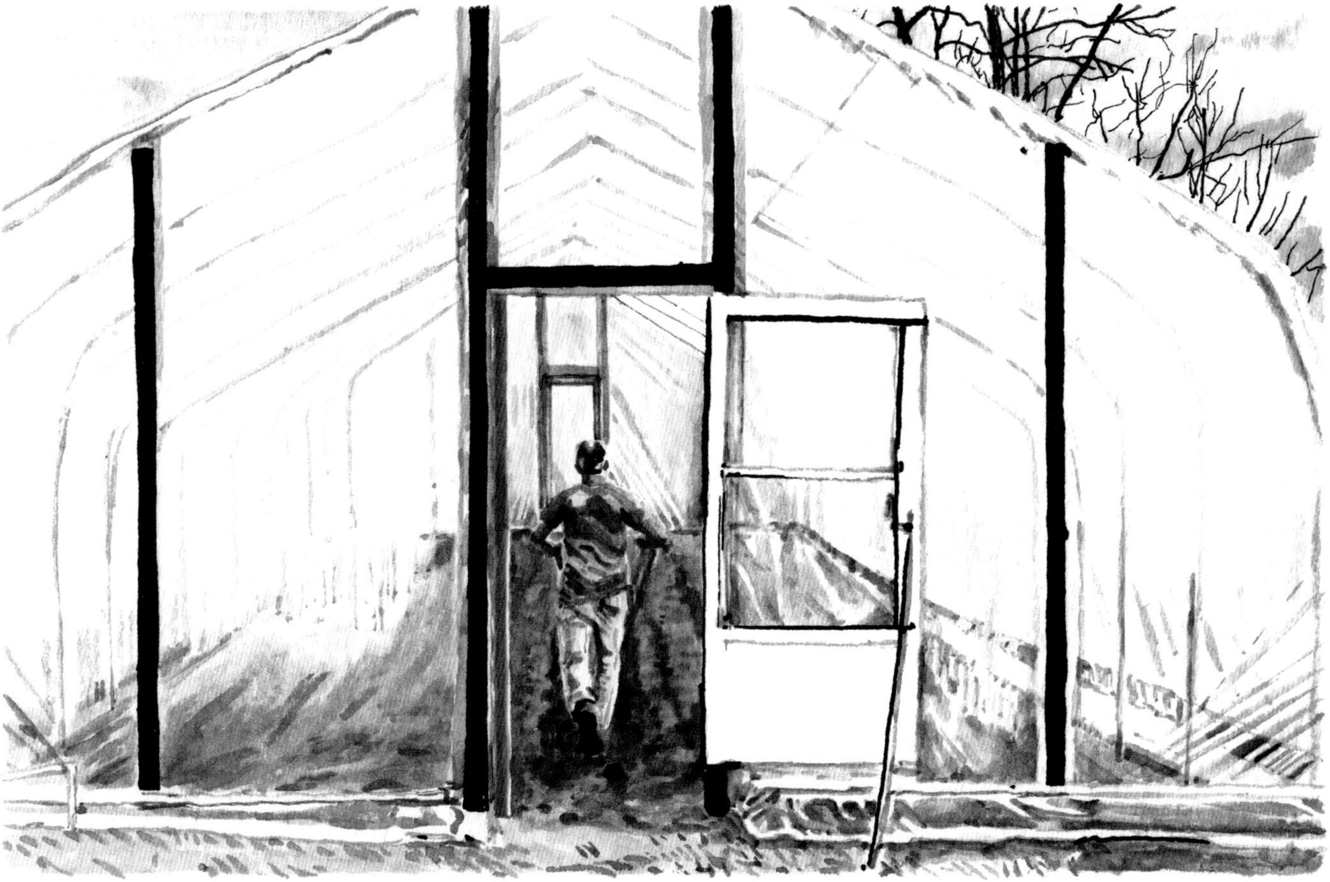

Sunday, November 17

After a day of steady rain, Crooked Creek has swelled and swallowed our bridge. Grandma Cate is bringing Phoebe back from an overnight in Lexington, so I wait on the road beside the creek. The water is not too high, but it's safer to walk across than to drive. I bring a pair of tall boots with me for Phoebe.

We keep getting mailings from FEMA informing us that we live in a flood zone, and that our flood insurance will continue to rise. At first we scoffed: the fields sometimes flood, but the house is on higher ground. Floodwaters have never come close to the bottom step of our porch. That's changing, as each year's floods grow more frequent and intense.

I dreamed recently that, during an epic flood, the writer and climate activist Bill McKibben floated through the farm on a makeshift raft. He was on his way to Dubai, he said, where he was giving a talk. I made him a bed in the treehouse, where he gratefully spent the night. The next morning he floated away, traveling—courtesy of climate change—with no discernable carbon footprint.

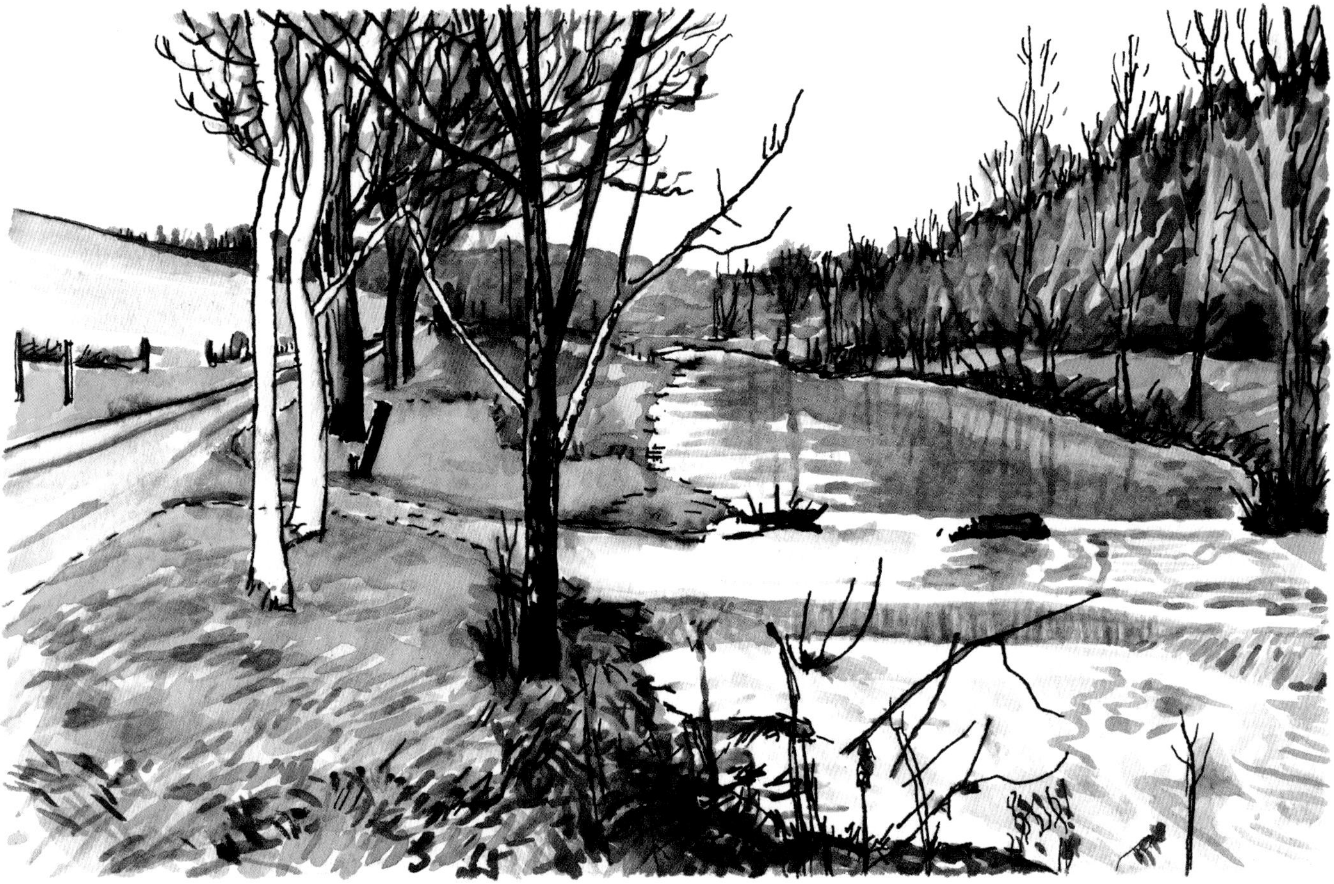

TUESDAY, NOVEMBER 19

We set posts for the new deer fence, which will surround the gardens nearest to the house. David's been working on the fence every day, while my work has taken me away from the farm often in recent weeks. Like many aspiring young farmers, David and I sought advice from Wendell Berry before we made the headlong leap into farming. "Write your own script," Wendell said. He also encouraged us to maintain an off-farm source of income. "It's too stressful on the land and too stressful on a marriage otherwise."

We've had marginal success at maintaining an off-farm source of income, and have felt, some years, the stress that lack of money puts on the land and on our bond. The patchwork of freelance jobs I've pieced together is limited by geography and my inclination towards solitude. I have just landed two oral history projects, though, that will keep me traveling a fair amount over the next year and enable us to experiment with our farm business. I don't know what this will mean for the tomatoes, but we will be making some revisions to the script.

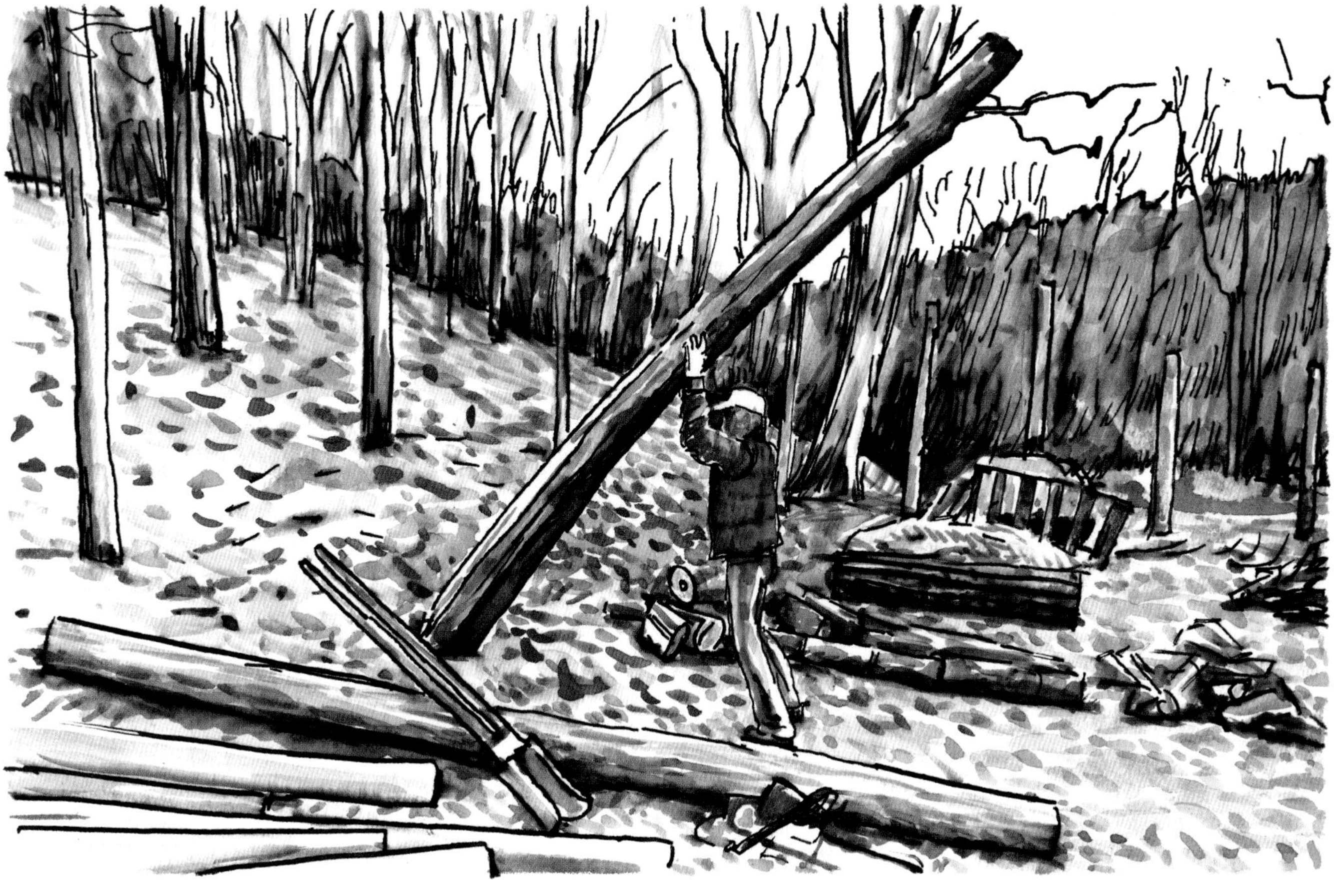

THURSDAY, NOVEMBER 21

The gateway arch of the deer fence, leading into the woods, has been erected. The posts need to be cut to even lengths: they'll all be about eight feet high, since deer can jump over anything lower.

Farming is, to an extent, a practice of erasure, an imposition of limits. We decide what forms of life we want to keep out and what we care to propagate and nurture. We try to hold the line, but the farm is a drunken boat in the wild sea of nature, and there is this constant spilling, out and in. We struggle to maintain control, and yet we are grateful for the spilling. We know the farm would die without it. An impermeable fence will kill what it contains.

Sunday, November 24

It's deer hunting season, and fences and property lines matter more than usual. Sometimes I don't walk in the woods when I hear gunfire, even when I stay on our own land. I hear nothing, so I walk. On the ridge, I see two men with guns on the other side of the fence. I say hello and walk on. Just before dusk, the valley is divided into islands of light and shadow, and the clouds are lit from below. Wind blows through the trees, and I root my feet and sway and lean and flutter my fingers.

Back at the house, the phone rings. It's one of the hunters. He advises me to wear orange when I go out. "I know you're on your land," he says, "but you can never be too careful." I thank him, but I'm bristling. A man I don't know has just told me what to wear to keep myself safe. He scolds me for not making myself more visible to men like him so that they won't accidentally kill me.

My sense of identity, over time, has staked itself to the edges of our fenceline. A wild form of movement takes my body when I walk in our woods: sidekicks, half-moons, warriors, moves I don't have a name for, because I've allowed myself to believe that I am free here. That this place is mine.

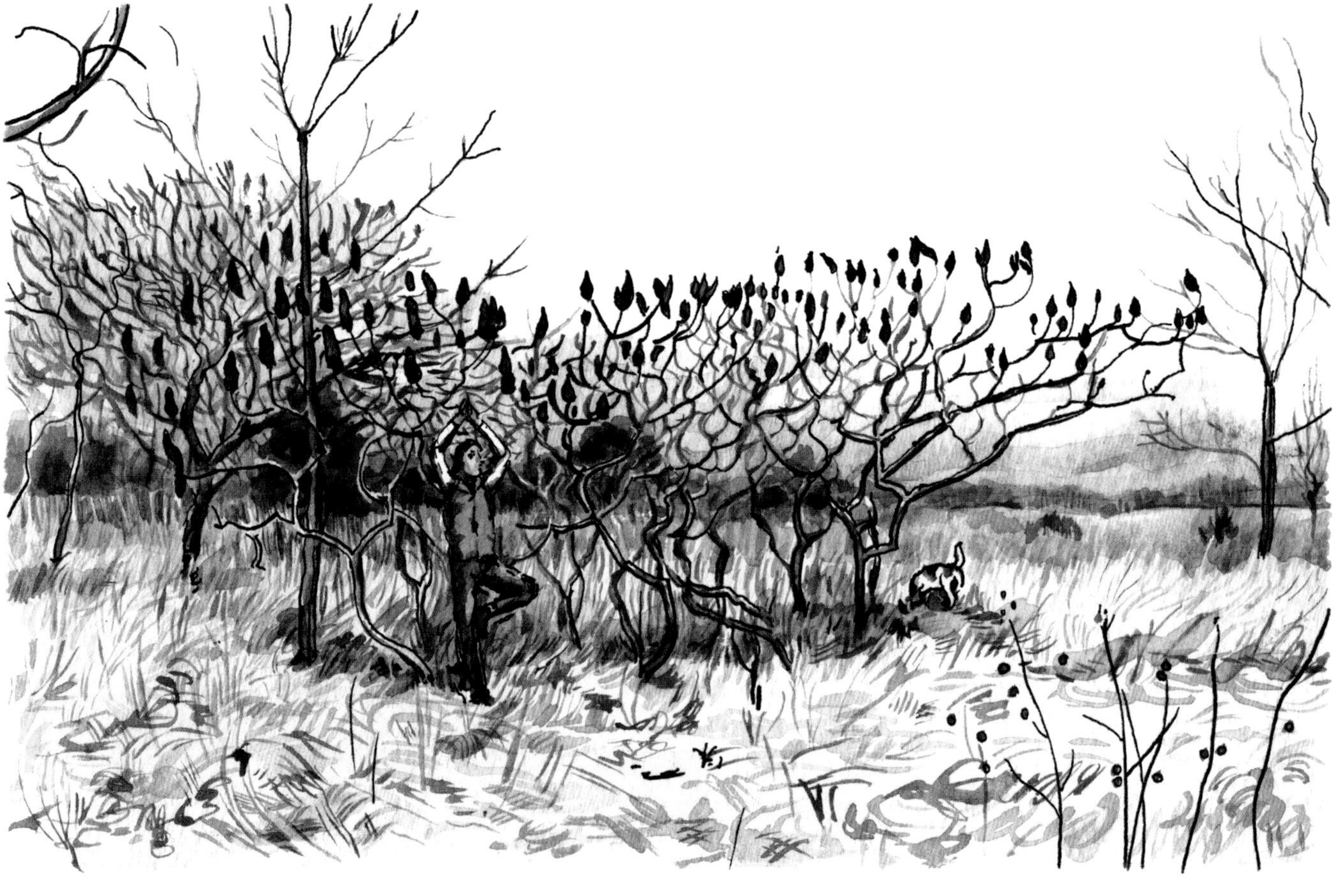

Saturday, November 30

We had thirteen guests here for Thanksgiving. I roasted my first-ever turkey: a heritage breed, locally raised. People expect turkey at Thanksgiving, and I wanted everyone who came to be happy. But everyone was not happy. I had warned my mother about the turkey, and she brought a vegan alternative. Still, she removed herself from the kitchen while I arranged the raw bird in the roasting pan. Phoebe stepped into the room while I slid the pan into the oven. "Nana's in the bathroom, crying," she said.

My mother appears to be a flexible person, but I have to admire how stubborn she is around the ethics of eating animals. If I've ever done anything to hurt her more than put a dead cooked turkey in the center of a table and given thanks for it, I don't know what it is. I did not have the patience with her tender-heartedness that I ought to have: It seemed to me she was being melodramatic and lugubrious. My snippy condescension was one more thing my poor mom had to suffer through on Thursday.

So here we are, back to building the deer fence. Mom wouldn't like to hear David call deer "giant rats on stilts." I don't like it myself; to me, deer are heart-stoppingly lovely. But after years of battling with them over the garden, deer have lost much of their charm for David.

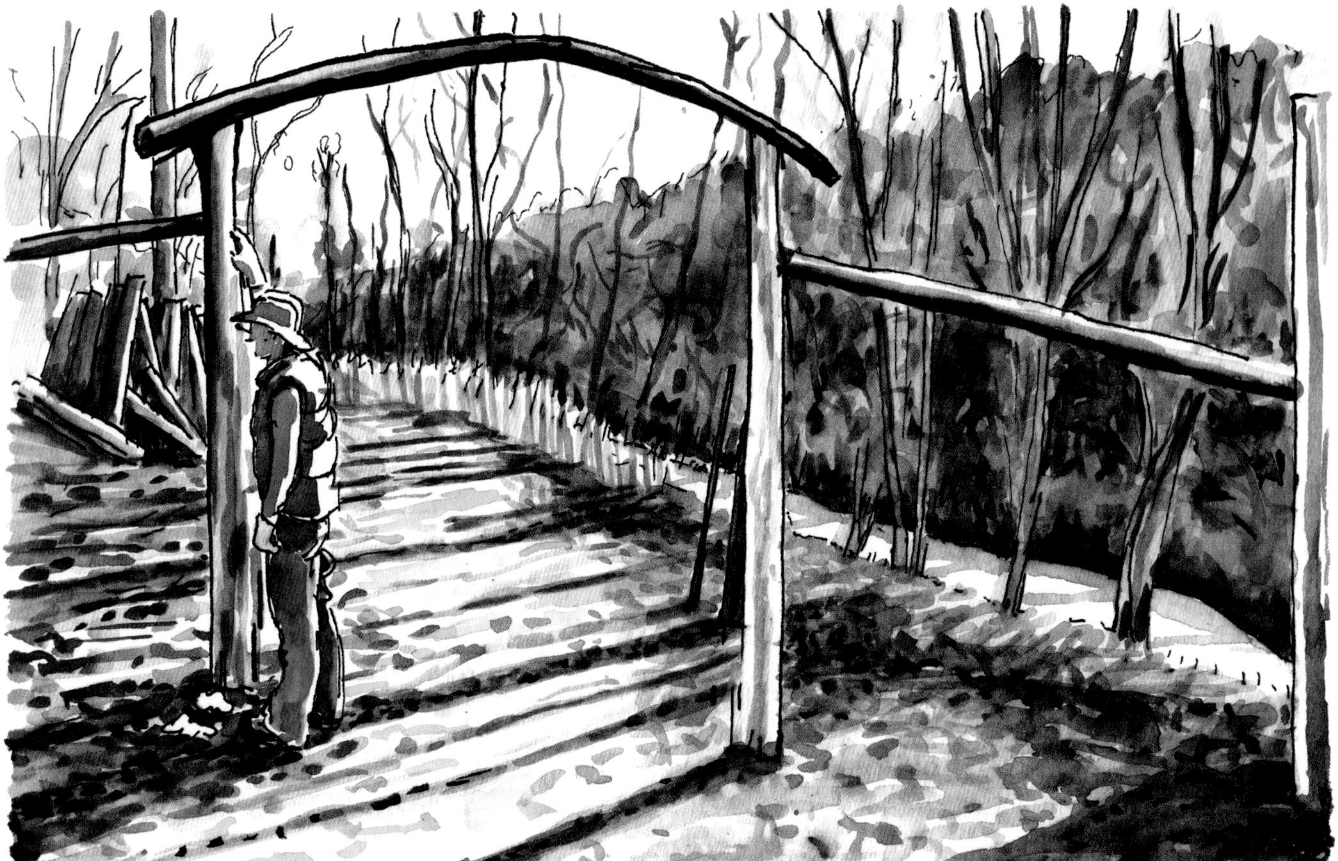

MONDAY, DECEMBER 2

"From the earliest times, human civilization has been no more than a strange luminescence, growing more intense by the hour, of which none can say when it will begin to wane and when it will fade away," W.G. Sebald wrote in *The Rings of Saturn*, a book I read while sitting close to the hearth over the course of several long winter nights, warmed by our steady contribution to the strange luminescence.

Two trees, an ash and an oak, had to be felled to make room for the deer fence. David has cut all the wood to stove-lengths. When Phoebe gets home from school, we gather and stack it in the barn. We burn things: that's what sets us apart from the songbirds, snakes, raccoons, vultures, frogs, herons, insects, and countless other creatures who share this land we call home. We burn gas and oil to power the chainsaw to cut the trees more quickly than we could with a handsaw. We burn more gas in the truck to haul the wood to the barn, and then we burn the wood itself. Back at the house, we flick a switch and burn coal cut from the heart of a mountain. We burn time, releasing heat that was slowly meted out to the tree by the sun.

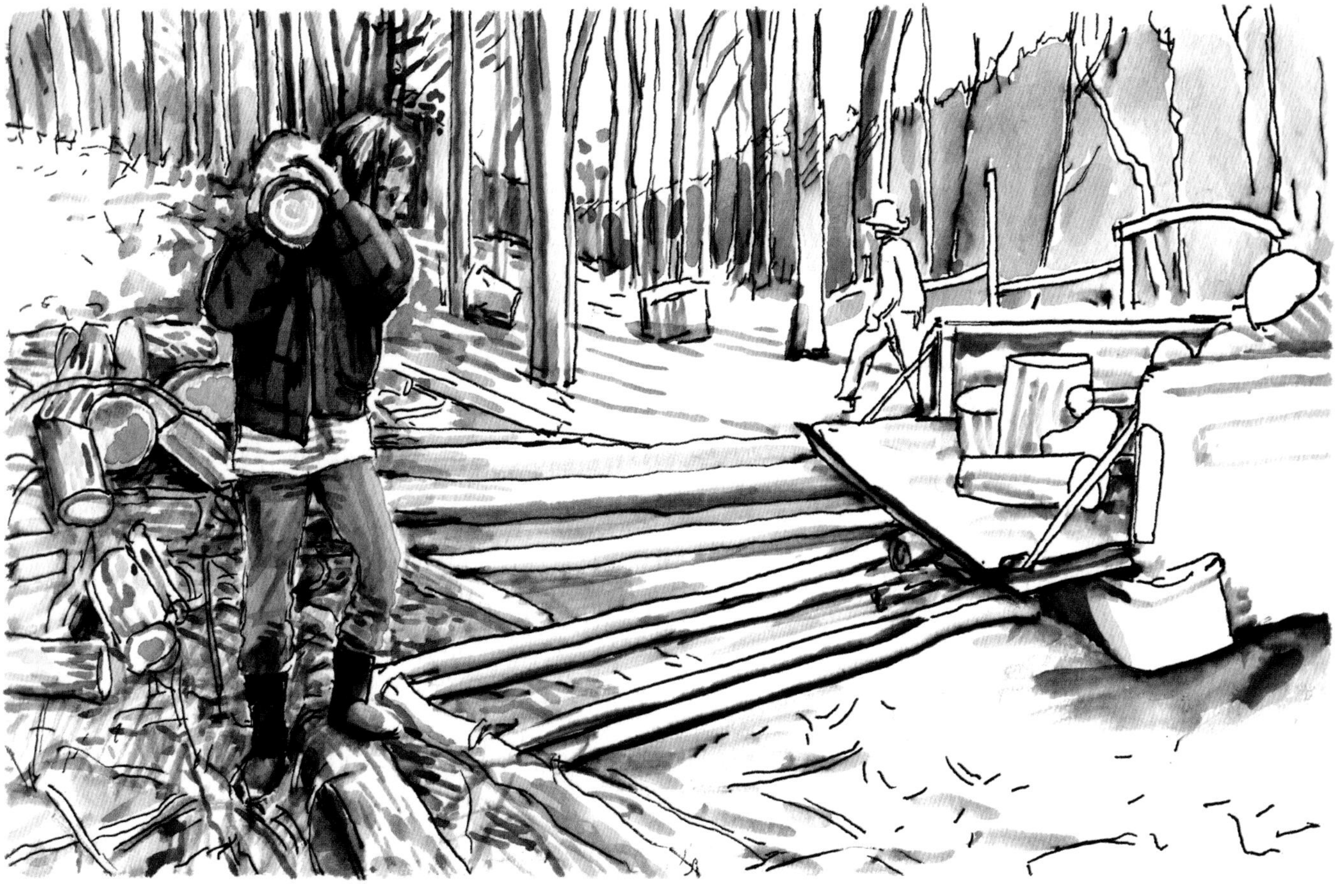

Friday, December 13

The ground has frozen during this last cold week. No more digging holes for fence posts. Work moves into the greenhouse where we replace windows on the house's south facing wall: goodbye to the huge single-pane panels we salvaged from a friend's house remodel; hello to new, efficient double-paned glass. It's in the twenties outside, but the greenhouse, heated only by the sun, is comfortably warm. Scraps of pale blue insulation board we've kept for years finally find their place in the walls. Maybe I'll be able to work in my winter studio without hands and feet going numb.

People often ask, "What do you do over the winter?" The best answer might be that we experience what it's like to begin to catch up—just to begin—and that experience gives us the vitality necessary to go on. Summer work is a scramble to stay in place, to merely stay apace of the season. This work is different. It's a long-term game. I wish we had time to work this way throughout the year: building the soil, clearing the creek of trash, improving things, rather than watching them fall apart. But that's just not the way it is, not the way it's ever been. I might as well aim to touch all the contours of our lives in this place, the beauty and wreck of it, while I have the chance.

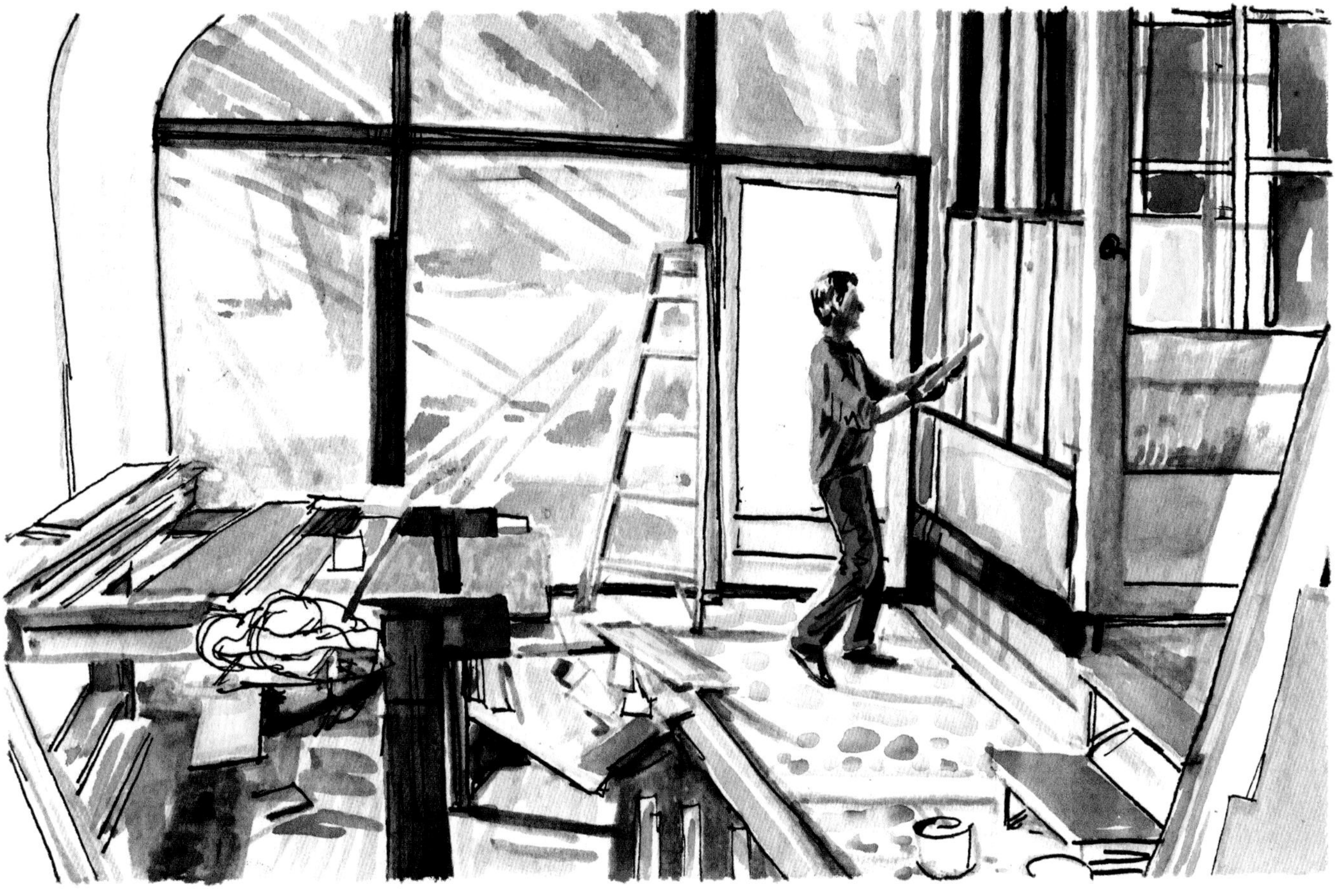

EPILOGUE

More than two decades ago, when David and I became farmers, we wanted to work toward repairing the ever-growing rift between people and land, starting with ourselves and our home. We believed—and we still believe—that the world needs more small, diversified farms, and that it would be an honor to be counted among them.

Yet by the time I began work on *Landings*, I wondered how we would survive in this place. It had been fourteen years since we moved to the farm—years of toil and exhilaration; of grappling with poverty and basking in plenitude; of raising a family in a community struggling with the loss of its own local economy. Our existence felt increasingly paradoxical. On one hand, even the notion of a *rift between people and land* belies the complexity of our lived experience here. It doesn't account for the joy, delight, and awe of our creaturely lives on Earth. On the other hand, the rift, on a planetary scale, keeps growing ever wider. To sustain my commitment to the farm, it was necessary to embrace my surroundings with more intention, to use art as a means of celebrating the struggle enmeshed in staying put.

Before I came to this point, art had largely been a refuge from the pressures of farm life, not a means of embracing it. After I decided to start drawing our daily lives, I began to carry a camera around with me, which I secretly called my *commemorator*, as in *co-memorator*: collaborator in memory-making. Look at the incline of this hill; look at how many different colors I simply call *green*; look at how a small shift in perspective changes an entire composition. When I could find the time, I looked through the photographs I had captured and started to draw. Drawing was, in a sense, a flesh-and-blood extension of the work the camera had begun, as if the path between my eye and hand was a developing bath in which the images steeped. After they became part of my body, I drew them out in ink and watercolor on paper. I never composed in pencil, but jumped in with a wobbly broken pen dipped in ink. Revisions remained visible—reminiscent of how, looking at the lines of this land, we can see how it has been altered by generations of human presence.

The year of *Landings* was a turning point. After fourteen years of intensive farming, the land needed rest, as did our bodies. We began to phase out marketing our produce through Community Supported Agriculture, opting to work increasingly with restaurants instead, which gave us flexibility as we experimented with what came next. For a time, my freelance work made up for our diminished farm income. We were familiar with the elaborate, largely improvisational dance of *making do*.

Meeting our daughter's educational needs was a constant challenge. We home-schooled through her middle school years, a wonderful and exhausting adventure that none of us could imagine sustaining through four years of high school. Finally, we settled on an imperfect solution: On weekdays, Phoebe would live with my mother in Lexington to attend a public school there with a strong art program.

A few months into Phoebe's freshman year, my mother was out walking when she was struck and killed by a car. After that, David managed the farm while Phoebe and I lived together in my mother's house. I returned home whenever I could, but we lived divided lives. I was profoundly uprooted and ravaged by grief.

Meanwhile, the farm itself was in crisis. Within a year of my mother's death, over the span of six weeks, we experienced the three most devastating floods we had seen since moving to the farm twenty years before. We knew that these floods were almost certain to grow more frequent and severe as the effects of climate change take hold. Our lives felt increasingly precarious.

That same year we had a new president, and much was made of the role the rural populace played in electing him. I had heard urban friends and family members deride country people for their unwillingness to leave their home places in favor of more cosmopolitan lives and economic opportunities, as if loving the land were a sign of backwardness, and as if urban centers are paragons of enlightenment.

There is a profound confusion at the root of this attitude. Of course it is true that many of us who live in rural places are the beneficiaries of an unjust and exclusionary system. Time and time again, our white supremacist government has run oppressed people off the land, or prevented them from owning land in the first place. Black farm ownership is at an all-time low, and Indigenous tribes continue to fight for full sovereignty on what land remains in their control. Yet a similar dynamic is at work in urban areas, where racist redlining still prevents people from owning homes in areas where land ownership is a form of generational wealth creation.

Paradoxes abound: there really is no rural-urban divide, and yet the perception of one poisons our culture. Every person in every city is dependent upon the health of rural places. The destruction and degradation of the earth and its creatures cannot be separated from the degradation and destruction of human civilization.

Growing up, Phoebe was keenly aware of these conflicts. She left her hometown in pursuit of educational opportunities, yet found that her city-based school placed little value on connections with the land. "I want to find a way to leave and come back, a way to study within rural traditions and the professional academic world, and a way to make a difference both within my small Kentucky home and in the world at large," she wrote in her college application essay.

As I write this, we have recently returned from delivering her to New York City, where she is attending Columbia University on a scholarship. By some combination of luck, privilege, and skill gained through experience, David and I are still on the farm, rebuilding and rediscovering our lives together.

❅

Working in the fields, I feel a fierce connection with the land. A sense of life force streaming up from the ground into my body, down from the air, in through my ears.

David and I talk while harvesting, strategize our lives. We laugh a lot. Maybe we'll rebuild upslope, where the floodwaters won't reach us. Maybe we'll dig into the hillside, to borrow some of the earth's coolness as the air grows hotter. Maybe we'll attach a sturdy anchor to the house and let it rise with the creek.

Walking in the woods, I think of the last time I walked in the woods, of the first time, of the friends I've walked with, of step-dancing along the trunk of the fallen cherry with little Phoebe when she was just learning to balance. That cherry tree is now broken, sinking into the ground. Today, I dance alone across a fallen maple. Pawpaw trees were all over this hillside just a few years ago—where have they gone? Oh, here they are, down by the creek. Pawpaws get around: they borrow the legs of possums and raccoons, who eat them and shit their seeds hither and yon.

Why do we spend so little time being amazed?

I woke this morning in the dark to the sound of frogs and crickets. I thought they sounded content, not afraid or alarmed, just full enough of life that they must sing some of it out.

ARWEN DONAHUE

ACKNOWLEDGMENTS

Our community of farm shareholders sustained our lives at Three Springs for almost twenty years. Their steadfast commitment not only helped pay our bills—they buoyed us, gave us hope. The brilliant restaurateur Ouita Michel's visionary support for local farmers has kept us going in more ways than can be counted.

Our neighbors Charlie and Helen Kiskaden have been models of kindness and generosity, as evidenced throughout these pages. Sandy Stone of the Cedar Hill Retreat Center passed away in 2022. In our last conversation, she told me that she had become a vegan and an advocate for farm animal sanctuaries. She expressed her hope that I would acknowledge that in this book. Sandy was always searching for ways to bring more grace into the world. We miss having her just down the road.

Kentucky's extraordinary community of writers, artists, and musicians informed this work and helped me articulate the connections between art and land. Special thanks to Barbara Kingsolver for writing her beautiful introduction, and to Wendell Berry and Bobbie Ann Mason for their generous readings and comments.

Without Sam Stoloff's generous guidance, *Landings* would never have been published. I am tremendously grateful to him and the Frances Goldin Agency. Thank you Rebecca Gayle Howell and Sarah Knott for your readings and insights. Thank you Meg, Katherine, and Kate at Hub City, for believing in this book and for bringing it to fruition with such care, intelligence, and alacrity.

To my family, Cate Wagoner, Analisa Waggoner, Judith Penelope (of blessed memory), Ron and Annette Wagoner, and Bill Donahue and Dana Densmore: thank you for your many years of love and support of our adventures in farming and art.

And most of all, thank you David and Phoebe—readers, subjects, and dearest of companions.

Donors

The Hub City Writers Project thanks its friends who made contributions
in support of this book and all Hub City Programming

Patty and Mack Amick
Marjorie and Kofi Appiah
Arkwright Foundation
Paula and Stan Baker
Harriet Ballenger Trust
Valerie and Bill Barnet
Bea Bruce
Judy and Brant Bynum
Camilla and Jeff Cantrell
Sarah Chapman
Mary Ann Claud and Olin Sansbury
Sally and Jerry Cogan, Jr.
Stephen Colyer
Kirsten and John Cribb
Magruder H. Dent
Coleman Edmunds
Carol and Ed Epps
Abby Fowler
Charles and Katherine Frazier
Susu and George Dean Johnson
Dorothy Josey
Cathryn Judice
Sara and Paul Lehner

Deborah F. McAbee and J. Byron Morris
Stacy and John McBride
Nan and Tom McDaniel
Nancy Milliken
Stephen Milliken
Weston Milliken
Milliken and Co. Charitable Foundation
Carlin and Sander Morrison
Dwight Patterson
Agnes Peelle
Julian and Beverly Reed
Pamela Smith
Diane Smock and Brad Wyche
Betty Snow
Sally and Warwick Spencer
Michel and Eliot Stone
Merike Tamm
Betsy Teter and John Lane
Melissa Walker and Chuck Reback
Kathie and Peter Weisman
Alanna and Don Wildman
Dennis and Annemarie Wiseman

Mitch and Sarah Allen

Tom and Ceci Arthur

Robert D. and Susan C. Atkins

Vic and Lynn Bailey

Susan Baker

Harold L. and Georgianna Ballenger

Tom and Joan Barnet

John and Laura Bauknight

Cynthia and Davis Beacham

Kathie and Roy Bennett

Elizabeth D. Bernardin

Billy and Page Blackford

Cindy and Louis Bottino

Mary Nell and George Brandt

William W. and Katherine K. Burns

Constance Caldwell

Harriet Cannon

Sarah and Randall Chambers

Anne and Al Jeter Chapman

Victoria T. Colebank

Rick and Sue Conner

Megan Demoss

Alice Eberhardt

Eugene Elrod

W Russel Floyd

Delie Fort

Joan Gibson

Barney and Elaine Gosnell

Andrew Green

Roger and Marianna Habisreutinger

Al and Anita Hammerbeck

Tom and Tracy Hannah

Daryll Harmon

John and Lou Ann Harrill, Jr.

James Hayes

Nancy Hearon

Elsa Hudson

Thomas and Juliet Johnson

Steve and Melissa Johnson

Ashby Jones

Daniel and Vivian Kahrs

Cynthia and Keith Kelly

Beverly Knight

John M. Kohler, Jr.

Anne Lander

Mary Jane and Cecil Lanford

Barbara Latham

Jack and Kay Lawrence

Wood and Janice Lay

Francie and Lindsay Little

George and Frances Loudon

Brownlee and Julie Lowry

Mary Speed Lynch

Suzan Mabry

Nancy Mandlove

Judy McCravy

Larry E. Milan

Don and Mary Miles

Boyce and Carole Miller
Cabell Mitchell
Karen and Bob Mitchell
Marsha Moore
Mamie Morgan
Susan Myers
Liz Newall
Corry and Amy Oakes
W. Keith and Louise Parris
Steve and Penni Patton
Jeremy Peach
Jan and Sara Postma
Mamie Potter
L. Perrin and Kay A. Powell
Betty Price
Terry Pruitt
Sharon and Garroll Purvis
Philip N. and Frances M. Racine
Eileen Rampey
John Ratterree
Elizabeth Refshauge
Elisabeth and Regis Robe
William and Carey Rothschild
Elena Pribyl Rush
Daniel and Bonnie Russell
Ellen and John Rutter
Kaye Savage
Susan Schneider
Joy Shackelford
Danny and Becky Smith
Pamela Smith
Chris and Tamara Smutzer
Brad Steinecke
Mary and Tommy Stokes
Tammy and David Stokes
Nancy Taylor
Cathy Terrell
Wendy Townes
Nick Trainor
Malinda and Charles Tulloh
Mark and Meredith Van Geison
Judith and Joseph Waddell
Anne and Andrew Waters
William Webster
Cathy and Andy Westbrook
Marie White
William and Floride Willard
Marianne Worthington
Bob and Carolyn Wynn

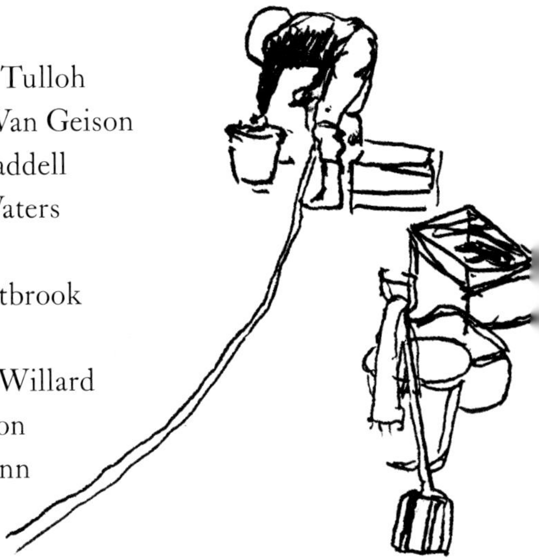

For more information about how to support the Hub City Writers Project and Hub City Press books, authors, and activities, please visit www.hubcity.org/support or contact us at info@hubcity.org

HUB CITY PRESS

PUBLISHING *New & Extraordinary* VOICES FROM THE AMERICAN SOUTH

HUB CITY PRESS is a non-profit independent press in Spartanburg, SC that publishes well-crafted, high-quality works by new and established authors, with an emphasis on the Southern experience. We are committed to high-caliber novels, short stories, poetry, plays, memoir, and works emphasizing regional culture and history. We are particularly interested in books with a strong sense of place.

Hub City Press is an imprint of the non-profit Hub City Writers Project, founded in 1995 to foster a sense of community through the literary arts. Our metaphor of organization purposely looks backward to the nineteenth century when Spartanburg was known as the "hub city," a place where railroads converged and departed.

MORE NONFICTION FROM HUB CITY PRESS

George Masa's Wild Vision Brent Martin

A Measure of Belonging ed. Cinelle Barnes

Gather at the River eds. David Joy and Eric Rickstad

Outside Agitator Adam Parker

Flight Path Hannah Palmer

Evenstar 12 / 20
LTC Caslon Pro 11.5 / 17.8